THE FAILURES OF ECONOMICS:
A DIAGNOSTIC STUDY

THE FAILURES

OF ECONOMICS:

A DIAGNOSTIC STUDY

Sidney Schoeffler

Associate Professor of Economics
University of Massachusetts

Harvard University Press · Cambridge · 1955

© Copyright · 1955 · By the President and Fellows of Harvard College

Distributed in Great Britain by
GEOFFREY CUMBERLEGE · Oxford University Press · London

Library of Congress Catalog Card Number 55–11953
Printed in the United States of America

TO MY PARENTS

PREFACE

A methodologist's lot is not a happy one. He is obliged by the requirements of his calling to carp, to criticize, to find fault, to disparage, and to throw cold water — and such activities do not often make for idyllic professional relationships with the other people concerned. It is often felt, and with considerable justification, that criticism is cheap and easy, that it is much more worth while to "lend a hand" in the ever continuing attempt to do better, and that any really competent man would want to be on the academic firing-line rather than spend his time and effort in "superintending" from the sidelines. The unhappy lot of the methodologist derives, therefore, from the circumstance that he often antagonizes the very people whom he respects and admires the most; and that he often wins the approval of at least some people for whose approval he does not care. And this somewhat melancholy situation is even aggravated by the fact that the methodologist will usually "pick" on the most creative and the most productive scholars in his field — since their work is the most important, it is also the most "worthy" of methodological analysis. There is a distinct element of intellectual patricide in methodological work, and this aspect of it does not help to win it social approval.

Some explanation is in order, therefore, as to why I nevertheless have chosen to devote my efforts to this despised activity. It is, quite simply, because I believe that much can be accomplished by methodological analysis in the present stage of the history of economics. I believe this despite the well-known fact that much of the effort in this field in the past consisted mostly of empty sound and fury and was quite barren of really fruitful results. The trouble with the early methodology was that it was premature. A discipline cannot start with methodology, or even be burdened with it in its early developmental stages. What is required at first is a great deal of intuition, *ad hoc* problem-solving, and just "groping around" in the empirical raw material. But today the situation in economics is quite different. We now have a substantial academic history behind us, and we have accumulated a great store of facts, theories, concepts, orientations, and procedures. The early stage is over, and the period of largely trial-and-error is probably over too. In other words, the time has come, I believe, in which something useful can be contributed by a critical investigation of methods as such. This essay, of course, does not even purport to be anything like a definitive job. The reader will be the judge whether it makes any contribution at all. But in either case, there is little doubt in my mind that a renaissance of methodological analysis in economics is both desirable and inevitable. The customary inverse relationship between the amount of methodological work and the amount of progress in economics no longer holds; today, the lag in methodology very likely is obstructing the further advance of economic analysis.

This essay is directed primarily at those of my colleagues, economists and other social scientists, who consider themselves to be professionally interested in the development of economics. It is also addressed to those others who are sufficiently concerned with the subject to be willing to do a little "digging" into it. My hope is, quite sincerely, not that my theses be accepted as they stand, but that they will induce other people to investigate further.

It is never easy, and usually impossible, for an author to make a full and honest declaration of his intellectual debts, human nature and the learning process being what they are. The list of actual "creditors" is always far greater than the author knows. As a practical matter, I can only attempt to acknowledge the more pressing debts.

This essay grew out of a doctoral dissertation in economics written at the New School for Social Research and submitted to the Graduate Faculty of Political and Social Science in 1951. It owes a great deal to the extraordinarily stimulating intellectual atmosphere pervading the New School, its classes and seminars. I have benefited very considerably from the guidance, advice, and criticisms of my thesis committee, consisting of Professors Adolph Lowe, chairman, Hans Neisser, Felix Kaufmann, and Kurt Riezler; and from the comments of Professor Alfred Kähler, who read the completed manuscript. Professor Lowe, in particular, has been unstinting of his time and wisdom and patience in helping to guide a somewhat unmanageable and obstinate young would-be scholar along the "proper" academic paths. (See also Appendix B.)

I have learned much (although some of them would deny it) from many people: people whose classes I have attended, whose works I have read, and with whom I have had the opportunity of talking about my pet schemes. My professors at New York University, at the University of Pennsylvania, at Columbia University, and at the New School for Social Research have been an almost unfailing source of inspiration. My present and former colleagues at the University of Massachusetts, especially Professors Philip L. Gamble, Gordon Donald, William Haller, Jr., Marshall C. Howard, Francis E. Hummel, Bruce R. Morris, Francis P. Murphy, Jerome Rothenberg, Richard T. Selden, and Allen Sievers, have been most stimulating, both by their advice and their criticisms. Mr. Haller, in particular, has given unstintingly of his time and erudition. As for writers in economics, logic, and related fields, the bibliography at the end of this book lists those whom I, in my own particular learning process, have found to be most interesting and instructive. An especial acknowledgment in this case is due to Professor Rudolf Carnap, to Professors Carl G. Hempel and Paul Oppenheim, and to the late Professor Felix Kaufmann.

Finally, I am grateful to Miss Dorothy A. Sullivan and to Mrs. Ruth Haller for their competent and patient help on the several versions of the manuscript, and to Miss Alice Pierce of the Harvard University Press for a thoroughly professional editing job.

SIDNEY SCHOEFFLER

Amherst, Massachusetts
October 1954

CONTENTS

Contents

THE FAILURES OF ECONOMICS:

A DIAGNOSTIC STUDY

The *Scientific American* for October 1951 contains, in separate articles, these two dramatically contrasting passages. The first is by the British physiologist Ernest Starling, who in 1923 declared to the Royal College of Physicians:

When I compare our present knowledge of the workings of the body, and our powers of interfering with and controlling these workings for the benefit of humanity, with the ignorance and despairing impotence of my student days, I feel that I have had the good fortune to see the sun rise on a darkened world, and that the life of my contemporaries has coincided not with a renaissance but with a new birth of man's powers over his environment and his destinies unparalleled in the whole history of mankind.[1]

The other quotation is from an article by Wassily W. Leontief:

If the great 19th-century physicist James Clerk Maxwell were to attend a current meeting of the American Physical Society, he might have serious difficulty in keeping track of what was going on. In the field of economics, on the other hand, his contemporary John Stuart Mill would easily pick up the thread of the most advanced arguments among his 20th-century successors. Physics, applying the method of inductive reasoning from quantitatively observed events, has moved on to entirely new premises. The science of economics, in contrast, remains largely a deductive system resting upon a static set of premises, most of which were familiar to Mill and some of which date back to Adam Smith's *The Wealth of Nations*.[2]

We all know of the astounding accomplishments of many of the sciences in the last generation or two. Not only physiology, but also physics, chemistry, genetics, mathematics, medical

[1] Quoted by Ralph Colp, Jr. in the *Scientific American*, Vol. 185, No. 4 (October 1951), p. 57.
[2] *Ibid.*, p. 15.

1

science, astronomy, and many other disciplines have been radically transformed during that period — sometimes several times — and have greatly enlarged their scope of understanding and their power of accomplishment. And in this period of intellectual ferment, of new horizons, of high-speed development and progress, the field of economics has advanced at only a snail's pace. Most economists are all too painfully conscious of still being in what Starling called a state of "despairing impotence" with respect to the subject matter of their study.

It has been over 175 years now that Adam Smith's *Wealth of Nations* has been part of the history of economic thought, and much longer since thoughtful people have concerned themselves with the whys and wherefores of economic life. Thousands upon thousands of scholars, as well as thousands of statesmen and men of affairs, have contributed their efforts to the attempt to understand the course of events of the economic world. And today this field of investigation is being cultivated more extensively, and more intensively, than ever before. How is it, then, that in all these years, and with all the undoubted talent that has been lavished upon it, the subject of economics has advanced so little?

Of course, a great many advances have taken place in the course of the development of economic thought, but quite certainly not nearly as many, or as important ones, as would seem to be warranted by the expenditure of time and effort along that line. We need only to look at the writings of the late mercantilists or, especially, at the writings of the early nineteenth-century economists to convince ourselves that, while empirical knowledge was scantier and theoretical concepts were cruder then than they are now, the basic method of analysis was scarcely different from what it is today. It is more than a little sobering to ask ourselves whether it really should have required all these long years and all these thousands of capable and brilliant men to carry the state of economic analysis the comparatively short distance from where it was then to where it is now.

While there have been some fairly sizable alterations in the theoretical terminology employed in economics during the last 100 or 200 years, the power of accomplishment of economics — measured in the pay-off terms of prediction and control — has changed but little. Economists could not predict the future course of economic events in the early days of the discipline, and they cannot predict the future course of events today. They could not foretell, with assurance, the consequences of given economic policies then, and they cannot foretell with assurance the consequences of economic policies today. And they could not formulate efficacious procedures for reaching given objectives then, and they still are not able to do so. Of course, there were many economists in the old days who believed they could do all these things, and there are many today who have similar confidence in their own abilities. But we need only to look at the arguments and discussions, then and now, that precede the adoption of a new policy measure — almost any new policy measure — to realize that equally expert men may, and usually do, reach diametrically opposite conclusions, that none of them can really assert anything with assurance, and that the element of subjective judgment (more accurately: prejudice) is the predominant factor, then and now, in any given prediction or policy conclusion. Even when professional opinion is virtually unanimous, we still cannot depend on it. Almost all economists, for example, wrongly predicted a sharp postwar recession for 1945–1946. The ability to predict and to take effective action implies a considerable intellectual grasp of the controlling principles of the subject matter concerned. It is that kind of mental grasp which has been attained in many of the other disciplines and which is still, after all these years, lacking in economics today.

The fallibility of the economist has earned him some rather widespread contempt and ridicule from various sections of the laity. "Practical" men, businessmen or government officials, who almost revere the doctor and the engineer, usually have scant respect for the prowess of the economist. They like to say, for example, that "if all economists in the world were laid end to end, they still wouldn't reach a conclusion," or that economists are ineffectual fuzzy-headed ivory-towerites who should be entirely ignored. This kind of contempt is not, unfortunately, quite undeserved. So far, the most spectacular accomplishment of economics has been its failures. The aforementioned forecasts, for the 1945–46 postwar periods, in which the almost unanimous consensus of professional economists was at the opposite end from the truth, is only one case in point. Here is another example:

J. A. Livingston, the financial editor of the Philadelphia *Bulletin*, has the interesting habit of asking some fifty of his fellow economists, every six months, to go out on a limb. He asks them where they think the Federal Reserve index of industrial production will stand six months hence.

Questioned in early June, his experts came up with this consensus: an eight-point rise in the FRB index over the second half of this year, to a level of 222. Thereafter, a three-point dip in the first six months of 1953, and a five-point decline in the second half of next year. The Livingston poll covers economists from labor, government and universities, as well as from banks, corporations and investment houses. Despite this diversity of background there has been a considerable uniformity in the economists' answers. Most of them have been wrong most of the time.

Some of their bloopers have resulted from unpredictable changes in factors outside business: the bullish combination of events in the summer of 1947 — announcement of the Marshall plan, a short corn crop, and the big wage rise in coal; the Korean War in June, 1950; the prolongation of the steel strike in June-July of this year. Very possibly the forecasters would have changed their 1952–53 estimates had they known how long the steel strike would last.

More significant, however, is the direction in which the forecasters erred. Three times in 1946 and 1947 they looked for a major downturn that did not develop, and three times in 1949 and 1950 they again were bearish and wrong. They missed the actual drop in business in between, in 1948, and were over-optimistic again in June, 1951, mainly because they misjudged the inventory situation.

Through most of the postwar period, and perhaps again now, the forecasters have been feeling ahead for a basic readjustment. They have pretty consistently underestimated the underlying strength of business, a hangover, perhaps, from the depression psychosis of the

1930's. Pessimism is almost inherent in some of the forecasting techniques — when business is good, it is easy to see which sectors of the economy might weaken but it is hard to project increases from an already high level in other sectors. Thus in 1949 and 1950 there were few experts who foresaw *both* the rise to record home-building and the expansion of car sales, which underwrote the recovery. Finally, to take the most sophisticated view of the matter, possibly the forecasters defeat their own forecasts by putting business on notice so far in advance that it discounts or overdiscounts the change they expect. Thus, warned of a recession in 1947, business cut some prices and so opened up new demands. Told to expect a boom after Korea, business overproduced and brought on the inventory readjustment.

The moral of it all? It could be that economic forecasters (perhaps like political forecasters) need to put more stress on imagination and less on being "sound" — to allow a little for the unexpected, speculate on new business developments like the 1950 housing boom, and keep an eye out for the way in which people, acting on the assumption of a given forecast, can thereby change it. Or, the moral may be, if the errant economists keep looking for a major downturn, long enough, one day they will be right.[3]

Many other instances of the fallibility of economics could be cited — but the melancholy facts are already well enough known.

Not the least significant evidence of the ineffectiveness of academic economics lies in the comparative successes of amateur and professional economists in the general fields of prediction and policy formation. Consider, for example, the following piece of news:

Over the week-end the average chest measurement of business

---

[3] *Fortune* (August 1952), p. 28 (Copyright 1952 Time, Inc.). It might be mentioned that, as Mr. Livingston reports in the *Sunday Bulletin* of June 27, 1954, the performance of his panel was dramatically improved in the period from the end of 1952 to the early part of 1954; and at the December 1954 meeting of the American Economic Association Mr. Livingston saw occasion to compliment the economists for their success in forecasting the recession and recovery of 1953–1954. But this improvement appears to be due to a fortunate accident, not to the use of better techniques of analysis. In mid-1954 the polled economists foresaw a *decline* in stock prices by the end of 1954, and then a "slight" increase by the end of 1955.

executives may easily have risen an inch or two as the result of a statement made by A. M. Raub of Dun & Bradstreet, Inc. Mr. Raub told a group of cost accountants that short-term business forecasting — that is, for periods of six to nine months — is more accurate when based on a sampling of the opinions of business executives than when based on studies by economists and government experts. Business executives, of course, have their order books, giving them a pretty accurate picture of the state of confidence in their fields. Government figures almost all deal with past performances . . .[4]

And in the field of public policy the most sensible recommendations are often made by businessmen or government officials whose principal training, if any, may have been in law, history, government, engineering, or some other noneconomic field. These "economic amateurs," after only a brief study of the facts in the case and of elementary economics, have proved themselves time and again to be the equals or superiors of professional economists in the effective formulation of economic policy.

It is necessary to inquire into the whys and wherefores of these failures of professional and academic economics before searching for the appropriate curative treatments. The present study attempts to contribute to this essential preliminary inquiry. But we may find — and this is the hope of this undertaking — that, as so often, the diagnosis is a highly important part of the cure.

[4] The *New York Times*, September 24, 1952.

CHAPTER 2: SOME SUGGESTED EXPLANATIONS

Professional economists have long been disturbed by the comparative lack of practical success from their efforts. In casting around for a plausible explanation of this unsatisfactory state of affairs, they have brought up a number of rather different ideas. The following are what would appear to be the most important of the suggested explanations. (The order in which they are discussed is not intended to reflect their relative importance.)

1. *The complexity of the economic world*

It is often pointed out that economic theory and economic analysis must *of necessity* deal with a greatly simplified picture of the economic system. The "real" system, with its millions of components and billions of interconnections and possibly trillions of transactions, is so fantastically complex that the very attempt at faithful realism in such a context is idiotic. The economist has no choice but to invent simplified constructs and to operate with them in his regular work. And, since his simplified constructs are inevitably somewhat unrealistic, his results cannot reasonably be expected to be in perfect, or even very close, correspondence to the events of the real world. That fact may be regrettable, but it is also unavoidable. The human mind is not infinite in its capacity, and it is obviously necessary to take its limitations into account.

It is also pointed out quite frequently that the physical sciences, with all their celebrated accomplishments, are equally helpless when confronted with analogously complex situations. The meteorologist, for example, finds himself with much the same type of problem as the economist. And even though his

sister physical sciences supply him lavishly with all their won-
derful results, his record of performance is equally undistin-
guished.

2. *The impossibility of experimentation*

Economists, in common with all social scientists, often com-
plain that their inability to conduct controlled experiments is
an almost crippling handicap in their search for useful facts and
laws. They may say, for example, that in dealing with an object
as complex in its internal structure as the economic system, the
most fruitful approach is a behavioristic one rather than a
micro-physiological one. A successful behavioral investigation,
however, requires controlled experimentation and that, unfortunately, is not possible in social science. In other sciences,
where such experimentation is possible, much progress has been
made by the use of the behavioral technique, even though the
internal structure of the system studied was almost as involved
as that of the economic system. In medical science, for example,
we have been able to find out such things as, say, the effect on
the human body of a deficiency of vitamin A. If we had had to
trace out the detailed physiological chains of consequences of
such a shortage, very likely we would still not have the answer.
Psychology, also, has adopted with considerable success the
method of controlled experimentation with the system — the
entire animal — as a whole. Indeed, it was psychology that
first developed a self-conscious behaviorism, mainly as a reaction to the difficulties involved in the various "internal" —
physiological or introspective — approaches.

There is at least one important field of study that has made
remarkable progress without the benefit of the possibility of
controlled experiment. But that science, astronomy, works with
a comparatively simple-structured subject matter and, moreover, has the advantage of being able to utilize the experiment-
ally determined principles of many other sciences, such as
physics and chemistry. It is therefore unreasonable to point to
astronomy as an example for the social scientist.

3. *The "free will" of human beings*

Many social scientists like to stress that, whereas the various natural sciences deal with a subject matter whose behavior is governed entirely by scientifically ascertainable laws of nature, they have to deal with the behavior of beings who are governed, at least to some extent, by their own noncaused "will." This will is "free," in the sense of not being a consequence of natural forces that are amenable to scientific study, and hence will necessarily frustrate any attempts at prediction by students of human behavior. It is therefore impossible, in principle, ever to reduce economic phenomena to rules and laws, and the failure in that respect should not, therefore, be a cause of unhappiness in economic circles.

This argument differs from the others stated here in being of religious rather than of purely scientific origin. It is often accepted as a matter of faith; but it has never yet been proved, on empirical evidence, to be true. The point is listed here as an important one mainly because a substantial number of people, including social scientists, believe it; and because, from a purely scientific view, it must be regarded as an unproved but possibly true (more accurately: not-rejected) hypothesis.

4. *The general indeterminacy of the universe*

This point is not very frequently raised by social scientists, but it is extensively discussed in other fields and it does have a direct bearing on the failures of economics. It is stated that the entire universe is basically indeterministic rather than deterministic, and that there is, consequently, an inevitable uncertainty about the flow of events in our world. We can only have probability knowledge of the future, never any certain knowledge. This particular stream of thought feeds on two rather distinct springs. First, there is the Principle of Indeterminacy in physics, commonly associated with the name of Werner Heisenberg, which proclaims the physical world — including the social world — to be governed by statistical laws, not "causal" laws. Second, there is the position arising from the philosophy of probability, largely originated by Hans Reichenbach, which regards certainty with respect to *any* synthetic proposition to be impossible. We can only have probable knowledge about the world; certainty is nothing but an extreme, and unattainable, form of probability. The consequence of either of these theories seems to be that no absolutely reliable statements about the future can possibly be arrived at, that any such statement only has a certain degree (less than one) of probability. There is always a chance, therefore, for a given forecast or policy recommendation to be wrong.

Even if this point is granted, it is not immediately evident why this basic indeterminacy and uncertainty should affect economics and social science so much more strongly than many of the other sciences. But that can be explained. First, since economics is concerned with a very complicated structure, it is subject to a large cumulation of the indeterminacies of the various component elements of the structure. Second, economics deals mostly with *unique* events, to which the application of probability laws is uncertain, whereas many other sciences (biology, chemistry, etc.) treat *large sets of similar events*, to which the application of probability laws yields straightforward relative-frequency statements. And third, economics is almost constantly concerned with the future, where the general indeterminacy is always the greatest.

5. *The self-defeating nature of social forecasts*

There are many adherents to the view that there is something inevitably self-defeating about economic (or, more generally: social) forecasts and economic policy recommendations. It is believed that the very act of arriving at and acting upon a prediction will so alter the course of events in the economic system that the forecast will, because of that alone, turn out to be false. Similarly, the adoption of an otherwise well-conceived policy will so influence the behavior of the various economic agents in the system that the actual effect of the policy will be different from the intended one. The social scientist is a part of the system that he studies, and his behavior usually influences the system in many disconcerting ways. The various participants in the system often orient their own conduct according to the activities of economists, and they may, in doing so, change their behavior patterns in unanticipated ways. As an example of this phenomenon we need think only of the forecasts of prices on the Stock Exchange or of governmental counter-cyclical policies.

It should be mentioned here, however, that the effect of the forecast or of the policy on the behavior of economic agents frequently works in favor of rather than against the economist. It is well known, for example, that many a pessimistic forecast turned out to be true simply because people believed the forecast and, by their subsequent retrenchments, brought about the predicted state of affairs.

6. *The difficulty of an open-minded, neutral, scientific approach*

In every social science it is extremely difficult, if not impossible, to achieve the open-minded, detached, objective approach that is essential for success in scientific endeavors. The perception and understanding of human and social events is almost unavoidably colored by the morals, the emotions, the religious attitudes, and the motivations of the perceiver. The natural sciences have been much more fortunate in that respect; they have not had to contend with nearly so many obstacles of this kind in their search for knowledge and clarity. It has been shown that preconceived ideas, especially when supported by strong motives, influence not only the interpretation but also the very perception of the events of the world. The economist, not being a "detached intelligence" but rather an interested part of the system he studies, reaps the full disadvantage of this peculiar characteristic of human nature.

7. *The "aspectual" nature of economics*

Many economists, especially the adherents of the various branches of the neoclassical school, believe that in order to make any headway at all it is necessary for them to limit their attentions to only selected aspects of human behavior. They believe, for example, that economics is and should be concerned with the institutions and processes through which human beings, in social groups, adapt their limited resources to their multitude of conflicting ends. Neither the ends nor the resources are to be explained by the economist. That is the job of psychologists, physiologists, and sociologists on the one hand and of geologists and demographers on the other. The economist is to be concerned entirely with the intermediate process — the process of adjustment. He must take both the resources and the ends to be "given" unexplained data. It is not his to ask why men like to wear socks, but only to study the consequences of that desire.

If this attitude with respect to the scope of economics is indeed the proper one, then the futility of economics is in large part a matter of voluntary choice by economists. The good neoclassicist deliberately refuses to pay attention to the most important links in the chain of causation through which the present exercises its influence on the future. It is not surprising, therefore, that he is not a successful forecaster and policy maker, whatever his other accomplishments may be.

8. *The incompleteness of economics* ⅄

F. S. C. Northrop takes a position quite similar to the above one in explaining the persistent lack of success of economics.[1] He begins by laying down the general criterion that "a theory of dynamics exists for a given science when its concepts are sufficient to designate the specific state of a system at a given time and its postulates permit the deduction of a specific state for any future time [p. 2]."

Economics, he continues, does not qualify under this criterion; it falls short with respect to both of the necessary conditions. First, its concepts cannot provide us with sufficiently de-

---

[1] "The Impossibility of a Theoretical Science of Economic Dynamics," *Quarterly Journal of Economics*, LVI (1941-42), 1-17 (Harvard University Press).

tailed descriptions of the individual states of the system. Economics, in its effort to attain publicly valid (intersubjectively controllable) theory, was prevented from accepting the exact preference maps of individuals as data; these maps can be, if at all, only subjectively known. It had to content itself with merely specifying that each individual has some order of preference or other. Therefore, "The first reason for the failure of contemporary economics to attain a theoretical dynamics now becomes evident. The initial requirement for such a dynamics is a theory providing concepts which define the state of a system at any given time, not merely with respect to its generic but also its specific properties [p. 9]."

Second, Northrop states, economic theory does not permit the deduction of future states of the system. This, he believes, would be possible only under a regime of mechanical causation, and such a type of causation exists only in systems which obey conservation laws. But conservation laws do not exist in economics; the total volume of wants, for example, does not remain constant through time.

This completes the essential outline of Professor Northrop's main argument. But Northrop does not have an entirely negative view of economic theory. Even though contemporary theory cannot predict, it can, when supplemented by other information, be of some use.

When the generic properties of the economic system designated by its postulates and their deductive consequences are coupled with its specific empirical characteristics given by contingent empirical information undesignated by theoretical concepts, the theory does enable one to foresee in part the more probable economic developments [p. 14].

Consequently, the person equipped with a knowledge of the theory is located midway between the position of the pure empiricist in economics, who must merely observe and theoretically deduce nothing, and the theoretical physicist who, given the present state, can, by his theory, predict everything [p. 15].

9. *The process of gradual approximation of reality* X

This argument often follows the before-mentioned one about the complexity of the economic system. It is alleged that it is necessary for economists to spend a great deal of their time in drawing deductive consequences from oversimplified and un-realistic assumptions — that without such an approach there is no hope for economics at all. The complexity of the system is such that any other line of approach would soon find itself completely overwhelmed by the masses of variables encountered. Economists therefore should and do employ a rather cautious and roundabout method of attack on their subject matter: they begin with the study of entirely imaginary and simplified economic systems and gradually, by changing their basic postulates, approach more and more closely the otherwise incomprehensible reality of the economic world. This process of gradual approximation has not yet gone very far — hence the "unrealism" of much of modern economics. But there is no reason for despair; the important thing is to be sure that the line of progress is in the right direction, and there seems to be little doubt that such is the case.

The process of gradual approximation to reality is also seen as a substitute for the experimental method. As Professor Higgins expresses it,

Within the deductive stage [of the method of economics], the method of 'successive approximations' is used. That is, the analyst begins with a model that is deliberately simplified, to isolate a particular relationship and so make analysis possible. Complications of the real world are removed by assumption, and then re-introduced one by one; at each step, conclusions are modified in whatever manner is logically necessary. This process is the economist's substitute for physical experiments; it is only the simplest kinds of elementary observation that permit laboratory experiment under control, and the use of statistics is limited by scarcity of reliable and comparable data. Consequently, the economist is compelled to rely in large measure on what the Austrians have called 'Gedanken-experimenten' or 'logical experiments.' [2]

[2] Benjamin Higgins: "What do Economists Know?" (Melbourne: Melbourne University Press, 1951), p. 10.

Comments on these explanations

There is little doubt that these explanations, especially when taken together, do account in large measure for the relative backwardness and ineffectiveness of modern economics, and do explain a good many of the behavior patterns of modern economists. But it is also true that the force of the arguments is often exaggerated. The disadvantages of the inability to experiment, for example, while unquestionably serious, are to a considerable extent overcome by recent inventions in statistical method. The modern techniques of analysis of variance and of covariance, for example, go a long way toward helping the economist disentangle relationships that formerly required controlled experiments. The difficulties resulting from "free will," assuming its existence, are not necessarily as crippling as they are often made out to be; even free-willed beings are subject to a large number of biological and physical laws. The scope of the free will, if any, is so much circumscribed by these laws that it need not at all be a serious obstacle to the scientific treatment of human behavior. The point dealing with the self-defeating nature of social forecasts and social policies appears to be a fallacy: there is no evident reason why a forecast of human behavior should not take cognizance of the effect of the forecast itself. This effect does, of course, make social forecasts more difficult than, say, weather forecasting; but there appears to be no convincing reason why it should make them impossible. Equally dubious is Northrop's contention that we can forecast the behavior of only those systems that obey conservation laws; there is no a priori reason, to my knowledge, why that should be so.

The most significant observation that we might make about these various explanations of the current state of economics is that they tend to place the principal blame on the refractory nature of the subject matter of economics rather than on the nature of our approach to that subject matter. This is, of course, a typically human attitude — it is always easy and pleasant to ascribe our failures to factors beyond our responsibility and control. It is not, however, a very fruitful attitude, no matter how plausible and valid the arguments may be. It is always equally valid (or equally invalid) to say that our difficulties are due to the weakness of our mode of attack on the refractory subject matter, and it is a very much more useful point of view. If a pair of scissors won't cut, we can say with equal justice that the material is too strong or that we haven't made the scissors sharp enough. But it is evident that the second explanation is more likely to lead to improvements in the situation.

It is the object of this study to analyze in what ways economists have fallen short in their methods of investigation and in their techniques of concept formation and reasoning. It is taken for granted that their field of investigation is a most difficult one and that the various points presented above are substantially correct. But we shall deliberately strike the attitude that the ineffectiveness of modern economics is the fault of the economists — even if it means slighting some really obstinate obstacles — always in the hope that this attitude will eventually yield the best results.

CHAPTER 3: SOME IMPORTANT METHODOLOGICAL
WEAKNESSES OF ECONOMICS

The main point of this chapter may be summarized in the following fashion: *The progress of economics has been and is so painfully slow because the concepts, the analytical tools, and the investigative tools employed by economists have been and are basically incompatible with the subject matter that economists study.* Economists have been and are doing something akin to working on steel with wood-working tools, studying the nucleus of the atom with a stethoscope, or trying to type an English message on a Chinese typewriter. As a result of this peculiar method, the activities of most of them are foredoomed to ineffectiveness insofar as useful applications are concerned. Something, to be sure, is accomplished by their work — but hardly enough to justify the strenuous efforts involved.

Economists have been and are engaging in these strange and sterile activities because, for diverse reasons, they have traditionally preferred to use in their endeavors whatever tools of thought and of investigation were already at hand rather than do their own tool-constructing. The creative methodological work that economists did do — and there was and is, of course, a considerable amount of it — was usually in the line of improvement of the borrowed concepts and methods rather than in pioneering attempts. Unfortunately, the tools that were taken over were usually designed for some quite different tasks than those which confronted the economist, so that the economist, in using them, maneuvered himself into the state of perpetual ineffectiveness that has been his main worry and concern ever since.[1]

[1] It has often been a source of surprise to me that so many economists like to point with pride to the fact that economics uses the same scientific method

Some of the details of the noncorrespondence between the structure of the intellectual equipment of the economist and the structure of the economic reality with which he has to deal are given in the following examples. Each states a type of concept or a form of reasoning commonly used in economics which appears to be unfitted for application to economic reality. To be listed are (a) its distinguishing characteristic; (b) a concrete illustration of the particular type of concept or form of reasoning;[2] (c) the purpose for which this concept or reasoning process is suitable; (d) the reason why economic reality is not in its domain of suitability; (e) a name for the kind of disharmony between concept and reality involved in the example. (The examples are not listed in order of importance.)

Example 1. *Mechanical behavior models*

(a) Distinguishing characteristic: The behavior of some organism or organization is expressed as a function of given environmental factors.

(b) Illustrative case: The theory of the firm. The theory of the firm, in any of its various forms, is a technique of computing how a firm will react, by its output and by the price it charges, etc., to such "environmental" given factors as the demand curves for the products which it turns out, the supply curves of the input factors, the production function under which it must operate, legal constraints, the liquidity position, etc. Some of the recent theories of the firm are quite complicated and make every effort to be realistic. All of them, however, insofar as the present writer is aware, postulate a fixed pattern of motivation (profit maximization, protection of asset position, avoidance of risk, etc., or some specified combination of these),

-----

as physics, biology, and others of its more glorious academic sisters. I suppose this is a way of excuse-making for the poor record of economics, and is usually combined with the customary assertion that its subject-matter is so very much more difficult. Very few economists view this similarity of method with the alarm they should.

[2] Most of these illustrations will refer to one of the exhibits discussed in detail in Chapters 5 and 6.

and are constructed in such a way as to yield, for each possible set of given factors, a unique and determinate response by the firm.

(c) Mechanical behavior models of this kind are useful instruments of analysis in all situations where the active elements are such that they will always respond in similar ways to similar situations — in other words, where the response indicated by the model is "necessary," not "voluntary" in some sense. Only in those situations can we place the kind of confidence into the results of the theory which is necessary for dependable prediction. Wherever this necessary invariance does not obtain, the results of the theory do not reliably correspond to the facts of the real world. We can never be sure then that the active agent will continue to behave in the future as it is expected to behave according to the theory, and we cannot therefore place full trust in the conclusion of a chain of predictive reasoning which depends upon such an assumption.

Examples of situations where mechanical behavior models are applicable are: chemical systems, biophysical systems, and the types of structure analyzed in classical physics.[3] It was undoubtedly for the analysis of such situations that mechanical-type models were originally developed. Economists simply took over the concept and adapted it for their own use.

(d) Unfortunately, however, the conditions under which the application of a mechanical-type behavior model is most useful do not exist in those aspects of the world which are studied by economics. The manager of a firm is not, for example, a chemical substance which reacts in a perfectly invariant way to given environmental situations. The organization which he controls — the firm — is not nearly as "well-behaved" as, to take another example, an astronomical organization. It may maximize (or minimize), or it may not; and we have no way of definitely knowing ahead of time what it will, in fact, do. The attempt to

[3] The assumption in the theory of the firm that the entity somehow seeks a maximum is evidently taken directly from the similar assumptions of classical physics, and, since the assumption seemed quite reasonable in economics, it probably paved the way for the adoption of a large number of other physical concepts.

describe its behavior by one of these mechanical models may be convenient and desirable for many purposes, but it does not make for successful prediction, or any other kind of successful application.[4]

(e) We may call the endeavor to describe a nonmechanical reality by a mechanical model *artificial mechanization*.

Example 2. *Batteries of homogeneous active agents*

(a) Distinguishing characteristic: An organization is defined as consisting of an entire collection of similarly structured and similarly motivated active agents.

(b) Illustrative case: The perfectly competitive industry. (Also: the entire group of profit-maximizing firms.) In the theory of perfect competition, an industry is visualized as consisting of a set of entirely homogeneous active agents, called "firms." Each firm is considered to be a mechanical-type organism, and all firms have the same mechanical properties.

It is true, of course, that no economist today regards the theory of perfect competition as descriptive of anything in the real world. But many economists do believe the theory to be the proper skeleton of the description of reality, a skeleton which merely needs to be modified for whatever specific circumstances there may exist in a given case. It has about the same methodological status as has, in classical mechanics, the theory of motion of particles in a vacuum. The present comment applies fully even when the theory is understood in this way.

(c) A battery of homogeneous agents is a particularly useful concept only, needless to say, where the agents are in fact homogeneous and where they occur in batteries. Such situations are not too frequent. The best examples that come to mind are: a chemical substance consisting of a set of similar molecules,

---

[4] If we ignore the possibility of free will, then we can indeed conceive of the manager of a firm as a mechanical-response type of agent. But then we should need an altogether huge number of variables to "explain" his behavior. It seems quite impractical to attempt to construct such very unwieldy models.

an electronic device containing a battery of similar tubes (an amplifier, for example, or an electronic computer), or, perhaps, a swarm of insects.

(d) Fairly obviously, business firms, even those within the same industry, are by no means homogeneous in their behavior. Each one is at least partially guided by unique customs, unique environmental factors, a unique managerial temperament, unique motivations, and a unique way of interpreting its economic situation. In studying the aggregate behavior of a battery of firms it is dangerous, therefore, to assume a complete similarity of behavior patterns. The deductive results of such theoretical analysis will not correspond to the actual occurrences in the world.

(e) We may denote the assumption that what is in fact heterogeneous is homogeneous, *artificial simplification*.

Example 3. *Empirical behavior equations*

(a) Distinguishing characteristic: The relationship between two or more variables is established by an inductive statistical procedure. It is usually expressed as a regression equation of a dependent variable upon one or more independent variables.

(b) The consumption function is the most prominent example in modern economics of empirical behavior equations. It expresses the dependence of aggregate consumption on national income, disposable income, and/or whatever other variables the analyst considers to be important. A great number of different consumption functions have been computed for the United States economy; among the most notable recent examples are those of Duesenberry and Modigliani.

(c) Regression equations of this kind are useful for purposes of prediction wherever (and only wherever) the empirically ascertained relationship is a stable one. In other words, the would-be prophet, in order to use the equation for his purposes, must be quite sure that the equation will continue to hold true, as stated, in the future. When that assurance is lacking, the forecasts or policies which are at least partially built

upon the given equation are undependable. Fields in which
empirical regression equations have proven themselves to be
useful are: genetics (for example: the dependence of characters
in the offspring on the relevant characters of the parents); agriculture (for example: in the study of the relationships between
various crop-determining factors and the quantity of the yield);
medicine (effect of various drugs on the physical state of
human beings); psychology (effect of various environmental
conditions on, say, the speed of learning); or chemistry (the
effect of pressure and temperature on the speed of a certain
type of chemical reaction). In each of these cases empirical
regression equations are useful instruments of forecasting because there is every reason to believe that the mechanism
through which the relationship expressed by the equation operates will remain constant in the future. It does not matter very
much here whether that mechanism is known in full detail to
the analyst or is largely unknown to him; the important point
is that he be quite sure that it will not change. The geneticist,
for example, can place strong reliance in his regression equations because he has every reason to believe that the structure
of the mechanism of inheritance in a given species is constant,
not variable. The agricultural experimenter puts his trust in
the constancy of physical law and the constancy of the structure of the plant he is investigating. The medical researcher can
rely on his findings because there is little doubt as to the constancy of the anatomy and the physiology of man. And the
chemist can believe in the continued applicability of his equations because of the invariance of the properties of atoms and
molecules. It is for purposes of the type just enumerated that
the appropriate statistical procedures were and are being developed.

(d) The economist, as so often happens, has taken over for
his own use the tools and concepts that have been constructed
for use in other sciences. Thus, he started to employ, almost
without change, the statistics developed for biology. But, unfortunately, as also so often happens, the conditions of suitability for the application of these tools and concepts are much

less pronounced in his field. Regression equations are fine for macro-biology but not for macro-economics. In biology, as has been mentioned, the invariance of the behavior patterns of the elements studied is assured by the constancy of their structure; in economics, the invariance of the behavior patterns of the elements studied is not assured, because the behavior-determining structure is variable, not constant.

In the case of the consumption function, for example, it is the set of socio-economic attitudes of the various individuals in the society that governs, in large part, the relationship between their consumption and their incomes and asset-holdings. These attitudes are quite sensitive to social pressures, military and political events, personal experiences, habit formation, conditions of work and of residence, and many other similar factors. It is therefore not only true that we have no strong reason for supposing consumption functions to be constant over time, but, further, we should certainly expect them to change. It should not have been such a gigantic surprise to economic forecasters in 1945 and 1946 that the postwar consumption function was entirely different from the prewar function. The war produced a drastic restructuring of those behavior patterns and attitudes that govern the consumption-income relation.

Economic statisticians might argue that a shift in an expressed relationship among economic magnitudes is not necessarily a sign of a variation in the underlying mechanism, but might merely reveal the fact that not all relevant variables had originally been taken into account. If all relevant variables are included in the formulation of the equation, the statisticians could add, then the necessary constancy will certainly exist. Consequently, they would conclude, regression equations are, in fact, suitable for application to economic analysis if only they are correctly used.

As stated, the above is of course an unanswerable argument. Indeed, it is a truism. If really all relevant variables are taken into account, and if we accept the general hypothesis of the "lawfulness" of the world, then the resulting equation must necessarily be the representation of a constant mechanism. But the difficulty arises in the attempt to specify the complete set of all relevant variables; the number of these variables may be astronomical. There is little hope of deriving useful equations under these conditions. Also, and this is an important point, if we do go down to all the determining variables of consumption, individual or aggregate, we are no longer in the domain of economics as customarily defined. The relationships governing the behavior of individuals, consumptive behavior or otherwise, belong to the field of *psychology*, and the variables which enter into these relationships are the variables of natural science, not of economics. In other words, in order to reach the constancy of mechanism which must be the foundation of a regression equation, we must leave the frame of reference that is the basis of modern economics and adopt the more fundamental and more inclusive frame of reference of the natural sciences. But while we remain within the economic frame of reference we have little warrant for using statistical regression equations for purposes of prediction or policy formation.

(e) We may denote the unwarranted assumption of the invariance of a regression equation over time — the treatment of a temporary relation as a general and invariant law of nature — by the name *artificial generalization*.

Example 4. *Classification and description of types*

(a) Distinguishing characteristic: Organizations, institutions, typical patterns of events, and other entities which are of importance to economic analysis are classified according to some scheme, described by types, or conceptually systematized in other ways.

(b) Examples in economics of this type of activity are: the classification and description of various types of economic fluctuations (as is done, for example, by the National Bureau of Economic Research), the typology of economic systems (socialism, fascism, etc.), and the classification of business firms into industries.

(c) Taxonomy seems to be quite harmless in most any

domain of investigation. But it is more useful in some domains than in others. It appears to be most useful when the following conditions are satisfied:

(1) The various classes within the scheme of classification are clear and distinct. Given any object which is defined under the classification, it is possible to ascertain, unambiguously, to which class it belongs.

(2) The objects belonging to any given class have some important property in common and differ in that property from all other objects. A property is "important" if it enters into the relationships studied by the science in question.

(3) The class-membership of objects is fixed, or is variable in predictable ways; preferably fixed. Objects do not vary easily or capriciously with respect to the class-membership-defining property.

These conditions are satisfied in many different fields; and in the sciences studying those fields taxonomy has played and is playing an important role. As examples we need only to think of the classification of plants and animals into species, genera, families, etc., and the classification of chemical substances into elements, compounds, types of elements and compounds, etc.

(d) Many economists, following systematizers in other fields, have become enthusiastic devotees of taxonomy. Unfortunately again, however, their field of study is not very promising material for useful classificatory activity. The typology of economic systems, for example, cannot serve well as a foundation for predictive economic laws. The set of existing economic systems does not satisfy the three conditions stated above; and, as a result, the future behavior of the systems cannot reliably be predicted on the basis of laws whose incidence depends on the class-defining property. There usually is considerable doubt as to just what class a given system belongs; and, even when the present class-membership is clear, the future class-membership cannot be known with any degree of confidence.

A closely related hardship often besets those economists who specialize in the careful description of the members of various classes of phenomena. The members of the class may undergo change without notice, and thereby leave the description with only historical significance and no predictive importance. Thus the National Bureau of Economic Research may well succeed in describing the entire complicated pattern of the "average" business cycle; but, even where the coming of another cycle can indeed be predicted, the description may be entirely inapplicable to the actual course of that future cycle. When a new member of a biological species is born, we can well predict what it will look like; but when a new business cycle is born, it may quite possibly unfold in some unprecedented way.

In many cases in economics, schemes of classification are a positive hindrance to further development. The various types under that classification may become stereotypes of thought (illustration: "socialism") and thereby obstruct the scientifically rigorous investigation of the affected objects. In the worst cases, these objects may change faster than the habits of thought about them.

(e) We may denote the classification of poorly classifiable objects by the name *artificial systematization*.

Example 5. *Mappings of structural elements of the world*

(a) Distinguishing characteristic: The structure of some aspect of the world is "surveyed" and then represented by some kind of picture of it.

(b) Many economists like to represent the structure of the tastes of an individual by a map called an indifference surface or a utility surface. In a similar way, the structure of the possibilities of production is represented by a production surface.

(c) As was true in the case of the classificatory activity discussed above, mapping is usually a harmless activity. But there are situations in which maps are more useful than in others. Generally speaking, there seem to be two different types of conditions in which maps are of considerable aid to the scientist:

(1) The structure which is to be mapped is a stable, enduring one, so that the mapping expresses information which can be relied upon to remain valid in the forseeable future. Examples of such stable structures are: the topographical features of geographical regions, the constellation of stars in the sky, and the structure of the United States Government. Maps have been made of all of these structures and they all have very considerable predictive value.

(2) The structure which is to be mapped is a variable one, but the pattern of its variation can be traced by successive mappings. The entire series of maps then tells us something about the process of change of the structure involved. Examples: weather maps, and the maps used by urban ecologists.

(d) Utility surfaces do not have the kind of usefulness that arises in either of the circumstances just mentioned. Condition 1, for instance, clearly is not satisfied. Human beings are constituted in such a way that their attitudes — all their attitudes — are at least partially determined by their immediate environment. Inasmuch as that environment never stands still, their attitudes and tastes do not stand still either; and a map of any given structure of attitudes and tastes can become obsolete almost instantly.

Condition 2 comes much closer to being satisfied than does Condition 1. But the study of the changes in attitudes belongs to psychology, not economics. Also, and this is perhaps more important, the structure of attitudes is so volatile that there seems to be no practicable way of keeping track of it. Only the broad outline of that structure is as "mappable" as, say, atmospheric pressure.

In general, it does not appear that the mapping of volatile (actually or potentially volatile) entities is of significant aid to prediction. The analyst never knows how long a given map will remain even approximately accurate. Predictions based, at least in part, upon such maps are therefore undependable.

(e) We may denote the mapping of a for-practical-purposes "unmappable" structure by the name of *artificial fixation*.

Example 6. *Time-series analysis*

(a) Distinguishing characteristic: The actual time series of a given variable is decomposed into a set of independent separate movements. The hope is that the various component movements are regular or predictable, so that the sum series can sensibly be extrapolated into the future.

(b) Economists have taken quite strongly to time-series analysis and extrapolation, especially in the study of business fluctuations. The series of such variables as gross national product, industrial production, wholesale prices, or per capita real income are broken down into such component elements as trend, seasonal, Kondratieff cyclical, Juglar cyclical, Kitchin cyclical, and "random." The most extreme use of such time-series components for purposes of prediction is made in a book by E. R. Dewey and E. F. Dakin, called *Cycles: The Science of Prediction*.

(c) Time-series analysis is a valuable aid to prediction if — and only if — the series can be decomposed into a set of components the future behavior of which can more easily be predicted than that of the original series. Under what circumstances is the future behavior of a given component series predictable? Generally, when its movement is the result of forces which are both regular and dependable, which can confidently be expected to continue their regular course into the future, and which will continue to have a constant relationship to the given time-series component. These conditions are satisfied, for example, in the case of the prediction of tides,[5] of the frequency of seventeen-year locusts, or of the movements of the moon. In each of these cases we need have little doubt about the regularity of the causal factors, and our predictions are therefore worthy of confidence.

(d) The unfortunate fact here is, again, that time-series

[5] See Dewey and Dakin, pp. 166–169.

analysis is not nearly as useful in economics as it has proved itself to be in other sciences. Again, many of the conditions of validity are lacking. The future GNP, for example, can not be extrapolated in total, nor by components. Only in the case of the seasonal component can one have any faith that the basic determining forces will continue to operate in the future as they have operated in the past. But even there prediction is unreliable; while there is little doubt as to the continuance of the cycle of four seasons every year, the relationship between these regular climatic factors and economic activity is shifting. As we attain more and more control over our environment we become less and less subject to any environmentally imposed limitations on our activities. The result is that economic activity is acquiring ever more freedom from regulation by the forces of nature; and this means, in the present context, that one of the few sources of predictability of economic activity is vanishing.

The other components of a GNP time series have far less claim to reliable predictability than even the seasonal factor. Trends have often been known to break, and they usually break without prior notice to the economist. The various cyclical components are notoriously erratic. As a matter of fact, in the absence of any regular and dependable causal factors with a constant pattern of relationship to GNP, we have no very strong reason to believe in the future recurrence of past cyclical patterns. This is especially true in view of the extensive role currently played by the government in the economic arena.

(e) We may denote the analysis of time series in those situations where such analysis cannot lead to reliable predictability by the name *artificial factorization*.

Example 7. *Endogenous models*

(a) Distinguishing characteristic: The movement of a system is described by a set of equations such that, given some "initial position," the future and past courses of the system are uniquely determined. The behavior of the system is thus governed entirely by its own structure, that is, endogenously.

(b) In economics endogenous models have been and are being applied most frequently in national-income theory and in business-cycle theory. For a completely endogenous national-income model, see the section on Somers in Chapter 6.

(c) Endogenous models are valid representations of real systems only when these systems are truly endogenous. Their behavior over time must be a function of their own structure and must be completely independent of everything else in the world. The form of the structure, as well, must be independent of any given outside factor. In other words, the system must be *closed*. Whenever the system is as much as potentially susceptible to "disturbance" from the outside, it is no longer endogenous and its future behavior is no longer fully determined by the structural equations.

It is difficult, and apparently even impossible, to think of actually existing endogenous systems in the world. This world of ours appears to be an integrated entity, not a disjointed one. Happenings in any part of it can influence, directly or indirectly, happenings in any other part of it. Nothing less than the entire world itself can therefore be taken as endogenous and closed. But there might be some reasonable approximations to closed systems, such as, for example, a galaxy of stars, an individual atomic nucleus, or a perfectly isolated perpetual-motion machine.

Quite often a set of structural equations does successfully describe the behavior of a system for considerable periods of time. Thus, for example, some endogenous business-cycle models have held quite well for periods of up to twenty years. Mathematical models of man-made machines provide good representations of their behavior as long as nothing goes wrong with these machines. But any such success must be attributed to a fortunate accident; a forecaster can never be sure, in advance, that nothing will "go wrong" with the system.

(d) The economic system is not closed. Its behavior, both in detail and in the aggregate, is responsive at all times to sociological, political, military, geographical, meteorological, medical, psychological, and even astronomical occurrences almost anywhere in the world. Sheer accidents in strategic places can have widespread repercussions throughout the system. It is therefore extremely risky, insofar as economic prediction is concerned, to represent economic reality by an endogenous model. The applicability of such a model is unavoidably a fleeting thing. The only way in which an endogenous model can ever be constructed in the first place is by an artificial mechanization of the component elements and/or by an artificial generalization of the structural equations.

(e) We may denote the application of an endogenous, closed model to a nonendogenous, open kind of system by the name *artificial closure.*

Example 8. *Semiendogenous models*

(a) Distinguishing characteristic: The model is in every respect like an endogenous, closed model except for a few "exogenous," nondetermined variables. When the values of these variables are given, the model becomes closed.

(b) A nice, clear-cut example in economics of a semiendogenous model is Colin Clark's model of the United States business cycle (described in Chapter 6). Also, most general equilibrium theorists (of the Pareto-Walras school) like to represent the economic system by a semiendogenous model, the exogenous variables being the demand curves for the various products and the supply curves of the factors of production.

(c) The domain of validity of semiendogenous models is much like that of fully endogenous models. The structure of the system to be represented by the model must be completely isolated from all potentially influencing outside phenomena. The behavior of all endogenous variables of the system must be uniquely determined from within. Only the exogenous variables can have any contact with the rest of the world. In other words, a semiendogenous system is one which is influenced from "the outside" only through the channel of a few exogenous variables, and in no other way.

One possible example of a real semiendogenous system that

comes to mind is a perfectly insulated, perfectly rigid machine which is controlled from the outside by a set of push buttons.

(d) The economic system is not at all like a push-button machine. The environmental factors that determine the course of events within it do not make their effect felt at only a few selected points of entry, but also at every point "within" the system as well. There probably is no event anywhere in the system that is not to some extent exogenous. To illustrate: The weather does not only influence economic activity through its effect on the demand curves of consumers and the supply curves of factors of production but also affects the conduct of most "intrasystemic" acts in addition. Socio-psychological relationships among individuals do not only condition their behavior as consumers and as suppliers of factors of production but also codetermine their conduct of the intrasystemic operations. Semiendogenous models are therefore unreliable for predictive purposes in economics; they presuppose an internal stability that does not in fact exist.

(e) We may denote the application of a semiendogenous model to a system of open structure by the name *artificial semiclosure*.

Example 9. *Partial consideration of variables*

(a) Distinguishing characteristic: A process of reasoning is carried on concerning the behavior of a set of variables in which the not-immediately-concerned properties of these variables are ignored entirely. We may, for example, consider the position of an object without paying any attention to its weight, its color, its value, its ownership, etc. We may talk about the physical size of a harvest without considering at all its value, its quality, its distribution of ownership, the attitudes of the people toward the product involved, its soil-exhausting properties, its effect on the balance of military power, or any of its thousands of other characteristics. We may discuss the insecticidal properties of DDT without considering at all the economic consequences of its production, the psychological effects on the people who use it, its influence on the further progress of biological science, and so on.

(b) Economics, as every other field of human discourse, abounds with examples of partial consideration of variables. Indeed, it seems impossible to talk about variables of the world in any other way; we cannot possibly pay attention to all the infinite number of properties of the entities we need to consider. We have no choice but to abstract one or a few properties of the concrete realities we investigate or analyze. So, when we consider, for example, the prospective effects of a new tax law, we pay attention primarily to its revenue-raising properties, and often also to its inflationary properties, its political consequences, and its effect on business motivations; but we almost universally ignore such characteristics of the tax law as its effect on the tendencies in the interpretation of the Constitution, on the pattern of social relationships among the members of the population, on the birth rate and the death rate, on the dietary habits of the population, on the frequency and the nature of crime, on the morale of the military forces, on the morale and activities of scientific researchers, on the attitudes of book publishers toward the publication of "worthwhile" but probably unprofitable books, on the development of the personalities of the members of the coming generation as affected by traumatic experiences with their parents on tax-due dates, on population migration, and on virtually every other aspect of our socio-economic-ecological system. Yet, with a little imagination, it is quite evident that a tax law will have all of these types of effects and many more, and that these effects are of importance to us.

With a little imagination also, we can see that all the customary discussions and analyses of the effects of economic events or of economic actions are of this partial, fragmentary kind.

(c) It is quite difficult to specify under what circumstances partial analysis would be "correct and proper," not merely an actually or supposedly necessary evil. One fairly obvious case that comes to mind is the one where the variables under consideration really do not have any of these other properties. It seems safe to say, however, that this cannot possibly occur in the world in which we live. There are no entities in it which are merely disembodied spirits floating about in empty space. Every one of the infinite number of concrete "objects" is tied to the rest of the world by a multitude of bonds of interconnectedness and mutual influence, and the variation of any one of the properties of the object will certainly produce some concomitant variation in the other properties.

It might be said that partial analysis is proper wherever the nonconsidered effects, though existent, are a matter of no importance to us. In preparing to make a policy decision we cannot hope to study the entire world in order to predict fully the effects of the decision; it is therefore sensible to confine our attention to only those aspects of the world that are really important. When considering a tax program for the United States, for example, it is quite proper to ignore its effect on the size of the earthworm population in Afghanistan. The difficulty with this general attitude is that it ignores the extent of the interconnectedness of the various parts of the world. A variable whose fate is, by itself, a matter of supreme indifference to us may by its behavior affect other variables which do matter. It is even quite possible to conceive of cases where the nonconsidered consequences of a given action will have "reëntrant" effects on the "important" set of variables and vitiate the originally intended consequence of that action. One cannot safely ignore *any* variable on the ground of nonimportance.

But, a "practical-minded" analyst might insist, can't we afford to ignore those aspects and effects of an action which are very small, and confine our attention to only the large consequences? On the face of it, this suggestion seems most reasonable. Nevertheless, there is a serious difficulty here too. There is no criterion that has been discovered up to now (at least to my knowledge) which can distinguish unambiguously between "small" effects and "large" effects. Differences between two states which in themselves appear to be insignificant frequently have rather large-scale consequences.

There is what has been called (by R. von Mises) the "small-cause, large-consequence" phenomenon. Very many constellations of circumstances constitute "trigger" situations, where an apparently inconsequential event can touch off chains of consequences the magnitude of which seems entirely out of proportion to the seeming importance of the trigger event. As illustrations, we may think of such happenings as the birth of Hitler, the caliber of marksmanship of the assassin at Sarajevo, the temper of Mrs. Murphy's cow that led her to kick over the lantern, a single blond hair found by his brunette wife on a man's coat, or the quality of the breakfast and consequent state of mind of a Supreme Court judge who casts the deciding vote in a far-reaching decision. We may think also of the nail in Poor Richard's saying:

> For want of a nail the shoe was lost,
> For the want of a shoe the horse was lost,
> For the want of a horse the rider was lost,
> For the want of a rider the battle was lost,
> For the want of a battle the kingdom was lost —
> And all for want of a horseshoe-nail.[6]

The point may be carried to even greater extremes. The factors (if any) that determine phenomena at the subatomic level also generate an ever expanding circle of effects. Not only physical

[6] For the case of meteorology Professor Eddington has stated this fact as follows: In order to predict next year's weather, "We should require extremely detailed knowledge of present conditions, since a small local deviation can exert an ever-expanding influence. We must examine the state of the sun so as to predict the fluctuations in the heat and corpuscular radiation which it sends us. We must dive into the bowels of the earth to be forewarned of volcanic eruptions which may spread a dust screen over the atmosphere as Mt. Katmai did some years ago. But further we must penetrate into the recesses of the human mind. A coal strike, a great war, may directly change the conditions of the atmosphere; a lighted match idly thrown away may cause deforestation which will change the rainfall and climate." Sir Arthur S. Eddington, "Reality, Causation, Science and Mysticism," *Man and the Universe: The Philosophers of Science*, ed. Saxe Commins and Robert N. Linscott (New York: Random House, 1947).

This enumeration is, quite evidently, grossly oversimplified. It was formulated, for example, before Dr. Langmuir and his associates started performing their tricks with the weather.

processes but also biological ones are subject to direction by micro-phenomena (genes, glandular secretions, etc.).

It is not very apparent how a variation in the size of the earthworm population in Afghanistan will have significant repercussions on the position of the United States Treasury, but it is certainly not beyond the realm of possibility that such repercussions exist.

For the reasons just stated, the writer cannot present any illustrations of circumstances in which any aspect of the variables studied and any consequence of variation in these variables can properly be ignored. This convenient state of affairs would exist only if the variables concerned were somehow torn out of their existential context and made into, to repeat a previous metaphor, disembodied spirits floating in empty space.

Nevertheless, the basic problem still remains. We cannot possibly, in studying the effect of a given action, trace the consequences of that action all through the universe. In order to accomplish anything at all we obviously must cut corners somewhere. But if we do that, then we cannot reliably predict the consequences of the action even on the "important" variables, and we have no alternative but to place our trust in guesswork. Is this an unavoidable dilemma?

A possible answer here is that we need not simplify our analysis by taking the course of ignoring the rest of the world or any part of it; we can simplify it by considering the various possible repercussions, all of them, in a short-cut way.[7]

(d) Economic variables clearly are not disembodied isolated variables. Every economic event has sociological, psychological, political, scientific, meteorological, geographical, medical and other reactions; and every event in these other fields produces reactions in the economic sphere. Reëntrant effects occur continuously, and the small-cause, large-consequence phenomenon is a very common one. Therefore, any element of partial con-

---

[7] For a suggestion of how this might be accomplished, see Sidney Schoeffler, "A Contribution to the Theory of Prediction in Economics," Ph.D. dissertation, The New School for Social Research, 1952. The model of prediction presented in Chapter 8 also purports to point the way toward a solution.

sideration of variables in a predictive chain of reasoning inevitably undermines the reliability of the resultant prediction. In the case of the prospective tax law cited above, the sum of the side reactions of the adoption of the law, ignoring now their own intrinsic importance, will quite likely have as much of an effect on the long-run position of the United States Treasury as have the direct tax-assessing activities provided for under the law.

(e) We may denote the practice of ignoring the existential context of variables under consideration, of disregarding the interconnectedness of the world, by the name *artificial isolation.*

Example 10. *Assumptions verified by their logical consequences*

(a) Distinguishing characteristic: An empirically observed phenomenon is "explained" by a set of hypotheses which, if they were assumed to be true, would have the observed phenomenon as a logical consequence. The fact that the event did occur is then taken as proof (or, by more cautious investigators, as a justification for supposing) that the assumed hypotheses are true.

(b) Recent economics abounds with attempts to verify basic assumptions by testing their logical consequences against empirical observations. As a matter of fact, many economists tend to regard this procedure as the essence of the scientific method. As examples, we may think of the attempts to "prove" assumptions about multipliers and accelerators by comparing the theorems deduced from them with empirical time series; of the efforts to establish assumed behavior patterns of businessmen (inventory policy, for example, or profit policy) by checking inferences from them against available statistics; and of the attempts to reconstruct the "minds" of consumers in this indirect way.

The main motive for the use of this technique of analysis is quite clear. It is frequently much easier and much less expensive to utilize indirect evidence. And often the method enables us to take advantage of already available statistics and other information, thus making it unnecessary to embark upon new fact-gathering expeditions.

(c) This method of analysis, if correctly used, is, from a purely logical point of view, equally applicable in all fields of study. But the method is a tricky and dangerous one, and hence should be reserved for only those cases in which no practicable alternative is available.

Let us first see in what way the method is hazardous in its application. The point here is that its use implicitly involves a serious logical error: the so-called fallacy of affirming the consequent. We have no right to infer from the facts that (1) we know "B" to be true and (2) that "B" is a deductive consequence of set of assumptions "A," that (3) "A" is therefore true. There may be other sets of assumptions "C," "D," or "E," etc., that also have "B" as a deductive consequence. Simply knowing that "B" is true gives us no guide at all for choosing the correct one among the two or ten or many sets of hypotheses from which "B" could be inferred. To take a rather simple-minded example, if we find a dead body in our closet, we cannot conclude from that that President Eisenhower shot him, even though this hypothesis would fully account for the observed phenomenon.

As has been mentioned, the method under discussion should be used only where it is the only feasible one. A good illustration of such a situation is provided by nuclear physics. The interior of the atomic nucleus is completely inaccessible to direct observation, and hence the only way in which we can obtain information about the micro-structure of the nucleus is through indirect inference from its observed macro-behavior. As we all know, much has been accomplished in this fashion. But the conclusions reached by this technique, being subject to the fallacy of affirming the consequent, must always remain tentative and uncertain, and can be used only as suggestions for further research.

(d) The economist is in a more fortunate position than the nuclear physicist. He very seldom deals with variables that cannot possibly be observed directly (or through reasonably straightforward indicators). There is little warrant, consequently, for his use of the treacherous method of indirect inference. He need not, for example, study inventory policy by reasoning backward from inventory statistics — he can go to the businessman directly; and, for much the same reason, he is not compelled to approach accelerators through the available statistics on national income. He may, of course, save himself considerable trouble by the indirect approach, but it is doubtful at best if this saving is worth the risk of error that is entailed by it.

In one case at least, the economist must use indirect evidence: if he is to make any headway in the study of preference maps of consumers. But, for reasons stated before, even here it is hardly worth the trouble.

(e) We may call the practice of unnecessarily exposing ourselves to the fallacy of affirming the consequent *artificial indirectness*.

General Comment on the Methodological Weaknesses

The foregoing catalogue of the weaknesses which are common in economic analysis was not intended to be exhaustive or free from overlapping. It is neither. It lists only those conceptual difficulties which seem to constitute particularly grave handicaps to the development of a really useful and productive economics. Also there is some overlapping, which was necessary in the interest of clearer exposition. Further, there has been a certain amount of exaggeration in the preceding discussion, again, for greater clarity of the essential points.

It should also be emphasized strongly at this point that the listed malpractices of economic analysis are malpractices only from the standpoint of reliable prediction and policy-making. Many of the artificialities mentioned have performed and are performing very important functions in the development of economics. For pedagogical or investigative purposes, for example, it is frequently necessary to depart from strict reality; the human mind has difficulty comprehending a complex structure immediately without prior "conditioning" on some simpler structure. The investigation of hypothetical situations may provide insights which could not be attained otherwise, and which can subsequently be extended to more realistic situations. The artificial constructions themselves may be improved over time and thus lead to more suitable techniques of analysis which otherwise would never have come to exist. The development of a science is a dynamic process, and anything which facilitates that process, though itself not measuring up to the more exacting scientific standards, is useful and valuable.

Having now acknowledged the one-sidedness of our approach, let us restate briefly the central point of this chapter. The record of performance of economics in the field of prediction and policy-making has been and is so very poor because the concepts employed by economists are, with few exceptions, utterly unsuited to the requirements of their task. Economists have seldom attempted, with a view to the special nature of their field of investigation, to devise their own tools of thought. They have taken their mathematics and their deductive techniques from physics, their statistics from genetics and agronomy, their systems of classification from taxonomy and chemistry, their model-construction techniques from astronomy and mechanics, and their methods of analysis of the consequences of actions from engineering. But the subject matter of economics unfortunately is quite different from that of any of these other sciences. As a result, the structure of economic analysis is not isomorphic with the structure of economic reality. In attempting to bridge the gap, economists have become accustomed to committing a considerable variety of artificialities in their collection, treatment, and interpretation of data. They artificially mechanize, artificially simplify, artificially generalize, artificially systematize, artificially fixate, artificially factorize, artificially close, artificially semiclose, and artificially isolate. They employ an artificial indirectness. They assume the heterogeneous to be homogeneous, the complex to be simple, the complexly related to be simply related, the unknown to be known, the variable to be fixed, the open to be closed, the connected to be isolated, and the indeterminate to be determinate. Unavoidably, therefore, predictions about economic reality which are produced with the aid of these techniques are quite undependable, and professional economics has been and continues to be a relatively ineffectual debating society.

A. INTRODUCTION

It has been necessary, in the preceding chapters, to discuss at some length what the subject matter of economics is *not* like, and what techniques of analysis and investigation are consequently *not* suitable to it. It might be desirable now to say a little more about what the economic system *is*, in fact, like.

It should be clearly understood at the beginning that we are not, at this point, looking for a concrete description of the American economic system or of any other specific system, or even of system-types like "capitalism" or "socialism." We are, in contrast, interested now in some characteristics of economic systems that are common to all specific systems, actual and potential, and that are relevant in specifying the methods of analysis required for the fruitful study of any of them. In other words, we wish to investigate such questions as: Is the system self-contained, or is it subject to influences from its "environment"? Which aspects of the system are subject to outside influences and which are not? What, if any, are the structural constancies? What structural elements are flexible? Are the relationships among the "interior" variables static or dynamic? What are the connections between economic, sociological, psychological, and political phenomena? Obviously, only the outlines of answers can be — or need be — presented here.

We will, accordingly, focus our attention on what we may call the "formal structural properties" of an economic system. To explain what is meant by "formal structure" we might say that it is because of a similarity of formal structure that the same techniques of experiment and analysis are applicable to such concretely different problems as (1) the effects of different fertilizers on the yields per acre of wheat, (2) the effectiveness of different teaching methods on the learning of arithmetic, (3) the effects of the various vitamins on body weight, and (4) the performance of different metals in the filaments of vacuum tubes. In contrast, we can say that it is a difference in formal structure that necessitates the use of entirely different tools of analysis, even in such concretely related fields as classical mechanics and quantum mechanics.

One of our basic conclusions, in the following, will concern the nature of the concept of "prediction" as it applies to economic systems. When it is said (and, alas, it is said often) that the social sciences cannot predict, the concept of prediction that is usually in the mind of the speaker is that current in the physical sciences. When the astronomer predicts a solar eclipse, or the physicist a chain reaction, or the geneticist the color of a baby's eyes, or the chemist the formation of certain molecules, he utters an unequivocal prophecy of things to come; and, if the scientist in question is at all competent in his field, that prophecy is almost invariably borne out by the subsequent course of events. If prediction is understood in this sense, the social scientist is not, and never will be, able to predict. We have already noted the basic reason: the field of study of the social scientist does not exhibit the required structural constancies. But this does not at all mean that reliable forecasting is really impossible in economics and in the other social sciences. It does mean that the concept of prediction must be reformulated so as to conform to the peculiarities of the field of social inquiry before it can usefully be applied there.

Much of the past impotence of economics is due to the uncritical acceptance by economists themselves of the extreme physical-science notion of prediction, and to their adaptation to that notion. Some economists valiantly undertook to battle and conquer "prediction"; but fate did not treat them kindly. Other economists gave up hope entirely, and proceeded to spend their time on descriptive or "institutional" work. The efforts of both of these groups, as we shall see, were largely wasted as far as genuine predictability is concerned; not being oriented

toward a relevant notion of prediction, their work did not and
could not contribute as much as it should have to the development of economics.

It is necessary, before we can proceed further in laying the
groundwork for formulating a useful and relevant concept of
prediction in the social sciences, to go into some formal definitions of essential working concepts. In a few cases we shall
assign to a term a meaning somewhat different from its meaning in common parlance; but the advantages of that procedure
are intended to outweigh the resulting disadvantages. (Some of
the definitions are intermediate steps in the derivation of later
definitions, and will not themselves be used in the subsequent
discussion.) A more extensive discussion of the concept of prediction will be undertaken in Chapter 8.

B. DEFINITIONS OF CONCEPTS

Variable: A variable is any "object" whatever which continues through time and which assumes, at each instant of time,
one of the set of mutually exclusive values in its characteristic
range of variation. (One of these values may well be "zero" or
"none," or some equivalent.) Some examples of variables (their
ranges of variation indicated in the parentheses following each)
are: the price of wheat (dollars, o to ∞); the black queen in
chess (the 64 positions on the board); the utility surface of a
given individual (the infinite number of shapes); a given proposition (truth or falsity); a legal rule (in force or not); an individual's social position (Warner's six social classes); etc. We
place no limitation whatever on the type of entity that can be
considered to be a variable other than that it must have the
defining properties. It may in fact vary or it may remain constant; it may take on quantitative or qualitative values; it may
vary over a continuum or it may have a denumerable or finite
number of values; and it may be directly observable or not.
If an object has two or more ranges of variation that interest
us, it is considered to constitute as many variables as it has
such ranges of variation. A given person, for example, might

be regarded as being the following six variables: John Doe (weight), John Doe (age), John Doe (religion), John Doe (social status), John Doe (wealth), and John Doe (occupation).

System: Any set whatsoever of jointly considered variables, including the entire world or any lesser set, is a system. For the purpose of this study we shall always regard time to be one of the variables of a system.

State of system: A state is any logically possible combination of values of the variables of the system. In an n-variable system a state is always a set of n values, one value for each of the n variables.

History of a system: A history is any logically possible sequence of states of the system, such that there is one state, and one only, for each point of time (in the time interval considered). It is, in other words, a time sequence of states stretching over any given finite or infinite period of time.

Event: An event is any given alternation of a set of histories (that usually have some property in common).[1]

Range of a system: The entire set of logically possible histories of a system shall be called the range of that system. The range is the totality of different courses of events that could conceivably transpire in the system.

Information: Information, in relation to a given system, is knowledge concerning the behavior of the variables that constitute the system. An item of knowledge is information in this sense if, and only if, the following conditions obtain:

(a) It is *valid,* that is, established as being true. We are assuming now that we have available appropriate methods for distinguishing between true and false propositions, and that, in general, our methodology of science is capable of coping with questions of this sort. A proposition whose validity is neither

---

[1] An alternation of a set of histories is described by the proposition that one of these histories is the "true" one. The various histories are regarded as joined by the logical connective "or." A state of the system is an event — the event consisting of all the histories that contain that state — and so is a single history, or the entire set of histories, or any other set at all. (The probability of an event equals the *sum* of the probabilities of the component histories.)

established nor disproved is not considered to be information, on the ground that it would not constitute reliable material for purposes of prediction and policy formation.

(b) It assigns probabilities [2] to at least one event of the system under consideration. It may declare an event to be impossible [3] (probability of zero), or to be necessary [4] (probability of one), or to be probable in an intermediate way. In the minimal case, it may merely restrict the range of the possible probabilities.

(c) Its validity conditions are fully stated; that is, it holds true, as it stands, under all possible surrounding circumstances. There should be no unstated validity conditions a change in which could, without previous notice, make the statement untrue. The following are some examples of propositions which do not meet this criterion and therefore are not information in our sense:

(1) War is accompanied by inflation.

(2) An increase in national income leads to an increase in private consumption.

(3) The volume of an ideal gas varies in inverse proportion to its pressure.

(4) Children of broken homes turn to crime.

None of these propositions, while often true, is inevitably true — there are always possible circumstances under which it does not hold. A process of analysis based in part on such a proposition is therefore quite unreliable.

Some propositions which do hold unconditionally are:

(1) The maximum attainable speed in the universe is that of light.

[2] "Probability" should here be understood in the sense of a relative frequency. Empirical probability laws are based on this notion of probability. We treat the logical concept of probability (what Carnap calls "Probability₁") as pertaining to the logical consequences of our information. See Chapter 8 for details.

[3] This means that none of the constituent histories can occur.

[4] This means that one of the constituent histories will definitely occur.

(2) After decapitation, a human being is dead.

(3) It is impossible to make water out of helium and iron.

(4) George Washington was the first president of the United States.

Each of these statements is true no matter what other circumstances exist anywhere in the world. It cannot be upset by any developments whatever. It is therefore, according to our definition, "information," and can confidently be used in a process of subsequent analysis.

A conditional proposition can be turned into an unconditional one by including within the proposition a statement of the validity conditions. Consider, for example, the statement: "The volume of an ideal gas varies in inverse proportion to its pressure." If it is changed to read: "When the temperature is kept constant, the volume of an ideal gas varies in inverse proportion to its pressure," the statement becomes a law, and hence information. No matter what situation pertains to the rest of the universe, if the temperature of the gas is constant the indicated inverse proportionality exists.

It should be noted here that any proposition about the world that embodies an artificiality (as described in the previous chapter) is not information in our present sense.[5]

Information consists of definitions and of synthetic propositions, and synthetic propositions, in turn, consist of observations, static laws, and dynamic laws.

Definition: A set of variables A is "defined" in terms of another set of variables B if the values of A and of B must

---

[5] One exception to this extremely important requirement of stating the validity conditions of a proposition is imposed upon us by the finitude of the human mind. There is a point beyond which no further conditions can be stated, because we may be entirely unaware that there may be further conditions to be reckoned with. We have, in general, no conception of the existence and nature of a condition unless and until there is a certain change in it and it thereby intrudes itself upon our awareness. The law concerning the maximum attainable speed is a case in point — we have no notion of "super-physical" elements in nature whose changes might render this law invalid. We would say here that we are justified in assuming the universal validity of a law if we have pushed the enumeration of conditions to the at-the-time ultimate limit.

always, by our resolution, bear a given relation to each other. Example: Disposable Income = Personal Income − Personal Taxes.

Synthetic proposition: a synthetic proposition represents *empirically ascertained* information.

Observation: An observation presents information about the state of a system as it was at a given point of time or during a given interval of time. It may specify the existing state uniquely or it may give only fragmentary information about it.

Static law: A static law is concerned with the coexistence, at any given time, of values of the variables of the system. It assigns probabilities to certain states, and thereby to the events defined by these states. The aforementioned Boyle's law, in its simple form, is a static law: it assigns the probability of zero to many combinations of volume, temperature, and pressure of a gas.

Dynamic law: A dynamic law is concerned with the succession in time of the values of the variables of the system. Like any item of information, it assigns a probability to at least one event of the system; but these probabilities are based on sequences of values of the variables. (An example of a dynamic law is the law of physics which specifies the maximum speed attainable in the universe to be the speed of light.)

Space of a system: The space of a system, relative to a given body of information, is the range of the system together with the known probabilities of the various histories and events.

Exogenous variable: An exogenous variable, with respect to the space of a given system, is a variable of the system whose probability distribution of values (at each point of time) is not fully deducible from a knowledge of the distributions of the values of all the other variables. It is, in other words, a variable whose behavior is not fully controlled by the other variables of the system.

Endogenous variable: An endogenous variable, with respect to the space of a given system, is a variable of the system whose probability distribution of values, at each point of time, is deducible from the probability distributions of the values of the other variables. It is, in other words, a variable whose behavior is fully controlled by the other variables of the system.

C. TYPES OF SYSTEMS

We are now ready to examine the different kinds of formal structure which a system may possess. To avoid spending time on nonessentials, we shall consider only empirical systems containing observational variables — we shall assume, in other words, that all variables created by definitional identities have been eliminated. This can, of course, be easily done, and does not result in any loss of empirical information. And as another time-saving device we shall confine our attention to dynamic [6] systems only. Static systems, whenever they occur, can be visualized as being special cases of dynamic systems.

While we are discussing empirical systems, we are not considering them as they, in a metaphysical sense, "really" exist in the world. We are not concerned — because we cannot be — with the "true nature" of our systems. All we will analyze, and all we can analyze, is the systems as they appear in our always limited knowledge of them — as they are portrayed in our present set of "information." Thus, a variable that would be revealed as being endogenous if we had complete information regarding the laws that govern its behavior might, using the information available at any given time, be judged to be exogenous. It is also quite possible that a variable, regarded to be exogenous today, would be recognized as being endogenous tomorrow, other information having been developed in the meantime. The classification below should therefore be interpreted as applying to our mental constructs of systems rather than to the "real" systems themselves; and it should be kept in mind that different mental constructs might become associated with the same underlying "reality" as time (and science) progresses.

Our classification of systems provides for the following

[6] We use the words "static" and "dynamic" here in the sense that Samuelson uses them.

categories: (a) mechanically closed systems, (b) stochastically closed systems, (c) semiclosed systems (mechanical and stochastical), (d) conditionally open systems, and (e) essentially open systems.

Mechanically closed system: This is a system whose space contains only a single nonzero-probable history. Its precise state at each point of time is therefore known. All variables of such a system are endogenous, and its laws, static and dynamic, are of the "absolute" type (that is, the probabilities they assign to events are either "zero" or "one"). Its behavior is not subject to any sort of influence emanating from variables outside the system — the information relating the variables of the system to each other constitutes, in effect, a set of simultaneous equations that have only a single possible solution.

Stochastically closed system: This is a system whose space consists of a set of histories all of whose individual probabilities are known. Its precise state at each point of time, therefore, also has a known probability distribution. The system is closed in the sense that its "internal" probabilities are fixed, that is, not affected by "outside" factors. As in the case of mechanically closed systems, all variables are endogenous.

Semiclosed system: A system can be called semiclosed if it contains endogenous variables. It would become closed if specific probability distributions were assigned to the exogenous variables. The semiclosure is mechanical or stochastical depending upon the nature of the resulting closure.

Conditionally open system: We shall call a system conditionally open if all of its constituent variables are exogenous. No aspect of its behavior is determined strictly from within the system (according to our present information); its connecting relationships are too weak or too few.

Essentially open system: We regard a conditionally open system as being, in addition, essentially open if we have conclusive evidence supporting the belief that no additional information will ever suffice to semiclose or close it.

D. ECONOMIC SYSTEMS

The methodological faults of which we have accused contemporary economics in Chapter 3 (and will continue in Chapters 5 and 6) can all be ascribed to the penchant of economists to treat the economic system and its various subsystems, mistakenly, as being in some fashion closed. A few extremists go as far as to deal with the economy, at least in its macro-aspects, as if it were mechanically closed. The majority of analysts, while not following the extremists, do commit the methodological sin of considering the economy, the firm, the consumer, or whatever entity they are studying at the moment, as being semiclosed. As a matter of fact, almost the entire apparatus of traditional economic theory (and even of modern statistical analysis) is founded upon the assumption of semiclosure. The various analysts may or may not actually believe that the system is semiclosed, but in their work they habitually proceed upon this hypothesis.

A terminological clarification is in order before we proceed further. Up until now we have often referred to something called the economic system, without specifying precisely what we were talking about. As might be expected there is little agreement among economists as to exactly what the term does denote — what it includes and what it does not include. The question is seldom even explicitly discussed; it is usually only implied in other contexts. The delineation of *the* economic system is, of course, inevitably an arbitrary one, but we can define *an* economic system as being any set whatever of "economic" variables, where "economic" variables are taken to be those customarily studied by people called economists. Thus the Marshallian "firm" is an economic system, as are the industry, the set of national-income variables, the purely competitive market, or any other set of economic variables.

We are in a position now to state the principal single point of this chapter: *Any economic system, aside from purely definitional variables, is always an essentially open system.*

This assertion is easier to make than to prove. We will only try to mention some considerations that make the point at least plausible.

In order to be *mechanically closed*, the system (we are now speaking of the set of variables existing in the world, not of their replica in our minds) must either be completely isolated from the rest of the universe or it must exist in a fixed environment. As approximations to the completely isolated system we may think of a well-running watch somehow suspended in intergalactic space, or of a planetary system. As for the systems existing in a fixed environment, they are more difficult to visualize. Environments other than empty space do not ordinarily remain fixed, and even "empty space" isn't quite empty of changing forces. The environment would have to be such as to never jolt or disturb the system in any way, so as to never cause a breakdown or a shift in the fixed relationships among the variables of the system, and so as to never cause a change in the validity conditions of any of the information relevant to the system. It does not require an extensive argument to support the view that an economic system — any economic system — is not mechanically closed.

In order to be *stochastically closed*, a system must be almost as insulated from the outside world, or embedded in as sheltered and unchanging an environment, as a mechanically closed system. The relationships among its variables must, as above, be completely immune from all shocks and distortions; and the statistical universe from which the "disturbances" or "errors" are drawn must be a constant one. Again it is difficult to visualize such a system — perhaps an atom with its electrons, protected from cyclotrons and from other atoms seeking valence bonds, comes closest to this ideal.

There is a tendency among some econometricians to build stochastically closed economic models. These models, of course, have a considerable mathematical elegance to them, but they are founded upon tacit assumptions about the environment of their variables that bear scant resemblance to reality. The validity of such models depends upon an unchanging sociological, political, cultural, physical, and biological context of economic activity. Such a constancy has never yet been known to obtain anywhere; and we certainly have no reason for supposing that the future will be any different in this respect. The "error terms" of the stochastical equations, it should be pointed out, account only for the pattern of disturbances that existed at the time the original data were assembled and that emanated from the environment of the system as it then was; they are no longer representative of reality after that environment has changed.

A system is *semiclosed* either (1) if some of the relationships among its variables are of the "universal law-of-nature" type, and are not subject to possible break-down, evolutionary change or any other type of distortion, and if these relations are strong enough to make at least one variable endogenous, or (2) if it is embedded in a peculiar type of partially varying and partially fixed environment, such that the values of the exogenous variables may change freely but that the validity conditions (or rather the realization of the validity conditions) of the relations among the variables of the system remain undisturbed. As before, these relations must be strong enough to make at least one variable endogenous.

As an approximation of the first kind of semiclosed system we may think of a chemical system, whose exogenous variables are temperature, pressure, and the like, and whose internal relationships are the laws of chemical reactions. Once the exogenous variables are specified, such variables as "type of end product" and "rate of reaction" become endogenous. The second kind of semiclosed system would be exemplified by a thermostat system (that was somehow protected from mechanical breakdown), or an automobile speedometer (that was similarly protected).

An economic system, to be semiclosed, would have to be set in a strange environment indeed. In the case of the "firm," for example, the ever continuing changes in tastes, in human relations, in fashions, in the weather, in politics, etc., that occur all around the firm, might well affect everyone else's behavior and thereby such exogenous variables of the given firm as "marginal revenue" and "marginal cost of labor," but they would not touch the patterns of behavior of the firm itself at all. For this to be true the firm would have to be completely insulated from the general social process, and its managers immune to all kinds of human consideration. In the case of a typical national-income system, as another example, the swirling social forces which always operate on human beings would have a great influence on men during office hours, when investment decisions are made, but no effect at all after five o'clock, when matters of consumption are considered. In the latter case, the pattern of response to income (or to a few other variables) is usually taken to be protected from distortion. Everything we know about psychology and sociology speaks against the very possibility of existence of such half-slave half-free contexts of economic activity.

Little needs to be said about the possibility of either kind of semiclosed economic system. The relations among economic variables, as is obvious, are not universal laws of nature, but always, no matter what variables are involved, depend upon specific and transitory historical, sociological, and political factors.

It is evident, then, that no economic system can be either mechanically closed, stochastically closed, or even semiclosed. And, moreover, not only are economic systems conditionally open — they are essentially open. The various considerations mentioned above can hardly ever fail to be true. The very concept of "economic system" inevitably involves an abstraction from a more full-blooded and higher-dimensional reality. No matter what the specific circumstances, and no matter what the state of our information, economic systems can never be as self-contained or as insulated from environmental forces as closure would require.

CHAPTER 5: CASE STUDIES

The following case studies are intended to supply concrete detail to our general contention that most of current economics is beset by often crippling methodological weaknesses, and that the ineffectiveness of economics is largely due to these weaknesses. In each case, the methodological errors primarily involved are pointed out; but the main concern is with the analysis of why, in view of these errors, the contribution is misleading or dangerous in attempts at the valid prediction of the future, that is, for the derivation of information [1] about the future. This is not an unreasonable limitation of scope. Prediction, whether of the autonomous course of events or of the consequences of our policies, is an indispensable prerequisite for effective action. Anything that is usable for valid prediction, consequently, is also usable for effective policy-formation; and anything useless for valid prediction is similarly useless for policy application to the real world.

It should also be mentioned that the survey falls very far short of being complete. Some prominent branches of economics (for example, labor economics and monetary economics) are slighted entirely, and others are represented here only fragmentarily. Fortunately, however, an encyclopedic survey of the entire field is quite unnecessary for our purpose. As long as we discuss typical examples of current endeavor in economics we are doing all that we need here — any effort beyond that would amount to little but an uninformative repetition of the same points over and over again.

[1] The reader should recall to mind at this point our definition of information as given in Chapter 4. Note that we regard a statement about the future to be a prediction if, and only if, it contains information. Any other type of statement about the future is, at best, a guess, and therefore useless or dangerous for the formulation of policy.

As the reader will note, attention is by no means confined to the work of poor or incompetent economists; as a matter of fact, we have deliberately chosen the work of some of the most brilliant and craftsmanlike of the practitioners of the discipline, whose accomplishments are deserving of respect and admiration. It is their work that is most worthy of attention and analysis. The assumption is that whatever criticism can be levied at their work will apply even more strongly to that of the more mediocre men in the field.

In a sense, the critique is unfair to the authors discussed. No attention is paid, for example, to the fact that many of them are themselves either partially or fully aware of the methodological weaknesses which are pointed out. They may have had to work under severe limitations of financial resources, availability of data and concepts; and, in many cases, they were doing as well as could reasonably be expected under the circumstances. Further, they may not have had prediction and policy-making in mind at all when they wrote what they did — sheer description is a worth-while goal in itself, and likewise is deliberate over-simplification for pedagogical purposes. Finally, it may be that the contribution discussed here is quite unrepresentative of the author's range of thought; and the stated criticisms may hence be inapplicable to that author's other efforts. The subsequent comments, therefore, should not be interpreted as in any way constituting a personal criticism of the authors discussed or a disparagement of their often substantial achievements.

A. EMPIRICAL STATISTICAL INVESTIGATIONS

Example A–1. G. H. Moore: *Statistical Indicators of Cyclical Revivals and Recessions* [2]

The National Bureau of Economic Research has long been the foremost data-collecting and data-interpreting agency in the field of business-cycle research. And this organization, under

[2] Occasional Paper 31 (New York: National Bureau of Economic Research, 1950).

the initial leadership of Wesley Mitchell, has probably done more to spread the gospel of empirical, inductive procedures in economics generally than any other single group or person. The basic idea is that the best way to arrive at useful propositions in economics is to proceed inductively from observations of reality, and not by way of the arm-chair speculative technique. Before we spin theories, we should know as precisely as possible what we are talking about.

Mr. Moore's paper has been chosen as one of our exhibits of empirical research because it is a good illustration of the National Bureau's approach. In it, Mr. Moore reports on one particular phase of the National Bureau's long continuing, cumulative study of business cycles — the process of evaluation, selection, and interpretation of "business indicators."

The project consisted mainly of an intensive analysis of the cyclical variation of 801 different economic time series. Mr. Moore's summary announcement of his results up to 1950 is as follows:

This report is preliminary. We have not applied as many objective criteria to the selection of indicators as we plan to, and further work on problems connected with the use and interpretation of indicators is in progress. Nevertheless, the investigation points to certain general conclusions, with which we may acquaint the reader at the outset . . .

1. Economic processes, as represented by monthly and quarterly time series, differ widely in the timing of their fluctuations during business cycles. While there is a strong tendency for many processes to expand and contract at about the same time, in every cycle the cyclical turning points of different series are rather widely dispersed. For example, of 400 series especially selected for the regularity of their behavior during business cycles seldom more than 80 per cent were undergoing cyclical expansion (or contraction) at any time between 1885 and 1940. Their peaks and troughs clustered around peaks and troughs in aggregate economic activity, but each cluster was spread over a year or two or three. Indeed, by the time the last few series in a cluster reached peaks, the first troughs in the next cluster had usually begun to appear . . .

Record of Timing of Selected Statistical Indicators at Business Cycle Turns

Selected Indicator	Reference period covered	Number of reference turns covered	Leads	Exact coincidence	Lags	Rough coincidence	Average lead (−) or lag (+), months
A. LEADING GROUP							
1 Business failures, liabilities, indus. & comm., Dun's	1879–1938[a]	14 peaks	11	1	1	2	−10.5
		16 troughs	14		1	1	− 7.5
2 Indus. common stock price index, Dow-Jones	1899–1938	11	8		2	6	− 6.0
		11	8	1	1	4	− 7.2
3 New orders, durable goods indus., value, Dept. of Commerce	1919–1938	25	21	1	2	9	− 6.9
		30	24	1	4	10	− 4.7
4 Residential building contracts, floor space, Dodge	1919–1938	5	4	1	1	1	− 6.2
		6	5			2	− 4.5
5 Comm. & indus. bldg. contracts, floor space, Dodge	1919–1938	5	4		1	2	− 5.2
		6	4	1	1	4	− 1.7
6 Average hours worked per week, mfg., Bur. Labor Statistics	1921–1938	4	3		1	1	− 3.8
		5	3	1	1	1	− 2.6
7 New incorporations, number, Dun's	1860–1938	20	12	1	4	8	− 2.5
		20	15	1	3	4	− 3.5
8 Wholesale price index, 28 basic commodities, Bur. Labor Statis.	1893–1937[a]	11	7		2	5	− 2.6
		11	8	1	1	5	− 3.2

a War cycle observations are omitted.

B. ROUGHLY COINCIDENT GROUP

Employment in nonagricultural establishments; Bureau of Labor Statistics
Unemployment; Department of Commerce
Corporate profits, quarterly; Department of Commerce
Bank debits outside New York City; Federal Reserve Board
Freight car loadings; Association American Railroads
Industrial production index; Federal Reserve Board
Gross national product, quarterly; Department of Commerce
Wholesale price index, excluding farm products and foods; Bureau of Labor Statistics

C. LAGGING GROUP

Personal income; Department of Commerce
Sales by retail stores; Department of Commerce
Consumer instalment debt; Federal Reserve Board
Bank rates on business loans, quarterly; Federal Reserve Board
Manufacturers' inventories, in current prices; Department of Commerce.

2. By the application of objective criteria it is possible to select series whose timing in successive business cycles has been relatively systematic, and which therefore may be of value as indicators of revivals and recessions. That is, one can identify a group of series whose turning points have typically preceded the cyclical turns in aggregate economic activity; another group whose turns have typically coincided (roughly) with the turns in aggregate economic activity; and still another whose turns have typically followed those in aggregate economic activity; in many cases the reasons for the differences in behavior of different series are apparent, though a thoroughgoing explanation may be lacking . . .

3. Series in all three timing groups (leaders, coinciders, and laggers), when interpreted in the light of their past behavior and economic significance, may prove useful in anticipating and identifying cyclical revivals and recessions. The evidence each type of series supplies serves to confirm or qualify that supplied by the others, and together they may be expected to provide helpful signs of an approaching recession or revival, and especially to facilitate prompt recognition of such a development once it occurs. . . [pp. 2–3].

By a rather complicated statistical process, the 801 series were evaluated on the basis of the regularity of their conformance to the aggregate cyclical pattern and the regularity of the timing of their turning points in relation to the aggregate cycle. At the end of a series of eliminations of nonregular series, Moore was left with a group of 21 series whose behavior was the most regular and dependable of all the series studied. It turned out that none of even these series was an absolutely dependable leader or lagger — they all suffered at least a few failures. In order to give the reader some further idea of the type of statistical thoroughness which characterizes the work of the National Bureau, Moore's tabulation of his final results [3] is reproduced on the preceding two pages (in an abbreviated form).

Moore is quite conservative in his discussion of the useful-

[3] *Statistical Indicators*, pp. 64–65. We have given near-full detail for only the first part of the table; further detail would not add to the point we are making. The table is intended only to indicate the procedures carried out by the National Bureau in their treatment of data and the type of result they are looking for.

ness of his results. He realizes that the data in the table cannot be used, in a mechanical way, to forecast future revivals and recessions, that a great deal of caution and judgment is required in the process. He quotes from a previous National Bureau publication [4] on the same general subject:

> Another difficulty is that no sequence of average leads of time series in past cyclical revivals can tell what the exact sequence will be at the next revival . . . The variations are at times irregular; at others they reflect secular or structural changes. . . Such changes in cyclical timing are full of instruction to the student of business cycles. They are important also to the man of affairs; he must be alert to changes in the making, eschew simple formulas, test his judgments by study of numerous statistical series, and stand ready to revise his list of indicators as the economic environment changes.[5]

Moore believes that these comments still hold fully true, even though the present study is based on more extensive data.

> Nevertheless, there is some ground for confidence that objective use of these methods will at least reduce the usual lag in recognizing revivals or recessions *that have already begun.* If, after an expansion in a group of roughly coincident series, several begin to decline, careful study of the recent behavior of a group of leading series may yield convincing evidence that the decline is or is not cyclical, and that a recession is or is not under way. True, this is forecasting of a sort. But it is forecasting with a highly important element of confirmation, which works in two directions. The behavior of the roughly coincident series confirms or fails to confirm that of the leading series, and vice versa. . . In any case, if errors are to be minimized, painstaking study of the current and past behavior of the individual series, intelligent analysis of the factors that underlie their interrelationships, and judgment of the changing political and economic environment, will be required [pp. 76–77].

In our comments on this study, let us focus attention on the 21 listed indicators and their significance. We would certainly agree with Mr. Moore that the application of these indicators to economic forecasting requires the consideration of a great

---

[4] Wesley C. Mitchell and Arthur F. Burns, *Statistical Indicators of Cyclical Revivals*, Bulletin 69 (May 1938).

[5] Occasional Paper 31, National Bureau of Economic Research, pp. 75–76.

number of other factors. As a matter of fact, we would put it even more strongly than that: these results are close to useless for prediction unless the relationship of the indicated phenomena to other environmental variables is quite clearly indicated. It is not extraordinarily helpful to admonish the economist to use his judgment — he should be given a much more definite guide than that. And this is not a counsel of perfection; it embodies only the minimum requirements for prediction as we have defined it.

Our main point is, not unexpectedly, that Moore's final results are an observation, nothing more. We are told what happened in the time interval covered by the data, nothing more. We have no right to assume that the indicated lead-lag relationships hold for any other time period, future or past. The difficulty arises mainly from the fact that the study gives us no information about the validity conditions (institutional, sociological, technological, etc.) of the indicated relationships. Not knowing upon what other variables the relationships depend, and how they depend upon them, we have no criterion whatever by which to gauge their applicability to various other time periods. In other words, in order to constitute a dynamic law, the table requires completion. As a very minimum, the conditions of validity of a given lead or lag relation must be stated; it would be better, of course, to have knowledge of a law which gives information about the lead-lag relationship under all possible constellations of the environmental variables. If we then had a further law governing the movement of the system with respect to these environmental variables, we could really arrive at powerful predictions.

The National Bureau attempted to overcome weaknesses like the ones we have specified by designing the criteria of selection of statistical indicators with that purpose in mind. Of the criteria upon which they finally settled, the following three are the most relevant. (They are given in the form of a description of an ideal indicator.)

1. It would cover half a century or longer, thus showing its relation to business cycles under a variety of conditions.

2. It would lead the month around which cyclical revival centers by an invariable interval — say three months, or better, six months. . .

3. It would be so related to general business activity as to establish as much confidence as the nature of such things allows that its future behavior in regard to business cycles will be like its past behavior.[6]

With respect to the first criterion we can only repeat: it does not matter what or how long the past record of the proposed indicator is; we can apply it to the prediction of the future only if we can know that the validity conditions will obtain in the future. The fact that a series has performed dependably "under a variety of conditions" does not help us if we do not know what these conditions were and how they compare to the possible future conditions. The last of the above criteria is little more than another admonition to use our judgment — and that cannot substitute for the type of knowledge required for prediction. Even an ideal indicator, as defined by the National Bureau, would not be a dependable constituent of a predictive model. The attempt to use it for prediction would constitute what we have previously called an artificial generalization.

Many people tend to take the view that criticisms like the above are "academic," that some of the leading series have in the past been right about 80 per cent of the time, that 80 per cent is a pretty good batting average, and that therefore it is a "good bet" to continue to rely on these series in the future. There is no point, they say, to strive for perfection — the important thing is to be right more often than wrong. On the surface of it this argument sounds quite persuasive, but, nevertheless, our comment must still be the same as before: we have no way of knowing without the suggested "completion" of the data that the batting average will continue to be as high in the future as it has been in the past. A shift in external circumstances may well produce a drastic shift in the probability of success of a given indicator.

[6] National Bureau of Economic Research, Bulletin 31, p. 20.

The main source of weakness in the results of Mr. Moore's study probably stems from the very approach to reality employed by the National Bureau. One cannot get an explanation of events from a study of external manifestations alone — and the preoccupation of the Bureau with time-series analysis limits its attention to only external, superficial manifestations of the real stream of events. To use a loose analogy, it is somewhat like trying to understand a football game by studying the geographical path of the ball during the course of the game; or, to use a more famous analogy, like studying the mechanism of a clock by analyzing the record of its tickings. Such an approach leaves us blind to the real determining variables — the "causes" — and therefore cannot lead to the kind of knowledge which is most useful in prediction.

An epistemologist might retort at this point that, generally, all of our information is of "external" characteristics, that the "inner nature" of all phenomena is inaccessible to us, and that we must, consequently, always be satisfied with the knowledge of mere "properties" of the real objects. Our rejoinder to this objection would be that the indicated limitation upon our knowledge exists only at what we might call an ultimate limit of observation. In nuclear physics, for example, we have no choice but to study the clock by its ticks; but in horology we can do much better than that. Economics is clearly more like horology than like nuclear physics. Undeniably, however, the results of Moore's study are, even in their present form, an extremely valuable contribution to economics. By providing us with a great deal of new information about reality, they serve as all-important clues in the search for static and dynamic laws. Even though they themselves cannot play a role, in their present "incomplete" form, in the derivation of reliable predictions, they make a large contribution in the preliminary "creative" process.

Example A–2. *The Business Investment Programs study*

Ever since the strategic role of business investment in the development of the business cycle has come to be appreciated, economic analysts have been trying to obtain forecasts of the future volume of that investment. In order to satisfy this demand, the Office of Business Economics of the Department of Commerce and the Securities and Exchange Commission have, in recent years, conducted a joint annual survey of the investment programs of American business firms for the next year.

The following quotations are from a typical report on such an annual survey, the report for 1950.[7] They constitute a good brief glimpse of the results obtained from and the procedure employed in the survey.

American business, exclusive of agriculture, plans another year of large capital expansion, although the aggregate investment will be less than the high figures of the previous two years. Expenditures for the construction of new plant and the purchase of new equipment are scheduled at $16.1 billion during 1950. This is $2 billion, or 11 percent less than in 1949. . .

These results are based on reports submitted between mid-January and mid-March in the annual survey of plant and equipment expenditures and sales conducted jointly by the Office of Business Economics and the Securities and Exchange Commission. The data presented in this article are estimates for all nonagricultural business based on a sample composed of most corporations registered with the Securities and Exchange Commission and a large number of unregistered manufacturing companies, unincorporated as well as corporate, reporting to the Office of Business Economics. [p. 6]

The writers believe that there is good reason for having high confidence in the forecast so obtained, especially when one possibly disturbing factor is taken into account:

In evaluating the 1950 investment intentions of business, attention should be drawn to the degree of accuracy with which businessmen have anticipated their actual outlays in the past. In 1949, aggregate

[7] Lawrence Bridge and Bernard Beckler, "Capital Investment Programs and Sales Expectations in 1950," *Survey of Current Business* (April 1950), pp. 6–10.

expectations of business were almost fully realized as nonagricultural business firms spent $18.1 billion, within 1 per cent of the amount that they had anticipated spending at the beginning of the year. In corresponding surveys covering 1947 and 1948, planned outlays were 14 per cent below those realized in the former year and 3 per cent below those realized in the latter year.

The experience in these annual surveys augmented by the more numerous quarterly surveys suggests that the degree of accuracy in businessmen's projections of their dollar expenditures on plant and equipment is closely related to movements in capital goods costs. In 1947, when businessmen underestimated their outlays by 14 per cent, the price rise for capital goods during that year was of the same order of magnitude. In 1948, with a smaller increase in capital goods' costs and a greater availability of supplies, businessmen were able to forecast their expenditures with a greater degree of reliability. [p. 8]

We might comment, in passing, that the "reliability" of the forecast was no greater in 1948 than in 1947; it was just more accurate. This greater accuracy is to be attributed to luck, and not to any procedural superiority. Before the event both forecasts were equally dependable (or, better, undependable); it just turned out that, by good fortune, there was less "disturbance" in 1948 than in 1947.

Despite their optimism, the authors are quite conscious of the shakiness of their forecast:

Though movements in prices are not likely to affect perceptibly the investment plans of business this year, there are two factors which may cause actual expenditures to diverge from expectations. First, changes in economic conditions do have some effect on investment plans . . . Second, . . . there is probably some understatement . . . for any period well in the future, since businessmen generally tend to be conservative in their budgets or stated plans and are less likely to report their more tentative plans over the longer term. [p. 8]

As is known now, the actual investment volume in 1950 diverged substantially from the planned volume. There were, indeed, substantial changes in economic conditions which forced a considerable modification of existing plans — the Korean affair stimulated a much higher volume of capital expenditures than was previously expected. This experience constitutes a very good revelation of the basic weakness of this type of forecast in general. It depends upon too many assumptions of constancy, where there is no justification (other than the heuristic one) for adopting these assumptions. The survey findings are observations of current mental states of businessmen, and have no dependable relevance to the future. People do change their minds. Future behavior is not limited or constrained to any significant extent by current opinions; we cannot therefore exclude any possibilities of future behavior on the strength of information about current opinions.

The office of Business Economics has sponsored a study [8] of the performance of these forecasts and of the reasons for discrepancies between planned and actual investment expenditure. The authors of this study summarize their findings as follows:

A special questionnaire sent to a sample of companies with large percentage differences between actual and anticipated expenditures in 1949 indicates that for these firms changes in the sales and in the earnings outlook accounted for nearly half of the cases where actual expenditures in 1949 were lower than those anticipated. . .

The most significant factors tending to increase planned expenditures were changes in the plant and equipment supply situation, changes in plant and equipment costs, competitive conditions, new products, and the failure to report small capital outlays and items whose acquisition was regarded as uncertain [pp. 11–12].

We cite these results here because they illustrate, again, why investment plans are no dependable guide to actual future investment. It would seem that, if we know what the principal "deflectors" are, we could make adjustments to the declared plans of the business firms and thereby obtain better investment forecasts. But, unfortunately, adjustments based upon studies of this sort do not lead to dependable forecasts. The reason: the factors which "caused" a change in plans in one year (or a series of years) need not be the factors which will

[8] Irwin Friend and Jean Bronfenbrenner, "Business Investment Programs and their Realization," *Survey of Current Business* (December 1950).

cause changes in the next year. Human behavior of the relevant type is responsive to whatever factors happen to appear in a given year, whether they are new or not. The results of 1950 bear this out; the factors which were, according to the study, important in 1949 (or the previously mentioned factors in 1947) did not explain the changes of plans in 1950, or in any of the subsequent years. Clearly, the use of the investment forecasts in subsequent economic analyses constitutes what we have called artificial generalization and perhaps also artificial isolation.

Example A–3. *The macro-theory of demand*

In contrast to the micro-theory, which is concerned with the details of the disposition of income, the macro-theory of demand only tries to explain the aggregate expenditure on consumption by the entire group of consumers.[9] Because of its less ambitious scope, the macro-theory is not beset with quite as many pitfalls as the micro-theory,[10] but it still manages to include most of them.

The most famous of the consumption functions is that of Keynes. It is a very simple one; it expresses consumption as a function of current national income: $C = f(Y)$. Other writers who have used this function have often modified it somewhat; Robertson, for example, made consumption a function of income of the preceding period, and others used the disposable income rather than the national income. Some criticisms apply, however, to all forms of this function, and it is with these that we shall be concerned.

These consumption functions clearly are not laws. Obviously they do not hold true under all possible conditions; and, even if there really exist some conditions under which they do hold, these are not only unspecified in the formulation of the function but are never even hinted at. Therefore, it follows that the

---

[9] Often, also, it tries to account for the aggregate expenditure on the major groupings of commodities.

[10] See Example B–1 below.

function cannot be used in predictive models without committing an artificial generalization.

Several economists have tried, in various ways, to improve the consumption function by including additional consumption-determining variables. They have usually turned to empirical data for suggestions on what the relevant variables are. Two of the outstanding attempts in this direction, those of Modigliani [11] and Duesenberry,[12] have come to the same general conclusion: that the greatest preceding disposable income has an important effect on current consumption expenditure. Professor Duesenberry's version of this thesis, in brief, is as follows:

> We have three important sets of facts about the relations between saving and income: (1) the data on aggregate savings and income in the period 1869–1929 collected by Kuznets; (2) the budget studies of 1935–36 and 1941–42; (3) the yearly data on aggregate savings and income for the period since 1929 published by the Department of Commerce. The three sets of data are inconsistent if the two hypotheses under consideration [mentioned below] are accepted. The Kuznets data do not show any tendency for the proportion of income saved to rise with income. The budget study data show that the savings ratio increases with income. The Commerce data also indicate that over the trade cycle the savings ratio varies with income, but the numerical results are not equivalent to those of the budget studies [pp. 1–2].

The two hypotheses to which he refers are those which underlie most of aggregate-demand theory: "(1) that every individual's consumption behavior is independent of that of every other individual, and (2) that consumption relations are reversible in time."

By an ingenious and highly competent analysis, and by the use of additional data, Duesenberry then shows (a) that these assumptions are unrealistic, and (b) that upon the substitution of more plausible assumptions the apparent inconsistency in

[11] "Fluctuations in the Saving-Income Ratio: A Problem in Economic Forecasting," *Studies in Income and Wealth* (New York: National Bureau of Economic Research, 1949), XI, 271–438.

[12] *Income, Saving, and the Theory of Consumer Behavior* (Cambridge: Harvard University Press, 1949).

the empirical data can be accounted for. His principal points are that consumption behavior is largely determined by a person's social environment, that a very strong drive toward consumption arises from the general desire to maintain one's social position, and that a person's *relative* position in the income distribution governs the status of consumption he wishes to maintain. In the long run, therefore, the aggregate savings ratio is independent of the absolute level of aggregate income, and "Cet. par. the propensity to save of an individual can be regarded as a rising function of his percentile position in the income distribution. The parameters of that function will change with changes in the shape of the income distribution [p. 45]." The cyclical movement of aggregate consumption is also influenced by the social-position motive — people usually try to defend that standard of living which corresponds to their highest preceding level of income.

If we supplant the previously cited assumptions of most demand theory with the more realistic ones that (1) an individual's consumption depends upon other people's consumption, and that (2) previous experience influences current consumption (denial of reversibility of consumption relations), we obtain a consumption function which includes the highest preceding disposable income as a determining variable. This is Duesenberry's conclusion:

> If in periods of steadily rising income the savings ratio is constant while in depressions the ratio depends on current income and previous peak income, we can explain saving with the relation $S_t/Y_t = 0.25Y_t/Y_0 - 0.196$, where S_t and Y_t are current savings and disposable income respectively and Y_0 is highest previous disposable income [p. 4].

Our first comment is the usual one: Duesenberry's savings function is not a law. Its continued validity is not independent of other events in the world, but is conditional upon some kind of structural constancy in the system. We say this unhesitatingly, despite the fact that, with this function, the computed values of savings and consumption have a high correlation to the actual values in the period covered, and that the function yielded a number of good forecasts. These data can mean only that some relation similar to that given by Duesenberry existed in the period covered by the data; they cannot assert anything about previous or subsequent time periods. Again, we are not even told under what circumstances we can expect this function to hold, except for the rather unhelpful implication that the function held for the conditions that prevailed during the base period, whatever they were.[13] Not knowing what the relevant conditions are, we cannot try to study their future movement, and we cannot attempt to discover what changes in the function would be induced by these movements. Duesenberry's function cannot be used in predictive models.

Duesenberry is by no means unaware of the need for finding a function which is as invariant as possible with respect to changes in other variables. As a matter of fact he explicitly discusses this problem (pages 71–76), and he appears to be quite conscious of the sources of weakness of his savings function. He believes, however, that if we can find relations which are invariant with respect to all variables except the psychological and institutional ones which govern the form of the consumption-income relations of individual families, we can make "satisfactory" predictions with their aid. This is, he says, because these basic relations tend to be fairly stable. All aggregate relations, therefore, which can be deduced from household relations have a high order of invariance. (He calls such relations "fundamental aggregate relations.")

In comment, we can only repeat what we have said before. Duesenberry is undoubtedly right in saying that his fundamental aggregate relations are dependent upon socio-psycho-institutional constancies. But he is overly optimistic in his attitude toward these constancies. Without knowing exactly what the variables are, and then knowing by what dynamic laws their

---

[13] A few of these conditions are, however, suggested. Duesenberry found that, in the period covered, the aggregate savings ratio was insensitive to change in some theoretically important variables, such as interest rates, expectations, and preference parameters.

movement is governed, we have no right to make any assertion about them. Laws and only laws are trustworthy as bases for predictions.

It is not unlikely at all that the entire attempt to discover dependable aggregate demand functions is, from the point of view of prediction, somewhat misguided. Consumption behavior is a stupendously complex phenomenon; and any manageable consumption function would therefore inevitably be characterized by both artificial isolation and artificial simplification. The very process of arriving at such functions renders them ineffectual. An aggregate economic function induced from empirical data on aggregate behavior can tell us, at best, only approximately what happened in the time period covered. It cannot say why things happened as they did, and it certainly cannot claim to specify how things must necessarily happen in the future. Empirically derived aggregate behavior functions are observations, not general laws, and they do not in any way narrow down the range of possibilities for the future.

In one respect, Duesenberry points the way toward progress in this field. He used the empirical findings on the behavior of "economic" variables not only for the derivation of equations, but also as a source of hypotheses on the socio-psychological determinants of economic behavior. This is perhaps the way in which empirical statistical research can become most useful for prediction. Even though we cannot derive laws from these data, we can get clues on where to look for laws. Once the statistical analysis has authorized us to reject the null hypothesis on the interrelationships among a group of variables, we can then start our search for the relevant laws.

Example A-4. *Input-output models*

One of the most notable of the recent developments in economic theory was the invention of input-output models by Wassily Leontief. These models have since shown themselves to be a powerful tool of analysis for a variety of purposes, and are now the object of much theoretical attention and the guide for a great deal of empirical research. And there is also a very good chance that they will prove to be valuable constituents of predictive models.

Input-output models, or, more generally, Leontief matrices, are a technique for investigating the individual and joint variations of certain sets of interdependent variables. The relevant theory was initially expounded by Leontief in a series of books and articles.[14] The most important points in connection with Leontief matrices are well summarized by Leontief himself:

A large statistical "input-output" table describing the qualitative inter-relationships between all the various branches of production, transportation, distribution, and consumption for one particular year constituted the factual basis of subsequent analytical procedures. The entries in this table are arranged in a checkerboard fashion, each row and the corresponding column of figures bearing the name of a separate industry — Grain Farming, Steel Works and Rolling Mills, Railroads, and so on. The entries along any one row show the distribution of the total output of the particular industry among all the other branches of the national economy. Thus the figures entered in the "Steel Works and Rolling Mills" row represent the amounts of the product of this industry directly absorbed by, say, Grain Farming, by the Railroads, by the Automobile Industry, etc.

The last entry in each row shows the total output of the industry (in this particular example this would be the total output of Steel Works and Rolling Mills), i.e., it represents the sum total of all the other entries along the same row. Government, Households, and Foreign Countries are treated as separate industries, that is, as separate branches of the economy. If read by columns the same figures show the quantities of the various kinds of inputs absorbed by each individual industry. The Steel Works and Rolling Mills column shows the amount of coal obtained by this industry from Coal Mining, the amount of Transportation received from Railroads, and so on down the column to the amount of labor (labor hours) obtained from the Households, which are also treated as a separate "Industry."

Detailed input-output tables describing the inter-industrial rela-

[14] Notably in: "Output, Employment, Consumption, and Investment," *Quarterly Journal of Economics*, LVIII (1943–44), pp. 290–313; "Exports, Imports, Domestic Output, and Employment," *ibid.*, LX (1945–46), pp. 171–191; "Wages, Profits and Prices," *ibid.*, LXI (1946–47), pp. 26–39.

tionships within the industries have been constructed for the years 1919, 1929, and 1939, the latter compiled by a special Inter-industrial Relationships Unit in the Bureau of Labor Statistics.

The amounts of the products of each one of the other sections of the economy absorbed by any particular industry (i.e., the magnitudes of the entries in one particular column of the input-output table) depend, first, upon the total level of its own output and, second, upon the quantity of each kind of input absorbed per unit of that output. The subsequent theoretical analysis is based on the fundamental assumption that the latter relationships are technologically determined and thus can be treated as structural constants. Given the actual magnitudes of these "technical coefficients," a system of linear equations can be set up describing the interdependence between the outputs of all the separate branches of the national economy. This system makes it possible to compute, for example, the direct and indirect dependence of the output (and the corresponding labor requirements) of any one industry upon the final (i.e., consumer or investment) demand for the product of any other industry.

The same set of technical input-coefficients determines also the price or rather the price-wage-profits structure of the national economy. It can be described in terms of a system of simultaneous value-equations — one for each industry. The price of any one kind of output equals its unit costs of production augmented by the unit profits. The *unit* costs are nothing but the sum total of the technical input coefficients of the particular industry, each multiplied by the price of the respective cost factor. Solved for the price of any one commodity, this system of equations makes it possible, for example, to determine the direct and indirect dependence of one particular price on the wage and profit rates prevailing in all the different branches of the economy.

The apparent difficulty of handling very large numbers of simultaneous equations — until recently the most widely cited obstacle to construction of (relatively) non-aggregative empirical general equilibrium systems — has been easily overcome through the use of modern large-scale computing machinery.

In treating technical input coefficients as independent structural parameters, this approach assumes them to be independent of the prices of the respective cost factors and thus eliminates from this particular general equilibrium model the "substitution effect" of the marginal productivity theory. This can be considered to be its fundamental weakness.[15]

The assumption of technical coefficients which are independent of prices is not the only such weakness of the model. It also assumes, as is well recognized, the absence of technological changes, and the absence of "interferences" with production (factors which cause, for a given input, a lower than customary output). Each of these assumptions adds a damaging element of artificial isolation to the model.

But let us ignore these points in order to come to what are for our purpose the most important comments. The model provides an excellent technique for the integration of observed facts and, as such, constitutes a really "grand" observation. But, as was true in the case of the consumption function, it is no more than an observation — it is definitely neither a static nor a dynamic law. It simply presents a given body of information about a particular year without giving any hint at all as to the validity conditions of the indicated relationships (other than that they held in the indicated year under the state of technology and physical plant then prevailing, whatever these may have been). Not knowing what the validity conditions — all of them — are, we cannot tell when changes in these conditions necessitate a change in the model. If the technical, institutional, physical and other relevant conditions were fully stated, and if we ignore the unrealistic assumptions mentioned above, then the matrices would be full-fledged laws, and be ready for use in predictive models.

In order to maximize the usefulness of input-output analysis, we should, ideally, carry through the following rather elaborate procedure. First we should derive, from engineering data, a matrix for each of the possible sets of conditions, not only for the set which happens to obtain at present. Then we should search hard for dynamic laws governing the movement of the system with respect to these conditions. We would then have a

[15] "Econometrics," *A Survey of Contemporary Economics* (Philadelphia: Blakiston, 1949), pp. 407–409. (Reprinted by permission of Richard D. Irwin, Inc., copyright holder.)

combination of a set of static laws with a number of dynamic laws, and would thus be able to make some very considerable headway in predicting the future.

There seems to be no insurmountable difficulties either in the reformulation of the matrices to conform to our requirements or in the "generalization" program. We would be dealing with fairly clear-cut physical limitations and with socio-psychological laws of behavior, not with potentially ephemeral aggregate behavior equations. It is this fact which contains the greatest promise for a successful use of Leontief matrices in predictive models.

B. MICRO-MODELS

A great proportion of modern economic analysis is concerned with the behavior of the various parts and segments of the economic system. The hope seems to be that an adequate understanding of the principles of economic behavior of individual persons, of individual firms, or of industries will ultimately permit a synthesis and thereby an understanding of the behavior of the system as a whole.

Economists have made much progress in this cellular analysis of economic activity — perhaps more than in any other branch of economics. It is quite probable that the ultimate synthesis will eventually be developed. It is also true, however, that the various micro-models which have been constructed so far are not of the kind that is suitable for use in reliable prediction. As we shall see, they all suffer from rather severe cases of artificial mechanization.

Example B–1. *The micro-theory of demand*

Demand theory usually pictures the behavior of an individual consumer as being determined by three major factors: the structure of his tastes as represented by his "preference map," the structure of prices, and his income. The individual is regarded as choosing the most "desirable" point on the preference map which is attainable to him with his present income — the point of tangency between an indifference surface and the iso-cost surface which represents his income. The more sophisti-cated versions of demand theory often make allowance for such other demand-determining factors as expectations of future prices and incomes, asset holdings, etc., but the basic structure of the theory remains unchanged. Usually, also, cash is included as a dimension in the construction of the preference map in order to bring saving desires into the scheme of analysis.

There has been, and is, a good deal of controversy as to whether preference maps can be drawn with a cardinal measure of utility or whether we have to be satisfied with an ordinal measure, and as to whether preference orders are internally con-sistent. Since the present point would be the same in any case, however, we may simply assume the existence of well-ordered, self-consistent preference scales.

The concept of a preference map is a fine example of a con-struct which plays a large role in economic theory and which nevertheless is, in its present usual form, entirely useless for purposes of prediction. Suppose, for illustration, that we have somehow ascertained the precise form of the preference map of a given individual at a particular instant of time. There is no way in which we can use this information for predicting the future consumption behavior of this individual. We never have a right to assume, as is so often done, that the map will continue unchanged over time, and that we therefore can use it, for ex-ample, to deduce how the consumer will react to price changes. Indeed, it very likely is impossible that this constancy should ever occur. This fact is sometimes expressed by saying that movements along the preference map are not reversible in time. A change in the price structure is seen as inducing a movement along the map, and this shift to a new pattern of consumption will so alter the shape of the map that, if prices should return to their former level, the consumer will not return to his original pattern of consumption. We have no quarrel with this proposi-tion as far as it goes, but we do say that it depicts very inade-quately the analytical weaknesses of this construct.

Preference maps change not only in response to price-induced alterations in actual consumption; they change with any alterations either in the external environment of the consumer or in his internal state. And these alterations go on continually — the world never stands still. The preference maps, therefore, also undergo continual changes; and to assume the contrary is to fly in the face of most of the well-established principles of psychology and sociology.

The attempt to use them for predictive purposes unavoidably involves an artificial fixation. But it is quite possible, in principle at least, so to enlarge this construct that it does become a useful aid in prediction. If we regard a given preference map not as an enduring structure of some sort, but instead as an observation, at a particular instant, of a variable, our attention is directed immediately to the constraints on the movement of this variable. We should then make a study of the dynamic laws of habit and attitude formation and change, and apply these laws to this specific purpose. There is little doubt that such laws actually exist — physiology and psychology have uncovered many dynamic constraints upon the "freedom" of human behavior. If we then incorporate these results into our conceptual model of the consumer, we have something that qualifies under our definition of law, and which therefore can be included in the bases of predictions. It is a little difficult to say just what the resulting theory of the consumer would look like without actually working it out, but it is clear that it would be considerably different from what it is now.

Whether or not dynamic laws of preference change can be discovered which are of sufficient strength to yield useful predictions is an empirical question and cannot be decided here. Our guess is that it would depend on our definitions of commodities. We should have considerably more success if we define commodities very broadly, like "clothing," "housing," or "amusement," than if we use very narrow classifications, like "blue rayon tropical suits" or "balcony seats for 'Gone with the Wind'." Our mores decree very uncompromisingly that we wear a suit during business hours, but they do not specify exactly what kind of suit. Obviously, the attitude toward suits in general is constrained by more powerful dynamic laws than the attitude toward particular styles or designs.

Let us look next at a construct which is derived from preference maps, the demand function (or demand curve) of an individual. In its customary form it is written: $d_i = \phi (p_1, p_2, \ldots, p_i, \ldots, I)$, where d_i is the quantity purchased of commodity i, p_i is the price of commodity i, and I is the individual's income. Being derived from preference maps, the demand function is, of course, afflicted with all the infirmities of these maps. Accordingly, the demand function, if regarded as a function, is a psychological monstrosity. It cannot represent any possible pattern of human behavior; and consequently it cannot serve in predictive models. We have said that this is true if the demand function is treated as a true function — if it is intended to show how the movement of the dependent variable is influenced by those of the independent variables. This view involves the counterfactual assumption of constancy in the preference map, and is therefore inapplicable to reality. If, on the other hand, we interpret the demand function only as an instantaneous picture, then it might, if reënforced by appropriate dynamic laws, be put to use. Unfortunately, economic theory almost invariably operates with demand functions in the counterfactual manner.

Many theorists have decided to treat the demand function in a somewhat different way. They by-pass the preference map entirely; and instead of using the preference map as a co-determinant of demand they go back to the variables which presumably govern the shape of that map.[16] Georgescu-Roegen,[17] for example, suggests that we consider, besides the current prices of the various commodities, their past prices. His point is that past prices influenced past consumption behavior, and that past experiences determine the present attitude toward

[16] Their reason for this approach does not concern us here; it is usually a desire to confine their attention to "observable" variables.

[17] "The Theory of Choice and the Constancy of Economic Laws," *Quarterly Journal of Economics*, LXIV (1950), pp. 125–138.

goods. Duesenberry [18] points out that we need to consider past incomes as well as present incomes because current consumption habits have been formed in the past and are therefore the result of the previous standard of living. He also shows that we must pay attention to the consumer's relative position with respect to the distribution of income. Other writers recommend the inclusion of other variables in the demand function, such as the rate of interest, expectations of future prices and future incomes, present and past advertising expenditures, current stocks of goods, cash holdings, etc.

These enlarged demand functions undoubtedly are improvements over the primitive kind which depends upon the constancy of a preference map. They make allowance for many of the forces which determine preferences, and thereby they have something to say about the changes in these preferences. Yet, it is very doubtful that this type of generalization of the theory of demand will lead to dependable laws of economic behavior. Consider, for example, a demand function which includes all of the above-mentioned determinants of demand as independent variables. This function still depends on an assumption, and, moreover, an assumption which is very unlikely ever to become realistic. The assumption here is that the indicated functional relationship will remain invariant over time; and, as before, we have no factual justification for believing so. This demand function is therefore definitely not a law, and to consider it to be so is to commit an artificial semiclosure.

The development of the theory of demand illustrates a point which, if it were not so familiar, would be quite remarkable. Let us take another look at the list of variables which have been proposed for inclusion in the demand function. Notice that all of them represent so-called "economic" magnitudes. And this is in the face of the clearest sort of evidence that "noneconomic" variables like weather, geographical residence, cultural attainment, religion, interpersonal associations, or the before-mentioned physical stimulation, exercise a very considerable influence indeed on the disposition of income. Why then this utter

[18] In *Income, Saving, and the Theory of Consumer Behavior.*

blindness toward such important factors when, on the other side, so much attention and analysis is lavished upon the "economic" ones? Perhaps it is due to a subconscious aversion toward non-numerical variables. Perhaps it is due to a peculiar kind of vicious circle: the theorists build their concepts around the variables about which there are data available, and empirical researchers, in turn, gather information only about the variables which have been suggested to them by the theorists. Or perhaps it is an "internalization" of the compartmentalization of science so complete that the very apperception of reality has been affected. In any case, these gaps serve to render the demand functions highly conditional and therefore undependable for purposes of prediction.

The most promising modification of the theory of demand still seems to be the one mentioned before — the search for dynamic laws of attitude and behavior change and the incorporation of these laws into the system of analysis. They should be supplemented, of course, by static laws of the instant-by-instant determination of human behavior.

We have already said, by implication, most of what need be said about market-demand functions. They are weak because they are derived from weak bases. We might mention yet another point in this connection. Duesenberry has shown very well [19] that the derivation of market-demand functions by the summation of individual-demand functions involves the assumption that the actions of different consumers are independent of each other, and that this assumption is clearly counterfactual.

Market-demand functions, like the others we have discussed here, are examples of a very common type of concept in economics, one that we might call *"ceteris paribus* constructions." They involve the assumption that it is possible to imagine some variables to change while all others remain constant. This is a very tricky assumption to work with. The world is a highly interconnected sort of thing, and it may well be that the seemingly independent variables are in some indirect way connected

---

[19] In *Income, Saving, and the Theory of Consumer Behavior.*

with each other. The assumption therefore invariably introduces an element of artificial isolation.

Example B–2. *The theory of the firm*

We shall now inspect a typical version of the theory of the firm. This theory is important for our purpose primarily because it constitutes a good example of economic theory of the purely deductive variety. We consider here a fairly simple, unrealistic, and static variant of the theory; but our comments will apply as well, though in somewhat lesser degree, to the more elaborate and dynamic theories.

The theory attempts to establish a number of laws which link the activity of a firm to certain conditions which are "data" for that firm.

The firm is viewed as producing p commodities, and using q input factors in the process. The "data" which govern the productive activity of the firm are:

(1) The demand curves for the p commodities (the competitiveness of the various commodity markets is reflected in the shape of the respective demand curves).

(2) The supply curves of the q factors of production (the competitiveness also being indicated by the shape of the curve).

(3) The production function, representing the state of technology and the relevant social and institutional constraints.

(4) The static profit-maximizing motive.

We are interested in the following actions of the firm (and these, and the necessary incidentals, are the only actions open to that firm):

(a) The quantities of each of the commodities it produces.

(b) The price (or prices) it receives.

(c) The amounts of each input factor bought.

(d) The price (or prices) paid for them.

By a process of pure deduction the theory discovers how (a) to (d) are determined by (1) to (4). It locates the "equilibrium points," investigates the stability of these equilibriums, and, in general, seeks to derive as many theorems as possible from the stated assumptions.

Much ink has already been mobilized to prove that the theory of the firm is much too limited to depict what actually occurs in the world. The theory does not take cognizance of most of the action-determining variables; it does not account for many of the different areas of action open to the firm; and it is built upon an entirely nonhuman concept of the motivation of behavior. It is too far removed from reality to serve in attempts at predicting reality. This is also true for the more sophisticated theories, which may take into consideration such additional factors as elasticities of expectation, selling behavior, modes of response to competitors' actions, or the firm's asset position. These constructions are all artificially mechanized and artificially isolated from reality, and, in view of the basic concept underlying them, unavoidably so. All of the theories which have come to the writer's attention are constructed in such a way that the "data" *determine a unique equilibrium position*; and this sort of theoretical construction is basically and fundamentally unlike the structure of open systems in reality.

Let us now for the sake of our further discussion forget the above objections and grant the empirical validity of the theory. Our question now is: Does the theory of the firm furnish us with *laws* for the purpose of prediction? The two relevant criteria for a law are: (1) invariance, or autonomy, with respect to all other variables, and (2) modification of possibilities. With respect to the first criterion, the theory easily qualifies. If the theorems (for example, the margin-equalization condition) are really deductive consequences of the stated assumptions, totally free of any surreptitious assumptions or errors of logic, then, of course, whenever the stated assumptions are "true," the theorems are true as well. This must be so whatever else the state of the world may be. But with respect to the second criterion, the theory of the firm unfortunately shows up much less brilliantly. Theorems contain no information that is not already contained in the postulates; they therefore do not modify any possibilities which were not already modified. The proposition, for example, that "the firm will equalize the ratios of marginal productivity to marginal cost of all the factors of production" tells us nothing that we do not already know from the proposition that "the firm will maximize profits." In other words, the space of a system cannot be changed on the authority of a deduced theorem, if the "postulates" have already been taken into account. The results of the theory of the firm are, therefore, not laws, and do not help us to make more useful predictions.

This leads to an interesting fundamental question concerning the role of deductive theory in general in prediction. If deductive consequences never add new information to a set of postulates, is it not true then that the entire discipline is nothing but a gigantic redundancy? The forecaster would merely have to make sure that the basic assumptions are really laws, and then would simply apply these same laws to the system, and thereby automatically make all the modifications of the space of the system that are warranted by the entire conceptual structure. In the case of the theory of the firm referred to above, after the data (1) to (4) have been applied to the system, all the other elements of the theory become, for the purpose of prediction, superfluous.

There is no doubt that, after the postulates have been taken account of, the various deductive consequences can add nothing more. This way of stating the fact, however, miscasts the role of economic theory. It becomes valuable, not as a source of laws, but as an aid in the process of translating laws into a form suitable for prediction. Most human minds are too feeble to recognize, at sight, the various logical consequences of even a mildly complicated body of information. And the process of predicting is, of course, a process of logic. Very likely, the assistance of a deductive theory is indispensable in the construction of realistically complicated predictive systems. In order to be of service in this way, however, economic theory will have to build upon "lawful" postulates and not upon convenient but counterfactual assumptions. And also, it will have to be worked out for all possible constellations of motives, of market conditions, etc.

An important corollary of the above conclusion is that the laws for effective economic prediction must come from outside the traditional boundaries of the field of economics. We have no choice but to rely upon other sciences to supply us with the laws which will affect the probability of movement within the "economic" realm. Sociology, for example, might tell us (if it can) how fast economic mores and institutions can change, and, perhaps, what economic phenomena are compatible with given mores and institutions. Psychology might disclose what modes of reaction to data we might expect and how fast these can change. The physical sciences and engineering would tell us what the production functions are and what possibilities of change exist; and the geologist would contribute information on the existence and location of natural resources. Economic theory enters only at the end of the process, to help us "translate" this information into its meaning for future economic developments.

Example B–3. *An inventory fluctuation model*

As part of their regular work, economists frequently have to develop "theories" for the purpose of "explaining" a set of observed phenomena. Data and observations are always incomplete in the sense that they do not reveal fully everything that happened. Only a few of the billions of phenomena, and only a few of the properties of these, leave an enduring and accessible record of their occurrence. If we ever want to "explain" an event, therefore, we must do a great deal of interpolating — we must use our imagination to "fill in" those aspects of the story leading up to the event which have not been, or which cannot be, observed. Theory construction, or "model construction," is very commonly employed in this procedure.

We have, of course, already discussed several theories, or

models, of economic phenomena. The present exhibit is designed to point up more vividly than the others, the creative, in contrast to the formal-structural, aspects of model construction. Our example is a very simple one; it is an attempt to account for the observed lag of inventory time series behind sales time series over the course of the business cycle.

In his book, *Business Cycles and National Income*,[20] Alvin Hansen presents a model which roughly explains — to his satisfaction — the observed data on sales-inventory relationships. Hansen acknowledges that his model was very largely inspired by the work of Lloyd Metzler in this field.

Two assumptions underlie this theoretical model: (a) businessmen tend to hold inventories in some fairly stable relation to sales; (b) businessmen's expectations with respect to sales typically conform to the condition of unity elasticity (i.e., sales are expected to continue to move in the same direction and at the same rate of change as in the recent past).[21]

Sales are seen describing, roughly, a sine curve during the course of the cycle. In such a curve there is a continual change in the rate of change of the curve — the part of the cycle above the two inflection points has a negative second derivative, and the part below the inflection points, a positive second derivative. Accordingly, the expectations of businessmen, which always suppose the second derivative to be zero, are always wrong in terms of subsequent developments; in the lower part of the cycle they always underestimate sales, and in the upper part, they overestimate. Their efforts to keep inventory in a constant ratio to sales are therefore continuously being frustrated. The actual level of inventory changes according to two factors: (1) purchases, which are based on expected sales, and (2) actual sales. If (1) is never properly geared to (2), therefore, the actual inventory change will never correspond to the intended inventory change, and the intended constant ratio to sales cannot be attained.

[20] New York: W. W. Norton & Co., 1951.
[21] *Business Cycles and National Income*, p. 471.

Hansen showed that the result of such a situation is that the cyclical movement of inventory stocks lags one-quarter cycle behind the cyclical movement of sales, and that the cyclical movement of investment in inventories, intentional or otherwise, coincides with that of sales. These deductions from the model, Hansen also finds, are in rough correspondence to the actually observed behavior of the variables concerned in the period from 1919 to 1941, and the model can consequently be regarded as an explanation of the actual course of events. Hansen explicitly recognizes that other factors besides faulty sales forecasts may help to produce the observed inventory lag; a firm may, for example, deliberately maintain its output for a while after sales have fallen off in order to avoid a premature disbanding of its organization. But he apparently does believe that the model described here constitutes the core of the explanation.

We have described this model here not because we are particularly concerned with the fate of inventories, but because we wish to evaluate the type of analysis employed there. Even though the reasoning pattern is formally similar to that of the theory of the firm, its relationship to reality is different. The theory of the firm proceeds from the basis of actual or assumed observed facts and arrives at deductions which supposedly tell us something new; in the inventory model, in contrast, it is the conclusions that correspond to observed facts, and it is the foundation of the model, the set of postulates, which is the supposedly new element.

The interpretation of Hansen's model, or similar models, as an explanation of reality involves, as we have previously noted, the logical fallacy of affirming the consequent. Even if it is true that a given set of assumptions leads to theorems that correspond to reality, it is not proven that these assumptions are the *only* ones which lead to such theorems; and it is not necessarily true, therefore, that the given assumptions correspond to characteristics of the real world. There are, in general, a very large number of sets of assumptions which are consistent with a given body of observed data. Without further evidence, we never have a right to prefer any one of these sets over any of the others. To do so nonetheless is to indulge in artificial indirectness.

The ideal procedure of building explanatory models would go somewhat as follows: (1) Specify the phenomena to be explained. (2) Define the set of all assumption-sets which are consistent with these phenomena. (3) Use all dependable facts (laws) which are available for the purpose of restricting that set. (4) Treat the *entire remaining set* of assumption-sets as the explanatory model.

The many model-builders in economics do, of course, use all sorts of supplementary evidence in their effort to arrive at plausible models. They test whether the behavior assumptions are "reasonable," whether the physical relations are tenable, or whether the several assumptions are mutually consistent in the light of existing institutional arrangements, etc. It would appear, however, that none of them carry out this process in a complete and adequate way, and the results, therefore, inevitably contain either the fallacy of affirming the consequent or an unwarranted exclusion of possibilities. For that reason, the explanatory models produced so far are not useful in the construction of predictive models: their assumptions are not laws.

Even in its ideal form the usefulness of the model is conditional. Assume that Hansen's inventory model is of this form. His two basic assumptions, then, are only observations, and not static or dynamic laws. They describe the behavior of inventory owners in the period covered by the data; they cannot by themselves assert anything about such behavior at any other time. Only if we can discover dynamic laws which restrict the possibility of change of that behavior can we use the assumptions for the purpose of prediction. Otherwise, their use involves an artificial generalization of the observations.

C. SEMIRIGOROUS FORECASTING TECHNIQUES

We use the term "semirigorous" to describe those techniques of predictive reasoning which have some of the trappings of rigor, but which nevertheless take liberties with matters of fact or matters of logic. A semirigorous technique may rely on some very undependable assumptions, it may reason in terms of non sequiturs, or it may do both.

Many of the examples of this technique have a surprisingly strong appeal to "practical-minded" people. A businessman feels constantly the need for a reliable guide into the future, but he also is strongly aware of the scarcity of such guides and of his own inadequacies in this respect. He may thus be in a proper frame of mind for embracing any plausible-sounding theory that may be presented to him.

Example C–1. *"Business forecasting" techniques*

We need say but little about the various mechanical or semi-mechanical devices which have been used, at different times and by different people, to foretell the future course of "general business conditions," or of specific time series. These business-man's forecasts are quite primitive methodologically, and there-fore do not present a very interesting field for analysis. Almost without exception they rest on a basis of very weak assumptions.

Hansen [22] has classified the methods used into three cate-gories: (1) the "overshoot" method, (2) the "lead and lag" method, and (3) the method of "weighing opposing factors." Each of these rests on its own type of unwarranted assumption.

The "overshoot" method involves one type of extrapolation of past tendencies into the future.

In its simplest form this method is based on the proposition that whenever business activity rises above normal, one may expect a reaction to set in sooner or later. And similarly, when business falls below normal, one may sooner or later expect a backswing. And the farther the departure from normal — in other words, the greater the "overshoot" — the greater the reaction which is bound to follow.

From this point of view, then, an important area for statistical

[22] *Business Cycles and National Income* (New York: Norton, 1951), Chap. XXX.

research is to study past fluctuations with a view to determining what is *normal* and to devise ways and means of continually projecting this normal trend so as to keep it up to date . . . And if one were doubtful about the precise accuracy of the estimated normal, one could take a somewhat less exacting position and merely seek to ascertain whether business was considerably above normal, at *supernormal* levels, or at more or less seriously *subnormal* levels [p. 580].

In the twenties, the "overshoot" method, in one form or another, was applied by such forecasting agencies as the Babson Economic Service, the Brookmire Service, and Moody's Service. The Babson Service, for example, used a variant of this method which places emphasis not only on the amplitude of the deviation from normal, but also on the duration of the deviation.

Thus the entire *area* in a chart (on which time is measured on the horizontal axis) above or below the normal trend line . . . was regarded as important. Indeed, under the law of action and reaction, it was assumed that any depression area could normally be expected to balance in size the preceding prosperity area [p. 581].

The assumption basic to the "overshoot" method is, of course, that past trends will continue into the future without break and that the cyclical pattern will retain its typical past shape. And, as usual, there is no reason to believe that this assumption corresponds in any way to an inevitable characteristic of our economic system. Trends do break, and patterns do change. As a matter of fact, the "overshoot" method failed miserably to foretell the sequence of events in the period after 1929.

The second method, the "lead-lag" method, was the mainstay of the famous Harvard Economic Service. It is based on the belief that the typical business cycle unfolds itself in a certain definite way, and that the component events occur in a regular and predictable order. Some of the time series, therefore, will always tend to lead the cycle, and others will tend to lag. Consequently, a leading series can be used to "call the turns" on various lagging series, and in this way acts as an "anticipator" of things to come.

The Harvard Economic Service classified various statistical series into three categories: (1) speculation, (2) business, and (3) money. The series included in Curve A, Speculation, were: (a) the prices of industrial stocks, and (b) New York City bank debits. In the B Curve, Business, were included: (a) bank debits outside of New York City, and (b) commodity prices. In Curve C, Banking, were included commercial paper rates. Generally Curve A was found to anticipate Curve B by from four to ten months, while Curve B preceded Curve C by from two to eight months [p. 582].

This scheme, as Hansen explains, was founded on a large-scale statistical study of the cyclical behavior of a considerable number of time series in the period from January, 1903 to July, 1914. The typical sequences of events, as uncovered in that study, became the basis of the 3-curve system, and were used for forecasting in the 1920's.

This "lead and lag" method, like the "overshoot" method described above, is clearly an invalid technique. Its assumptions seem to be particularly weak, and it is no surprise that it too failed in the hour of greatest need, the period following 1929. It based its forecasts on relationships existing before World War I, even though the nature of these relationships was such that any one of the major structural changes which continuously occur in our dynamic economy would suffice to upset them. It requires optimism of a very high order to place much confidence in a foundation as volatile as that.

In recent years, the lead-lag type of analysis has been refined considerably, mainly, as we have seen, through the work done at the National Bureau of Economic Research. It is now considerably more sophisticated than it was in the 1920's. But as we have also seen, the fundamental weakness, unwarranted assumption, has not been fully removed from this approach.

The third method, that of "weighing opposing factors," is not as formal and mechanistic as the previous examples. The method

consisted simply of listing, identifying, and measuring as far as possible the forces making for expansion on the one side and for depression on the other. An effort was made to appraise the relative strength of the opposing forces. Since the weight to be given to the various factors was a matter of judgment, no definite quantitative conclusions could be reached [p. 583].

Simply to describe this method is to indicate its unreliability. The effects of the various separate factors cannot be predicted with assurance; it is impossible to tell with assurance whether a given factor is "favorable" or "unfavorable." Also, it is basically fallacious to consider separately the elements of an interdependent system — whether a factor is favorable or otherwise depends on the total state of the system. "Judgment," in this respect is, in almost all cases, but a euphemism for an uncontrolled reasoning process. Subjective "weighting" processes cannot be relied upon.

Example C–2. *The Dow Theory*

The Dow Theory of stock-price movements is another good example of a specialized mechanical forecasting device. There are many different versions of this theory, almost as many as there are Dow theorists; it is therefore difficult to state of what propositions the theory is composed. Fortunately, however, from our particular point of view a "representative average" is adequate. We shall, accordingly, consider the version of the Dow Theory elaborated by Charles Dow, S. A. Nelson, and William P. Hamilton, the foremost theorists in this region of analysis. An excellent summary of their views is presented in *The Stock Market* by Professor G. L. Leffler; [23] and all of the factual material following is taken from Chapter 33 of that work.

The Dow Theory purports to be able to forecast the over-all broad movement of the stock market. It pays principal attention to the so-called "primary movements" in the market, which are the long-term cyclical tendencies in the movement of stock prices — the alternation of "bear" markets and "bull" markets. The other components of the stock-index time series

[23] New York: Ronald Press, 1951. (Copyright 1951 The Ronald Press Company.)

as analyzed by this theory, the "secondary" (short cyclical) and, especially, the "daily" movements, are of only subordinate importance.[24] The claims put forth by the theory are quite modest. It is admittedly unable to predict the length of a given bear or bull market, and it also gives no definite information about the amplitude of the cyclical swings involved. The main ostensible advantage of using the theory comes from its being able to tell when either a bull or a bear market has terminated, and when, consequently, the market has turned in the opposite direction.

The main points of the Dow Theory have been summarized by Professor Leffler as follows:

1. There are three movements in the stock market: (1) the primary movement, (2) the secondary reaction, and (3) the daily fluctuation of stock prices.

2. Primary and secondary movements may be forecast by the action of the Dow-Jones rail and industrial averages — "the most remorseless of barometers."

3. The averages do not forecast how long a primary or secondary movement will last, but their action does indicate when a new movement has begun.

4. Confirmation of a new primary or secondary movement is indicated either (a) by both averages making a line [drifting sideways with only narrow oscillations] and then breaking out of line; or (b) by both averages making new highs or new lows. Both averages must confirm each other.

5. The market is forecast solely by movements of the averages, which discount everything; there is no need to consider volume, to introduce other economic series, or to use extensive charts and records . . .

6. The primary purpose of the theory is to forecast the major trend — the bull or bear market; it may forecast secondary movements, but this is of little significance.

[24] According to Hamilton's calculations, in the period from 1900 to 1923 the average bull market lasted 27 months and the average bear market 15 months. As for the secondary movements, more recently called "technical corrections," other students have placed their typical length as between two weeks and a month.

7. The primary trend will continue as long as the averages confirm each other.

8. The theory is not a system for "beating the market," but rather one that can benefit the intelligent speculator who wishes to protect himself by a study of the averages as a stock market barometer [pp. 518–519].

Several studies have been made to ascertain the effectiveness of the Dow Theory in forecasting what it claims to be able to forecast. These studies have, typically, not been methodological, but, rather, compared a number of forecasts derived from the theory with subsequent actual developments. The findings indicate that the theory is sometimes successful in forecasting a bull or bear market, and sometimes unsuccessful. Leffler describes a few instances in which the theory was spectacularly unsuccessful. In discussing Alfred Cowles' study of Hamilton's editorials in the *Wall Street Journal* he says:

On February 15, 1926, the *Wall Street Journal* carried these very significant words in an editorial on the market:

"It can hardly be said that the averages at the moment look convincingly bullish, and a relatively small change in both of them would make them look decidedly bearish. The fluctuations at present are at least strikingly like those which have occurred in the past at the top of a long bull movement."

The Dow-Jones industrials did, indeed, drop 23 points the next month; after this reaction, however, they began their dizzy climb of 246 points as the greatest bull market of history roared to a crash. The Dow theory had failed to forecast this truly remarkable rise [p. 522].

The theory performed with a similar lack of distinction in forecasting the end, in 1946, of the World War II bull market:

. . . the industrial average was again at a new high of 212.50 on May 29. On June 13, the rail average also forged ahead to another new high of 68.31, or 0.08 points above the February figure. According to orthodox theory, the market was ready for another bull movement. Unfortunately, these last-named figures represented the peak prices of the averages for a period of four years. There was no further bull market, and the collapse came within two months [p. 520].

Proponents of the Dow Theory advance a great many reasons why the market does tend to behave as described by the theory. Though many of the reasons seem plausible, none of them point to anything that must inevitably happen. In other words, the Dow Theory is not based on well-established laws. Accordingly, the main propositions of the theory are nothing more than assumptions, and therefore the forecasts based upon them must exhibit all the familiar frailties resulting from artificial generalization and fixation. The malperformances of the theory in actual practice provide additional evidence of its undependability, but this further evidence is not necessary. The methodological evaluation is sufficient.

Example C–3. Edward R. Dewey and Edwin F. Dakin: *Cycles*: *The Science of Prediction* [25]

Messrs. Dewey and Dakin present us with a set of ideas on economic predictions which, formally, are very much like the ones current in natural science, but which differ considerably from the approaches conventional in social science.

It is the business of science to predict. An exact science like astronomy can usually make very accurate predictions indeed . . . Economics is now reaching a point where it can hope also to make rather accurate predictions, within limits which this study will explain. . . The reader will be introduced to a method of thinking about the future which — new though it may be to him — seems definitely to have proved of value. . . We shall find, as we go forward, that in this approach to economic phenomena we are abandoning the classical approach based on endless argument over cause and effect. It is hoped that the reader's reward will be the discovery that in economics, as in other sciences, we are apparently dealing with

[25] New York: Henry Holt and Co., 1947. For the purpose of this discussion we accept as accurate all of the evidence, statistical and otherwise, cited by the authors in support of their thesis. (The material reproduced herein is copyrighted by the publishers, Henry Holt and Co., and is reprinted by their permission.)

laws regarding rhythmic human response to certain stimuli that give a remarkable working tool to any man who is responsibly concerned with future outcomes. . . The ability to calculate probabilities is a vital part of all our modern scientific progress. . . The discovery that the law of averages applies to humanity — that certain activities of people, viewed en masse, fall into definite patterns, some of which repeat themselves with periodic rhythm — promises to be of great aid in making economics function as a true science. . . The result [of the statistical study of periodic rhythms] is not prediction, in the sense in which the word is ordinarily understood. If the reader nevertheless wishes to regard essential parts of this book as prediction, then it should be emphasized that the "forecasts" are written by the data themselves. They emerge as tendencies in the organisms being studied. They do not rest on the opinion of any man, or men. They are, in effect, the *probabilities* of tomorrow [pp. xi–xv].

After this introduction, Dewey and Dakin proceed to develop their point by the use of the techniques of time-series analysis. They show that the time series of many different phenomena in this world can be broken down into a number of components, each of which behaves in a regular and predictable fashion. The main problem is to isolate these components and to study their characteristics; and from there on it is just a matter of extrapolating a given time series into the future by synthesizing these regular and predictable components. The authors show quite convincingly that seemingly very erratic time series can be decomposed in this way and their future course (also seemingly erratic) be charted. The cyclical nature of a time series may not be apparent upon mere inspection because, for example, as the authors point out, a composite cycle of perfectly regular 3-, 5-, 8-, and 17-year components would repeat its over-all pattern only once every 2040 years, and that pattern is therefore anything but easily visible.

The authors show, first, that many growth phenomena exhibit long-term trends of the characteristic S-shaped variety. As examples, they present such data as the population of various countries, the growth patterns of individual organisms, United States manufactures, the iron and steel industry, and shipbuilding. After a growth-curve has been started and the general shape of the curve has become apparent, the future trend can be forecast, unless, of course, there is a break in the curve. The trend in United States cotton production, for example, was broken and a new trend started by the Civil War; and the trend in United States wool production was radically altered by the Tariff Act of 1924. (Inasmuch as the occurrence of such breaks is unpredictable from a study of the time series, the very projection of a trend is already an unwarranted assumption.)

As the title indicates, the primary concern of the book is with the analysis of the various cyclical fluctuations around the trend. The authors find periodic rhythms almost wherever they look. They present data on such natural rhythms as the abundance of Atlantic salmon, the offerings of lynx skins to the Hudson's Bay Company, the amount of ozone in the air at London, the mortality due to pneumonia and influenza, the amount of growth of redwood trees, the abundance of sunspots, and many others. In all of these illustrations the periodicity of the cycle is fixed and regular.

There are four major rhythms which Dewey and Dakin believe to be particularly important in the American economy. There is a 54-year rhythm, which manifests itself most plainly in wholesale prices, interest rates, and some production series. Another rhythm, of nine years' duration, is very prominent in wholesale prices, common stocks, and a large number of industrial series. A 41-month cycle is presented by the prices of many commodities and of many securities, by the rate of change of industrial production, and by other production series. Lastly, there is an $18\frac{1}{3}$-year rhythm in the variations of real estate and building activity, many industrial series, the marriage rate, wheat acreage, and a number of other time series. The over-all level of activity in the country can be forecast, according to the authors, by the summation of the various separate rhythmic movements.

The most startling aspect of this book is the drastic conclusions drawn by the authors. They believe that economic forecasting should be done *only* through the mechanical extrapolation of previously observed cycles — that all other approaches are doomed to futility. Their supporting arguments for this conclusion are quite persuasively presented.

The first point is that various apparent turbulences and disruptions that manifest themselves at various times do not interfere with a regular rhythmic pattern, but operate independently of it and perhaps even are the instrument of its recurrence. To show that rhythms may be entirely undisturbed by some surrounding phenomena, the authors say:

> We might ask . . . why the recoveries shown after the decline should show such parallels in a group of nations as diverse as these countries in the economic *mechanisms* they had prevailing after 1933. In that year, for instance, the New Deal began in the United States and Hitler took over in Germany. The United States began promoting reciprocal trade treaties, and Germany tried her hand at forced exports, backed by subsidies and the Schacht invention of several different kinds of marks. Britain moved toward preferential tariffs within the Empire, and France moved toward the Blum concepts of socialism. With all such divergencies of mechanism, the nations concerned went through the era with a consistent and continued similarity in economic outcomes.
>
> Even more to the point, the various nations, through all their depressions and ensuing political disturbances and recoveries of the 1930's, displayed in their economies the rhythmic patterns that one could have anticipated from observing their past patterns of response [p. 78].

A number of quotations from Schumpeter's *Business Cycles* are given in support of this general view. For example, the authors state:

> Of the rise in American prosperity that was attributed after 1933 to the measures of the New Deal — but which arrived strictly as might have been anticipated by anyone projecting the familiar economic waves of the past — Schumpeter declares shortly: "It would be contrary to all experience and common sense, though of course no logical impossibility, that a process which can be strictly proved to have been running its course since at least the sixteenth century and right to the end of 1932, should have come to a stop suddenly on March 4, 1933 [p. 79]."

This leads to their second main argument in favor of time-series extrapolation. Dewey and Dakin believe that, because of the infinite complexity of the world and the finitude of the human mind, a detailed causal study of events is a hopeless undertaking. The only way in which we can look into the future is to put aside the causal way of thinking, to look for past patterns of phenomena, and to project these patterns, without in any way inquiring into the whys and wherefores, into the future.

The study of rhythms has not yet proceeded beyond problems in correlation. Even to this point our progress has been wavering and uncertain. The greatest single piece of progress to date, in the study of economic phenomena, has undoubtedly been the recognition that we are in fact often dealing with *rhythms* rather than mere oscillations. This recognition has recently changed the whole focus of economic inquiry. Until it was reached, millions of words had been written in the quest for *reasons* for economic changes. Pursuing such a method of inquiry the old economics had made little progress toward becoming a true science. Rather, it became a larger and larger debating society, devoted to examining reasons why a given event should cause some particular result.

The mere abundance of such reason-why material — so great that no student could ever master it, reconcile it, and put it to practical use — was itself evidence that the method was fruitless. . .

With the discovery of rhythm in economic phenomena, some economic inquiry immediately changed direction. The question was no longer *why* we have business cycles, and *why* we meet recurrent economic slumps. Now the fundamental question was simply: Are the cycles really rhythmic? And if so, does the rhythm spring from within or without the economy?

To the first part of the query continued research has been able to give an affirmative answer almost beyond doubt [p. 141].

But there definitely are some factors which do tend to disturb a regular pattern of events. The authors mention, for example, wartime inflations as factors which are unpredictable in advance but which nevertheless have an effect on the price level. Apparently somewhat at a loss about the best way to treat such factors within their general framework of analysis, Dewey and Dakin do not present a very clear discussion of this problem. Their basic idea seems to be that the pattern can be depended upon to reveal the timing though not the amplitude of the cycles in the affected time series. The amplitude is a summation of the war-leverage effect with the "normal" components. In the words of the authors:

> The forces represented by our rhythms are quite evidently not the only forces at work in our society. There are doubtless many sporadic ones in addition. But the rhythms we have do show a regularity which persists, and usually dominates, regardless of what other forces are present on the scene.
>
> On many of the economic charts and wave patterns we know about, a period of war registers itself as a sort of volcanic explosion above the level of the prevailing trends. All the waves revolving around the trends are tossed high in the air, as it were. Yet the actual wave patterns — as patterns — are often less disturbed by war than one would expect. . . Still more: Regardless of the degree of disturbance, once the war "explosion" has subsided and the disturbances recede, the previously prevailing trends and levels have usually been re-established in our economy. *Previous wars did not, in themselves, alter basic underlying trends*, insofar as our statistical data show them [p. 207].

It is not easy to evaluate the significance of the ideas presented here, although it is quite easy to make a number of critical observations. We can point out, to start with, that the continuation of a past pattern into the future is not something that can be known — it can only be assumed; and we could support this contention with a list of historical examples of tendencies which lasted for very long periods of time, but nevertheless were, at one point, suddenly broken. We can also show that some predictions based on an extrapolation of the rhythms discussed in this book were very wide of the mark. Dewey and Dakin themselves, however, were sufficiently confident about the power of their method to have made a forecast of the state of business in the 1947–1952 period. (The book was written in 1946 and published in March 1947.) Their projection is based on the following data:

1. The underlying 54-year rhythm in wholesale prices is on the decline. It turned in 1925; the pattern is due to reach bottom in 1952.

2. The shorter 9-year pattern in wholesale prices — a rhythm that applies also to iron, steel, and stockmarket prices — which had its last high in 1937, reached for another high in 1946. The pattern was due then to turn down until 1951.

3. . . . the 3½-year pattern — almost universal in business — was forecasting a peak in 1947. . . Lows are due in '48 and '51.

4. The 18⅓-year pattern in building activity apparently reached its high about late 1942. . . In general, building and real estate patterns are due to decline to a low around 1953.

5. The 15-year pattern in the index of the purchasing power of beef cattle prices . . . was scheduled for a high around 1944, thereafter declining to a low due in 1951 [pp. 226–227].

After a warning that, because of sporadic factors, etc., no unqualified forecasts can be made, the authors continue:

Still, with all these qualifications, it is worth noting that the expectancies facing us do not suggest any lengthy postwar boom. On the contrary, the number of important rhythms that come to a low together around 1952 suggest the possibility of a growing postwar crisis. The reader now familiar with this method of analysis will not expect the crisis really to be avoided or halted by any preventive measures which the government might decide to take. . . Probably the most we can hope for would be some kind of palliative action if the blows fall [p. 227].

In very sharp contrast to the dire and well-reënforced warnings, the actual rate of economic activity in the 1947–1952 period has exceeded all previous peacetime records. Almost every one of the details of the forecast turned out to be drastically wrong.

So, on the face of it, the approach to forecasting advocated by Dewey and Dakin doesn't have very much to recommend itself to others. And, moreover, still another criticism can be made of it, this one on grounds of methodology. To be useful tools for prediction, the rhythms should be well-established empirical laws. A proposition, however, cannot be an empirical law if it contains "escape clauses," especially so if the escape clauses do not indicate the nature of the possible escapes. The rhythms are being presented to us as patterns that will persist into the future, *unless* something comes along to disturb the normal sequence. The various possibilities of disturbance are not indicated. The proposition asserting the persistence of the rhythms is therefore of the kind that cannot be proved or disproved by recourse to the facts; it is always possible, afterwards, to point to some disturbing factors which presumably accounted for an observed divergence between expected and actual happenings. Laws of this sort have been termed, by less friendly writers, to be meaningless; we have decided to call them assumptions.

For the same reason that disturbances can always be found to account for past "violations" of a law of this kind, the future occurrence of such disturbances is unforeseeable. The implications for the role of such laws in prediction are obvious. We can also dispose fairly easily of the authors' general contention that the projection of past rhythms into the future indicates the probable future, not the actual future. First, the authors do not indicate how the shape of the relevant probability curve might be ascertained. Second, even if they did, we would still have no grounds for believing this probability distribution to be stable over time. Dewey and Dakin's procedures clearly involve artificial generalization and artificial factorization.

It might well be, however, that there is something useful and worthwhile in this approach. We cannot use it as a substitute for causal thinking — even if for no other reason than that the "sporadic disturbances" do exercise a causal effect that must be considered in arriving at a forecast. But we can interpret the results of the time-series analysis as clues in our search for causal factors. The data cited by Dewey and Dakin in support of their thesis are quite persuasive — there seems to be something to it. If we can discover the law or laws which "explain" the various observed rhythms, they would make a very useful building block, to be used together with other building blocks, in the construction of predictive models.

D. MACRO-ECONOMIC MODELS

Macro-economic models, especially statistically induced econometric models, have achieved in recent years considerable prominence as analytical and predictive devices. And it seems safe to say, further, that most of the advanced thinking in the entire field of macro-economics today, whether specifically concerned with prediction or not, is carried on in terms of the model concept. Before launching into our discussion of the usability of this concept, in its various formulations, for the purpose of prediction, let us first get a clear notion of what a macro-economic model looks like. Lawrence R. Klein, one of the pioneers in the econometric technique of analysis, has presented us with an excellent brief description:

> The purpose in building econometric models is to describe the way in which the system actually operates. . . If we know the quantitative characteristics of the economic system, we shall be able to forecast with a specified level of probability the course of certain economic magnitudes such as employment, output, or income; and we shall also be able to forecast with a specified level of probability the effect upon the system of various economic policies.[1]

> We view the economic system as describable by a set of simultaneous equations expressing all the interrelationships among the measurable economic magnitudes which guide economic behavior. The variables in this set of equations are classified into two main types, endogenous and exogenous. The endogenous variables are those variables which are determined within the system of economic forces in a narrow sense, and they include such familiar magnitudes as output, employment, prices, profits, rents, interest. The exogenous vari-

---

[1] *Economic Fluctuations in the United States, 1921–1941* (New York: Wiley, 1950), Cowles Commission Monograph No. 11, p. 1.

ables are those which represent forces outside the confines of the economic system. They are determined by natural, technological, sociological, political, or institutional forces which are assumed here to be non-economic. It is, of course, not satisfactory to separate sociology and politics from economics, but our purpose in pioneering will be served best if we make assumptions which simplify our model as much as possible. Eventually we may hope to develop a complete social theory which leaves in the exogenous category only such variables as weather, earthquakes, and other "acts of God" [p. 2].

The appropriate procedure in forecasting by econometric methods is: (1) Construct a mathematical model of the economic system. The components of this model fall into four categories: technological equations, economic behavior equations, legal rules, and definitions. Technological equations are, for example, the input-output relationships, technically called production or transformation functions. These equations act usually as constraints upon the movement of the system. Allowance must be made in them for technological change. The economic behavior equations are those that depict the actions of the fundamental units of the system (households, business firms) within the framework of a particular type of market system and mode of production. Examples of economic behavior equations are the familiar profit maximizing equations of the firm or the consumer demand equations of the household. The legal rules act as constraints autonomously imposed upon the system by the government. A tax law is an example of a legal constraint. In mathematical form this law may state that taxes are a function of income. Taxes and income are variables of the equation system, but the parameters of the functional relation between these variables are determined by governmental action. Since households and business firms must operate within the framework of the particular legal rules in existence, these rules become constraints upon the economic behavior decisions of these units. Finally, the definitions are introduced for accounting purposes. They state, for example, that the rate of change in the stock of fixed capital equals net investment or that gross national expenditures equal the sum of expenditures by consumers, business firms, and government. The definitions express exact relations among the variables of the system, but the technological and economic behavior equations are not exact; they are subject to a multitude of disturbances. The agricultural production functions may not give the correct input-output relationship if there is a large uncontrollable disturbance in the weather; consumers may not spend according to their customary patterns if there are temporary shortages of necessities. Endless disturbing factors cause the observations to deviate from the equations of the system. The legal rules, in principle, could be made into exact relationships without error, but a complete representation of laws will often lead to complicated equations. Consequently, approximations are usually substituted for the true legal rules and these approximations are subject to errors of estimation. For example, the highly complex laws on personal income taxation cannot be exactly represented by a simple linear relationship between total taxes and total income for the entire community. The approximation function will have to make allowance for a margin of error.

(2) After the mathematical model has been established, the econometrician uses the past data to estimate the parameters of the equation system. The disturbing factors are always present, and it is possible to estimate the difference between the observations of the past data and the values of variables calculated from the estimated equations. From the difference, an estimate of the disturbances, the average variation of the disturbances in the past can be determined; this should give us some idea of the amount of variation to expect in the future. For the period of forecast some variables are usually known in advance — government expenditures, tax rates, population, lagged variables, controlled prices, etc. If the values of these predetermined variables are inserted into the estimated statistical equations, estimated values of the other variables in the system can be obtained for the forecast period.

A forecast from such a statistical model is not exact because the equations upon which the forecast is based are not exact. Essentially two types of error are involved, and proper allowance must be made for both. The econometrician estimates the parameters of his model equations from a sample of past data. The parameters are not known precisely because they are estimated from a finite sample (often small, say 20 years' observation, in econometric work). There are, however, mathematical statistical methods of estimating the sampling errors involved in the determination of the parameters of the model. In addition to the sampling fluctuations, there are the above mentioned disturbances in the equations of the system. The fluctuations of the disturbances can be estimated from the past observations. By combining the two types of error, a single error can be attached to the forecast of economic variables from the statistical model. This gives a range of forecast rather than a unique point. It is customary to make some assumptions about the population distribution patterns of the error terms, and if this is done, a definite probability can be assigned to the chance that the forecast will actually be in the computed range.[2]

Most econometric models are considerably less carefully elaborated than indicated by Mr. Klein's program. Klein himself does carry out his full program [3] and, moreover, combines it with some quite sophisticated techniques of statistical estimation. We shall, however, confine our discussion to the more simple models, primarily because the aspects of such models upon which we wish to concentrate are more directly discernible in these simpler versions. In justice to Mr. Klein's path-breaking efforts it should be clearly understood that the more crude of our criticisms do not apply to his own ideas.

Macro-economic models attempt to take cognizance of the effect of the structure of the economic system on its future behavior. In this they clearly constitute an advance over the analysis employed in previous forecasting attempts, as, for example, time-series extrapolation. But, as we shall find, the advance is not sufficient to outdistance the objections we have raised against the various older techniques described in the last chapter.

Most macro-economic models constitute an artificial closure (or semiclosure) of reality, and, on that ground alone, could be disqualified from participation in predictive attempts. Our first example is an especially clear-cut illustration of the point at issue.

[2] Comment published in *Studies in Income and Wealth*, XI (New York: National Bureau of Economic Research, 1949), pp. 352–354. Detailed examples of all the steps in this approach are given in Mr. Klein's paper, "The Use of Econometric Models as a Guide to Economic Policy," *Econometrica*, XV (1947), pp. 111–151.

[3] See his *Economic Fluctuations in the United States, 1921–1941*.

Example D–1. Harold M. Somers: "A Theory of Income Determination" [4]

The attention of a great many economic theorists has been focused, during the last two decades or so, on the forces which determine the level of national income (and of the various associated magnitudes) at a given time and over given periods of time. The most prominent single contribution to this school of thought has been, of course, the work of J. M. Keynes. But there were other important basic contributions too, notably the period analysis of Robertson, the process analysis of the Swedish school, the reaction-lag analysis of Kalecki, the statistical studies of Tinbergen, the econometric work of Frisch, the economic growth studies of Hansen, and a number of other pioneering researches. These leaders, and their many colleagues and followers, have furnished us with a fairly well-defined system of concepts for macro-economic analysis; one that has become the basis for most of the theoretical and empirical work currently being done in this field. Most economic forecasters, too, employ this general conceptual framework. It is therefore of considerable importance for us to appraise the results of this school of thought from the viewpoint of the requirements for valid economic prediction.

Harold M. Somers has done us a great service in this connection. He has assembled a great deal of what is best in the different contributions into a single model of income determination. By looking at his model, therefore, we can gain a good idea as to what macro-economists have been doing of late. In justice to Professor Somers it should also be pointed out that his contribution is more than an assembly job — it is an outstanding example of the technique of model construction.

After a discussion of the major contributions to the field, Somers arrives at the following eclectic result:

The complete model consisting of ten equations and ten endogen-

[4] *Journal of Political Economy*, LVIII (December 1950), pp. 523–541. (Published by the University of Chicago Press.)

ous variables follows. The model is broken down into Keynesian, Robertsonian, Swedish, and "additional" segments.

Keynesian segment:

$$Y_{r_t} = C_{r_t} + I_{r_t} \tag{1}$$

$$S_{r_t} = I_{r_t} \tag{2}$$

Robertsonian segment:

$$\overline{Y}_{r_{t-1}} = C_{r_t} + S_{p_t} \tag{3}$$

$$C_{r_t} = f(\overline{Y}_{r_{t-1}}) \tag{4}$$

Swedish segment:

$$S_{r_t} = S_{p_t} + S_{u_t} \tag{5}$$

$$I_{r_t} = I_{p_t} + I_{u_t} \tag{6}$$

Additional segment:

$$I_{p_t} = g(\overline{S}_{u_{t-1}}, \overline{I}_{u_{t-1}}, \overline{\imath}_t) \tag{7}$$

$$I_{u_t} = (C_{m_t} - C_{r_t}) + (I_{m_t} - I_{p_t}) \tag{8}$$

$$C_{m_t} = \phi(\overline{S}_{u_{t-1}}, \overline{I}_{u_{t-1}}) \tag{9}$$

$$I_{m_t} = \Psi(\overline{S}_{u_{t-1}}, \overline{I}_{u_{t-1}}) \tag{10}$$

The subscripts are: r, realized magnitudes; p, planned magnitudes; u, unplanned magnitudes; m, goods produced; t, periods of time. The variables are: Y, income; C, consumption; I, investment; S, saving; and i, interest rate.

We may trace through the process of income determination in this model. Given last period's unplanned saving and investment, equations (10) and (9) supply us with the volume of capital goods and consumption goods produced. Given last period's income, we obtain consumption in (4). With this information and planned investment in (7), we obtain unplanned investment in (8). Adding them together in (6), we get the realized investment. With the realized investment we obtained from (6) and the realized consumption we obtained from (4), we obtain realized income in (1). Then, using the realized investment from (6) again, we obtain realized saving from (2). And using realized consumption from (4) again, we obtain planned saving in (3). Using these in (5), we obtain unplanned saving. In this way we obtain income, unplanned saving, and unplanned investment.

Another way of describing the function performed by the various equations is to say that the Keynesian segment establishes the relationships that exist between realized income, consumption, investment, and saving; the Swedish segment defines the relation between planned and unplanned magnitudes; and the added segment gives us the determination of planned and unplanned investment. Combining these segments and using the model as a whole, we can determine income from period to period [p. 532].

We have already commented (Example A–3) on the usability of aggregate consumption functions in attempts at economic prediction. The same kind of criticism can be leveled against all so-called economic behavior equations — none of them can qualify as laws. To the extent that the above model consists of such equations, therefore, it is unsuitable for prediction.

A closely related set of difficulties in the model stems from the dynamic nature of many of the equations. (Those equations are dynamic which relate to each other variables with different time indices.) These equations do not refer to the calendar time with which we must be concerned in prediction, but imply some kind of operational time, which is measured in terms of intrasystemic happenings only, with no direct reference to the calendar.[5] The particular kind of time presupposed by Somers' model is one which (1) progresses in discontinuous jumps, and (2) permits no developments within each given period. It is no simple matter, and perhaps impossible, to discover a transformation equation which will enable us to move back and forth between this kind of operational time and calendar time and still stay within the requirements of valid prediction. Simplifying assumptions are often made concerning the transformation equation, such as that the unit period corresponds to the "typical" income-payment period (a week, for example); but it is obvious why such makeshifts are unsatisfactory if reliable prediction is to be our goal.

Most important, however, we can recognize here the all-pervading tendency in economic theory to attempt to represent

[5] For an excellent and penetrating analysis of the different kinds of time which underlie the various types of economic theory, see William C. Hood, "Some Aspects of the Treatment of Time in Economic Theory," *Canadian Journal of Economics and Political Science*, XIV (1948) pp. 453–468.

reality by a closed conceptual system. There seems to be an almost compulsive drive in this direction — the theorist seems to feel that he isn't doing a proper job unless he comes up with such a gadget. Somers, as can be seen, carries that tendency to its full logical conclusion. In his model no outside data at all are needed, except for initial conditions (and i). The whole thing is as mechanical as an idealized astronomical system. It is quite certain that neither he nor any other theorist of similar mind would claim that a model like the above is really an adequate representation of reality — they all are fully conscious of the elements of oversimplification. But they do apparently believe that the models depict the skeleton of the real flux of events, and that various details and individual circumstances can be superimposed upon that skeleton when the occasion calls for it.

Running the risk of being unnecessarily repetitious, we again assert that this point of view is mistaken in its very conception. There is a fundamental structural difference between open and closed systems, and any attempt to equate the two can only lead to results which, if used in forecasting, are utterly undependable.

Somers, for example, uses his model for the derivation of some propositions on the course of national income over time. He arrives at the following conclusions, among others:

A rigorous analysis of the necessary and sufficient conditions for the stability of income over time gives us the following conclusions:

I. The equality of realized and planned saving is sufficient and necessary for an equilibrium of income over time.

II. The equality of realized investment (saving) and planned investment is neither sufficient nor necessary for an equilibrium of income over time.

III. The equality of planned saving and planned investment is neither sufficient nor necessary for the equilibrium of income over time.

IV. The combination of conditions II and III is sufficient but not necessary for the equilibrium of income over time [p. 534].

For the above-mentioned reason, these theorems, while describing for us the properties of the given closed system, do not help us in prediction, and therefore not in policy-formation.

Notwithstanding its indicated limitations, the conceptual structure presented by Somers does suggest to us the main outlines of a valid and very useful contribution to economic prediction. The model shows what is perhaps one of the very few ways in which powerful dynamic laws can be derived directly from "economic data." The national income of a given period may not uniquely determine the expenditures of the next period, but it does impose definite limitations upon that amount. We need also to take account, of course, of accumulated funds and monetary factors, but the shell of the final form of the law seems to be the one given by Somers.

Most economists and econometricians are not quite as extreme as Professor Somers in building their models. Many of them seek to escape the most obvious of the artificialities by constructing the model from stochastical equations, others, by admitting a limited number of exogenous variables into their scheme, and still others, by using both devices. Our next example illustrates the use of the second of these methods. The resulting model is still, however, an artificial semiclosure of reality.

Example D–2. Colin Clark: "A System of Equations Explaining the United States Trade Cycle, 1921 to 1941" [6]

Mr. Clark is not using the econometric model developed in his article for the forecasting of the future, but rather for the "explanation" of the past. However, inasmuch as the logical structures of prediction and of explanation are identical, and inasmuch as the approach used in this model is quite typical of that of many modern econometric forecasting attempts, this model serves our purpose admirably.

Mr. Clark describes, at the outset, how he obtained the forms of the constituent equations of his model:

[6] *Econometrica*, XVII (1949), pp. 93–123.

It has . . . proved possible to co-ordinate the work and theories of others into a fairly simple system of linear equations which provide a satisfactory explanation of *quarterly* movements in the U. S. trade cycle between 1921 and 1941, the system being on the following lines:

1. Consumption is treated as a function of current income and of maximum *previous* income (function suggested by Modigliani to take account of our reluctance to revise consumption standards downwards).

2. Imports are considered to be a function of current income.

3. Investment in producers' durable equipment (all private fixed investment other than construction) is treated as a function of current income and of the stock of producers' durable equipment already in existence (the life of previous investments being taken as ten years).

4. Investment in construction is treated as a function of current income and of the stock of past construction (the life of buildings being taken somewhat arbitrarily at forty years).

5. Changes in inventories are regarded as a resultant of "goods put into stock" and "goods drawn from stock." The former is considered dependent on the business man's expectations of the state of the market, which can be expressed by a composite function of current level of sales, upward or downward trend of sales over the past year, amounts of goods already in inventories, and the financial situation. The latter may be expected to be a given fraction of current outlay, or sales, i.e., that proportion consisting of goods which by their nature require a fairly long period of production or storage.

6. Outlay and income are taken inclusive of transfer payments, on the grounds that an increase in income from this source may have a significant effect upon consumption.

7. Taxation was only taken into account through the change in the constant and slope of the consumption function which may occur when there is a considerable and sustained change in rates of taxation.

The current rate of money wages is used (as Keynes suggested that it should be) as the basic *numéraire* for reducing all money figures to real terms. This enables us to determine all the functions in real terms, and draws attention to the fact that changes in money wages are generally neutral in their effect on the trade cycle, apart from the effect of such changes on the *real* value of the stock of money, of exports, or of public expenditure.

The exogenous variables from which all movements can eventually be determined, are thus seen to be public expenditure, exports, quantity of money, and the stock of capital goods and inventories in existence at the beginning of the period. The quantity of money acts on the trade cycle through its influence on willingness to accumulate inventories but through no other channel.

All other variables — consumption, various types of investment, inventory changes, imports — are endogenous, i.e., *fully determined by functional relationships with the exogenous variables or with each other*. The exogenous variables on the other hand contain a greater or lesser element of independent movement, resulting from the judgment of public authorities, the bargaining strength of trade unions, and events abroad [pp. 93–94].

More specifically, Clark's model of the United States economy is constructed from the following variables:

C $\quad$ indicates personal consumption expenditures.

I $\quad$ indicates imports.

G $\quad$ indicates producers' durable equipment gross.

H $\quad$ indicates new private construction gross.

J $\quad$ indicates net change in inventories.

X $\quad$ indicates outlay or sales.

Y $\quad$ indicates gross national product or income (including transfer payments).

P $\quad$ indicates government purchases of goods and services and transfer incomes.

E $\quad$ indicates exports and net balance of invisible transactions.

X_{-t} indicates the value of X, t quarters previously.

$\bar{G}$ $\quad$ indicates the cumulated value at the beginning of the quarter for G for the past *ten* years.

$\bar{H}$ $\quad$ indicates the cumulated value at the beginning of the quarter of H for the past *forty* years.

$\bar{J}$ $\quad$ indicates the cumulated value of J (taken from the 1929 base point approximately determined by Professor Kuznets) at the beginning of the quarter in question.

$\bar{J}'$ is the difference between $\bar{J}$ and a downward trend line (which trend line is believed to represent the decreasing need for stocks owing to quicker communications).

B represents the amount of bank cash at the beginning of the quarter, converted to wage units.

B' is the difference between B and an upward trend line (representing apparently a greatly increased financial caution, or demand for liquid assets in relation to business done).

M ("Modigliani factor") represents the highest *previous* value of Y attained *a year or more* previously. (Rising income is assumed to take about a year to effect a lasting change in consumption habits.)

Y' represents the "full employment" level of production measured in wage units, i.e., a parameter changing with increasing population available for work, and changes in normal working hours [pp. 100–102].

These variables are then organized into "a system of 7 equations in the 7 endogenous variables C, I, G, H, J, X, and Y. The exogenous variables are P, E, and B' [p. 102]." After obtaining the values of the various coefficients from the best available data by means of the least-squares method, Clark arrives at the following set of equations. (By means of a computational short-cut, the number of equations has been reduced to six.)

$$(8')\qquad (C - I) = a'_1 Y + 0.322\,M + a'_0$$

$$(3')\qquad\quad G = 0.120\,Y - 0.0061\,\overline{G} - 2.32$$

$$(4')\qquad\quad H = 0.255\,Y - 0.0142\,\overline{H} - 3.57$$

$$(5')\qquad\quad J = -\,0.5\,X - 0.113\,\overline{J}' + 0.119\sum_{1}^{5} X_{-t}$$

$$+\,0.186(\sum_{1}^{3} X_{-t} - \sum_{4}^{6} X_{-t})$$

$$+\,0.136\,B' - 4.72$$

$$(6')\qquad\quad X = (P + E) + \theta_1 Y + 0.322\,M$$
$$-\,0.0061\,\overline{G} - 0.0142\,\overline{H} + \theta_0$$

$$(7)\qquad\qquad Y = X + J$$

(where for 1921–33, $a'_1 = 0.550$, $a'_0 = -8.16$, $\theta_1 = 0.925$, and $\theta_0 = -14.05$; while for 1934–41, $a'_1 = 0.283$, $a'_0 = -0.23$, $\theta_1 = 0.658$ and $\theta_0 = -6.12$) [p. 108].

(The above quantities are all expressed in billions of wage units per quarter.)

The parameters a'_1, a'_0, θ_1, and θ_0 are computed separately for 1921–1933 and for 1934–1941 in order to reflect the differences in the structure of the American economy between the two periods.

After having completed his model, Clark then takes the final step of computing the values of the endogenous variables for each quarter of the 1921 to 1941 period. The computation is carried on in quarterly steps. For each quarter, the initially given or previously computed values of the lagged endogenous variables, as well as the appropriate values of the exogenous variables for that quarter, are "fed" into the equations, and the values of the endogenous variables for that quarter are determined.

It is only fair to point out, before proceeding to our evaluation of the model described above, that the fit of the computed time series to the actual time series is a very good one indeed. It should also be said that this work has since been subject to much revision and improvement, which is still in progress. However, since our concern is with the method of analysis and not with the results, the model presented will serve well as a case study.

It is unnecessary for the purpose of this study to investigate the technical procedures leading up to the model. We are interested in the predictive value of the model, and it is possible for us to form a conclusion on that point without delving into such matter as the accuracy of the original raw data or the merit of the least-squares method of curve-fitting. Accordingly, we shall not investigate these matters at all, but instead will assume that all of Mr. Clark's information is correct and that his statistical procedures are without flaw.

The model is clearly a good one from the point of view of pure logic. The conclusions — the computed values for the time series of the endogenous variables — are fully deducible from the postulates — the set of equations and the values of the exogenous variables. The process of mathematical calculation constitutes a valid logical chain; so we need not pursue this aspect of the model any further. The model must stand or fall, therefore, as far as its reliability in forecasting is concerned, on the correspondence to fact of the propositions which form its basis. We have already conceded the accuracy of the given quarterly values of the exogenous variables; the whole problem therefore settles upon the question of the correspondence to fact of the six equations which define the structure of the model.

No problem exists with reference to equation (7); it is a definitional identity and, consequently, always true. The other equations in the set, however, are of an entirely different variety; they are what Klein calls "economic behavior equations." As has been described above, the form of these behavioral equations is derived from economic theory — it is from there that we usually get our ideas as to what variables influence what other variables of the economic system. Statistical estimation comes in on the second step, in establishing numerical values for the coefficients in the theoretically determined equations. There are, unfortunately, weaknesses in both of these steps which act to destroy the reliability of the entire model for purposes of prediction.

The *form* of the equations is such that only a very few of the variables which exercise an influence on a given endogenous variable are permitted to show their effect. This is not a criticism of Clark's model in particular. The total number of influencing variables is so enormous — in the case of the consumption function, for example, the behavior of each consumer is governed by a separate, and very large, set of variables — that a very drastic simplification is necessary in all econometric models. Probably all model-builders are aware that, in the process of simplification, a great deal is lost, but they are also aware that it is a completely hopeless attempt to list in an econometric equation all of the relevant variables. Unfortunately, in this case, necessity is not the mother of virtue. The makeshift arrangement of reducing the number of variables to "manageable" proportions unavoidably results in an undependable description of reality. There remains the ever present possibility that one or several of the suppressed variables will "assert" themselves, exercise an effect on the given endogenous variable, and thereby make its actual behavior deviate from its calculated behavior. Even within the time period covered by the model the actual values of many variables were occasionally quite far away from their calculated value. In an attempt at extrapolation this inadequacy of the model can certainly be expected to increase.

The stated numerical values of the parameters in the questions are also a source of weakness of the model. This is so because we are given no reason whatsoever for confidence in the *continuing* applicability of the given numbers. What these numbers are always depends upon the state of a large number of extrasystemic factors, and any change in these factors should be expected to change the values of the parameters. Such a change did occur, according to Clark's model, in 1933, and this change was a completely unpredictable one. It did *not* occur, again according to that model, at any other time; and this must have been the result of a constancy in the relevant outside factors, the existence of which was equally unpredictable in advance. The ever present uncertainty about the values of the parameters is not made any more bearable by the fact that we are given no hint whatsoever as to what the important outside influences upon these values are; the statistical estimation technique is completely blind to the chains of causation that exist in the actual world and which connect any given system of variables with the rest of the universe. The equations do not "explain" the phenomena of the world at all; they are only pictures of superficial, *and possibly momentary*, relationships. To hold otherwise constitutes an artificial generalization of the model.

We shall now make an inspection of two sets of ideas on the use of *stochastical* economic models. The further development and improvement of such models is regarded by many prominent economists to be the main hope for effective forecasting in the economic realm.

Example D–3. Jacob Marschak: "Economic Structure, Path, Policy, and Prediction" [7]

Professor Marschak presents us with a beautifully clear and concise statement of the principles underlying the more advanced probabilistic techniques of economic forecasting from econometric models. The following is a reproduction of the entire short article, reprinted here with Professor Marschak's kind permission.

I. *Policy and Prediction*

1. Knowledge is called useful if it helps to choose the *best policy* (action).

2. Best policy depends on (a) the things which one values as goals (e.g., for a firm, profit; for a government, national income, or budget surplus, etc.); (b) noncontrolled conditions (e.g., for a firm, weather and government policy; for a government, weather). The best policy is an action that maximizes *a*, given *b*.

3. To choose the best policy, it is necessary to predict (a) the effect of alternative policies under any given noncontrolled conditions; (b) the future noncontrolled conditions.

4. Thus, all useful knowledge implies prediction; and knowledge useless at one time may become useful later when new goals and conditions present themselves.

5. In human affairs (but also in large parts of technology), to predict is, in general, to estimate, for given conditions and for a

---

[7] *American Economic Review*, XXXVII (May 1947), pp. 81–84. This article does not represent Professor Marschak's most recent thought on the subject. See, for example, his article in *Studies in Econometric Method*, Cowles Commission Monograph No. 14 (New York: Wiley, 1954) for a more carefully elaborated treatment of the topic. We have decided to examine Professor Marschak's earlier article because it presents the "heart" of the matter in a more easily accessible form. (We are *not*, it might be restated, at all interested in the merit of any individual author, but only in the merit of certain procedures of analysis.)

given probability level, a probable range of the results of a given policy. This range is wide if the observations are few or subject to large errors, or if structural relations (see II) are subject to large random disturbances.

II. *Stochastic Economic Structure and Path*

6. The probabilistic character of economic prediction is due to the chance ("stochastic") character of economic *structural relations*.

7. Each of the structural relations describes either (a) human behavior (of a specified group of people), e.g., consumers' demand depends on their current and past income, assets, prices and on a "random disturbance," the latter being the aggregate effect of numerous, separately insignificant factors; or (b) technology, e.g., crops depend on acreage, labor, fertilizers, humidity, and a random disturbance; or (c) legal rules, e.g., price ceilings, tax laws, bank reserve regulations. Economic structure is fully described by these relations provided the character of the random disturbances (their variances, covariances) is given.

8. The number of structural relations must equal the number of economic (or nonautonomous) variables. In addition, structural relations contain noneconomic (or autonomous) variables. At any time, the probable range of values which an economic variable can take depends on the following conditions: (a) the economic structure; (b) the values of noneconomic variables.

9. Conditions can be noncontrolled (see 2 and 3 above) or controlled. Policies and controlled conditions are identical. Thus a policy fixes either some of the structural relations, or some of the noneconomic variables. However, certain government actions may lie outside of government control. For example, certain parts of the budget (interest on national debt) are determined by past values of certain variables; and tax rates may reflect political shifts which, in turn, are partly determined by economic conditions at or before election time. Such nonautonomous government actions will not be classified as policies; and relations stating what determines such actions may have to be included among structural relations (possibly using information gathered by political scientists). On the other hand, government policy may consist in deliberately invalidating such relations of the past and in fixing autonomously variables that were previously governed by structure.

The deliberate introduction of "automatisms" into the economic structure is a particular kind of policy; for example, adopting the legal rule that a change of level of employment or prices by given amounts should be followed by a certain change (stated in advance) in tax rates or public expenditures, with the object of stabilizing employment or prices; or the Bank of England's old rule to raise discount rate when gold flows out.

10. The path which an economic variable follows through time depends therefore on (a) economic structure and (b) on noneconomic variables.

Depending on the character of random disturbances the probable range of deviations from the most probable path will be larger or smaller; the most probable path may show *oscillations* if some of the structural relations are dynamic, e.g., if they contain time-lags or rates of change or acceleration — as in the case of "cobwebs."

III. *The Need for Structural Estimation*

11. Predictions for a future period, based on observations during a past period, are of different kinds according to whether both or one or none of the types of conditions 8 *a, b* changes within and between the two periods.

12. In particular, if structure is known to remain in the future what it was in the past, and if the noneconomic variables have constant values through both periods, the path of each variable would be predictable from the past, apart from random disturbances. In the presence of random disturbances, the problem is analogous to that of weather prediction.

13. If structure is known to be retained but the noneconomic variables have assumed and are going to assume changing though known values, it is possible to estimate for each current economic variable its dependence ("regression") on all noneconomic ones and on the past ("lagged") economic ones, and to apply this relation to the future. One can thus estimate the effect of policies that consist in controlling certain variables (tax rates, bank reserve ratios).

14. Finally, if structure is known to change in a given way, the prediction of the effect of this change requires the estimation of the original structure. In this case the study of past relations 7 *a, b, c,* is necessary.

15. Case 14 applies also with regard to the particular policy of introducing "automatisms" (see 9 above) of the most effective kind. For example, to fix in advance the best possible schedule relating tax

rates to the unemployment and prices of the previous month, it is necessary to know the lags and elasticities in the consumption equation and in other structural relations at a time when no such legal schedules were in operation. Only when such new device has operated long enough can structural estimation be replaced by the more "mechanical" type of predictions described in 12 and 13.

IV. *Economic Theory, Statistics, and Mathematics*

16. The statistical estimation of the structural relations 7 *a, b, c* is the "filling of empty boxes of economic theory." The theory is a set of hypotheses. Most of these hypotheses state which variables enter which structural equations, or state certain inequalities (e.g., regarding the signs or relative sizes of certain elasticities). They are based, essentially, on experience independent of the material which is to be used in estimation. This experience includes statements on rational (i.e., utility-maximizing) behavior and on deviations from it, on a plausible psychology of anticipations, on technological data, etc.

17. Economic theory is useful in the case 14 and useless in the cases 12 and 13. It can be presumed, however, that cases 12 and 13 seldom occur in practice. In particular, any policy that changes one or more of the structural relations of the past, gives rise to case 14, and necessitates structural estimation for prediction purposes. Structural estimation may seem useless until a structural change is expected or intended: it comes in very useful then. Thus practice requires theory.

18. All the foregoing statements are concerned with the logic of economic knowledge and its uses. This logic is the same whether or not mathematical symbols are used. However, mathematical presentation is of great help in testing the internal consistency of a theory (see 8 on the number of relations and variables); and it is hardly avoidable when the appropriate estimation methods are to be chosen and applied.

19. After stating the hypotheses about the structure, one may find that a certain collection of data will permit prediction only in the form of such a wide range of values as to make it useless for policy choice (since a wide range of policies will appear to yield equally good results). For this, mathematics cannot be blamed; it will merely reveal what otherwise might remain concealed. Mathematics does not suppress any information available for other methods; and it makes clearer when and how additional information must be

used (e.g., extending time series, supplementing them by cross-section data including attitude surveys, etc.).

The resort to stochastical equations in the construction of a model of the economic system is designed, primarily, to overcome that weakness of such models which stems from the suppression of relevant variables. Each equation, as before, still shows explicitly only the most important (according to some standard) variables; but the effects of the multitude of other influencing variables, instead of being ignored entirely, are now subsumed under a single "random disturbance." The various properties of that disturbance are intended to reflect the net importance and potency of all the variables impounded within it, and in this way to tell us everything we need to know (for all practical purposes) about these variables. True, say the proponents of these models, our equations no longer yield us definite unique values for the endogenous variables, but this definiteness would have been misleading anyhow. Now, at least, we know what the probability distributions of the deviations of the actual from the computed values are, and this knowledge is enough to fill the gap in our grasp of the system. As Professor Marschak declares, "Economic structure is fully determined by these relations [7, a, b, c] provided the character of the random disturbances (their variances, covariances) is given."

Our problem now is: Assuming, again, the data from which we proceed to be adequate and the statistical estimation procedures to be valid, do the resulting stochastical equations really constitute propositions about the world in which we can place complete confidence? Do these equations provide a firm basis for a chain of predictive reasoning? Are they laws or only assumptions?

In looking into these questions we can afford to ignore one of the problematic elements which are unavoidably present. Because of the fact that a statistician cannot study the entire universe of the deviations, he cannot discover the "actual" distribution of these deviations, but must estimate that distribution from a limited sample. As a result, we can only know what the distribution *probably* is; and therefore any given stochastical equation may quite possibly be "wrong."

Stochastical models suffer, however, from a more fundamental weakness, as we have noted before. They do not really remove the difficulty produced by the suppression of variables; they only push it back one step. The validity of a stochastical equation depends on *an assumption, that the universe of errors, from which the errors observed in the past and to be observed in the future are drawn, remains constant over time.* If this universe changes, the distribution of errors changes too, and the estimated stochastical equations lose whatever validity they originally had. We have no way of knowing that the required constancy will in fact obtain — we don't even have information on the "usual" behavior of such universes. Worse yet, the model contains no clue as to what the factors are to which the shape of the error universe is responsive. We cannot therefore study its characteristics without going back to the very variables which the model-builder wished to suppress in the first place.

Professor Marschak himself states a number of points which, if carried a bit further, lead to the above conclusion. He recognizes, for example, that "cases 12 and 13 seldom occur in practice." We would go further and say that these cases never occur in practice; we never know that either the noneconomic variables or the structure will actually remain constant. Professor Marschak clearly suggests to us what the weak aspect of the entire econometric procedure is by saying that the validity of all regression equations of current economic endogenous variables on noneconomic and lagged economic ones is conditional upon the constancy of the "structure." It is only an extension of this thought to say that the validity of the structural equations is, in turn, conditional upon another kind of constancy behind *them*, and that that constancy is conditional upon yet another one, and so on. It is therefore quite unfortunate that, in the specification of "structure," no clue is given under precisely what conditions the form of the equations will continue to hold, the parameters continue to remain true, and the distributions of the disturbances remain as given. Even the estimation of structure, then, does not enable us to make predictions (in our sense of the word).

The relationships expressed in the model therefore remain exposed to unexplainable and unpredictable shifts, which can occur, without notice, at any time. This difficulty is perhaps implicit in the very nature of statistical analysis. Statistical perceptions are, probably unavoidably, blind to the reasons for and conditions of the regularities and regressions which they uncover.

There is another, but related, weak spot in the above-presented set of concepts. Professor Marschak's mode of presentation of his ideas connotes that he regards the "structure" as being more stable than both the values of the noneconomic variables which codetermine the system and those of the economic variables which are determined by it. There seems to be no reason, and none is indicated by Professor Marschak, why this should be so. The source of this bias seems to lie, in part, in the physical form of the mathematical representation of the model. People who work with mathematical equations tend to form a mental habit of regarding the values of independent and dependent variables as being very volatile, the various parameters as being fixed, but not immutably so, and the basic form of the equation as staying absolutely constant. Another important source of the bias, one with a more "reputable" pedigree, might stem from the traditional view of the economic system as being a complex of *constant adjustment processes* which reconcile scarce and variable means to even more variable ends. A change in the social, psychological, physical, or technical environment was usually seen as affecting the economic system as a change in either demand or supply conditions, which were then reconciled, by the old and *unchanged* adjustment processes, to a new equilibrium position. Only seldom does one find a thorough analysis of an environmental change which alters the response properties of the system and which changes the form of the structural relationships within the system. It is probably important that economists accustom themselves to dealing with relationships which are potentially as variable as the values of the variables they relate to each other.

As a summary judgment, we classify the type of forecasting model described by Professor Marschak as being an artificial semiclosure of reality.

Example D–4.   Trygve Haavelmo: "The Probability Approach in Econometrics" [8]

In view of the great importance of statistical-econometric methods in economic forecasting, it seems warranted to take a look at yet another, but somewhat different, set of ideas on this subject. The paper to be discussed here is a very well-thought-out presentation of some rather fundamental principles of econometric model-building.

Mr. Haavelmo begins with the recognition of the fact that there are, in general, an infinity of variables influencing any given economic variable, y. But he believes that this situation can be simplified to manageable proportions by a distinction between the "potential" influence of one variable upon another and the "factual" influence. The former refers to the relative size of variation in y that might be induced by a *possible* variation in the influencing variable, and the factual influence is the result upon y that can be imputed to an *actual* variation in the influencing variable. Haavelmo states his faith underlying the construction of economic models as follows:

This distinction [between potential and factual influence] is fundamental. For, if we are trying to explain a certain observable variable, y, by a system of causal factors, there is, in general, no limit to the number of such factors that might have a *potential* influence upon y. But Nature may limit the number of factors that have a non-negligible *factual* influence to a relatively small number. Our hope for simple laws in economics rests upon the assumption that we may proceed as if such natural limitations of the number of relevant factors exist [p. 24].

[8] Supplement to *Econometrica*, XII (July 1944).

This assumption, Mr. Haavelmo believes, is a well justified one in economic research.

Whenever we try, a priori, to specify what we should think to be "important factors", our imagination is usually exhausted rather quickly; and when we attempt to apply our theory to actual data (e.g., by using certain regression methods), we often find that even a great many of the factors in our a priori list turn out to have practically no factual influence [pp. 25–26].

His recommended model consists, therefore, of a system of equations relating a number of variables having, for the period observed, significant factual influence upon one another. However, because of the many suppressed variables with potential but small factual influence, the equations cannot be "strict" functions, but must include a "general shift" whose properties represent the importance of the ignored factors. Accordingly, a "theoretical model" is

a restriction upon the joint variations of a system of variable quantities (or, more generally, "objects") which otherwise might have any value or property. More generally, the restrictions imposed might not absolutely exclude any value of the quantities considered; it might merely give different *weights* (or probabilities) to the various sets of possible values of the variable quantities. The model in question would then usually be characterized by the fact that it defines certain restricted subsets of the set of all possible values of the quantities, such that these subsets have nearly all of the total weight [p. 8].

The stochastical laws to be applied to the model would then be derived by the techniques of statistical estimation. (Mr. Haavelmo applies the Neyman-Pearson theory toward this purpose.)

This immediately raises the question, again, as to the degree of permanence of the probability laws which connect the variables of the model. If we try to make a prediction, these laws may break down in the time interval considered, and cannot therefore yield a worthwhile prediction. Mr. Haavelmo makes the following remarks in this connection:

A particular system of such relationships defines one particular theoretical *structure* of the economy; that is to say it defines a theoretical *set* of possible simultaneous sets of value or sets of time series for the economic variables. It might be necessary — and that is the task of economic theory — to consider various *alternatives* to such systems of relationships, that is, various alternative *structures* that might, approximately, correspond to economic reality at any time. For the "real structure" might, and usually does, change in various respects.

To make this idea more precise, suppose that it be possible to define a *class*, Ω, of *structures*, such that *one member or another* of this class would, approximately, describe economic reality in *any practically conceivable situation*. And suppose that we define some non-negative *measure* of the "size" (or of the "importance" or "credibility") of any subclass, ω in Ω, including Ω itself, such that, if a subclass contains completely another subclass, the measure of the former is greater than, or at least equal to, that of the latter, and such that the measure of Ω is positive. Now consider a particular subclass (of Ω), containing all those, — and only those — structures that satisfy a particular relation "A". *Let* ω_A be this particular subclass. (E.g., ω_A might be the subclass of all those structures that satisfy a particular demand function "A".) We then say that the relation "A" is *autonomous* with respect to the subclass of structures ω_A. And we say that "A" has a *degree* of autonomy which is greater the larger the "size" of ω_A as compared to that of Ω.

The principal task of economic theory is to establish such relations as might be expected to possess as high a degree of autonomy as possible [pp. 28–29].

Any relation that is derived by combining two or more relations within a system, we call a *confluent* relation. Such a confluent relation has, of course, usually a lower degree of autonomy (and never a higher one) than each of the relations from which it was derived, and all the more so the greater the number of different relations upon which it depends. . . [p. 29].

What is the connection between the degree of autonomy of a relation and its observable degree of constancy or persistence?

If we should take constancy or persistence to mean simply invariance with respect to certain hypothetical changes in structure, then the degree of constancy and the degree of autonomy would simply be two different names for the same property of an economic relation. But if we consider the constancy of a relation as a property of the behavior of *actual observations*, then there is clearly a difference between the two properties, because then the degree of autonomy refers to a class of *hypothetical* variations in structure, for which the relation *would be* invariant, while its actual persistence depends upon what variations *actually occur*. On the other hand, if we always try to form such relations as are autonomous with respect to those changes that are *in fact most likely to occur*, and if we succeed in doing so, then, of course, there will be a very close connection between actual persistence and theoretical degree of autonomy [pp. 29–30].

Having come as close as possible to this goal in model-construction, predictions are then made by assuming the joint probability law (consisting of all the stochastical relations), whether it is known or only estimated, to remain constant during the time-span covered by the prediction. "A statistical prediction means simply a (probability) statement about the location of a sample point not yet observed [p. 105]." And, ". . . in order to be able to predict there must be a certain persistency in the type of mechanism that produces the series to be predicted [p. 107]."

Before we go on to our comments on these ideas, it should be said that the above brief summary is very far from doing justice to Mr. Haavelmo's important paper. A wealth of ideas, which we have not even hinted at, is admirably developed and coördinated there. In particular, we have omitted entirely any mention of what was really the main contribution of that paper: the application of the Neyman-Pearson theory to the problems of model-building and prediction.

Comments: First, to clarify the terminology. The relationships of which Marschak spoke in his points (12) and (13) are, in Haavelmo's language, highly confluent relationships, and therefore of lesser (though conceivably of equal) autonomy than the structural equations. Marschak's "random disturbance" is the same thing as Haavelmo's "general shift." In general, the two sets of concepts are very similar, except that, within the papers discussed here, Haavelmo's ideas are more extensively elaborated.

Although Haavelmo recognizes that his stochastical equations are confluent with respect to many of the more fundamental relations, in his final formulation, he still proposes to incorporate these equations into the basis of a model. The continuation of the validity of these equations is simply assumed; and he gives no indication as to the external conditions under which this continuing validity would really be assured. In other words, like Marschak, he postulates a fixed universe from which the sample points are drawn. All of the above-stated comments on Marschak's article therefore apply to Haavelmo's ideas as well.

Another closely related assumption is involved in his faith that the variables with small factual influence will continue to have a small such influence. Haavelmo recognizes that the occurrence of surprises in this respect would invalidate a model of the type he suggests — even make such models impossible. As to the "justice" of this assumption, we can say that very frequently dormant variables with considerable potential influence do remain conveniently dormant for long periods of time, but that sometimes, in "periods of change," they do become active. At any rate, we never *know* when such activity will or will not occur; and, moreover, the ever present possibility of "upsets" of established relationships has sometimes been known to become a rather dramatic actuality.

Haavelmo does not regard the probabilistic nature of his model as a weakness. He bases his views on the opinion that all laws only assert probabilities (page iv) — the conventional laws making statements whose "probability is almost 1." He relies on economic theory and "fruitful hypotheses" to tell him where laws exist, and, without much thought to domains of validity, proceeds to the statistical estimation. The rest of the universe is isolated from the variables under discussion by the assumption that the variables of small factual importance will continue that way. We, in contrast, would not regard as a law any statement which is not universally valid. The statement must thus include in its formulation all variables which can possibly have an effect. (The unavoidable small-scale errors of measurement are easily dealt with by making the scales coarse enough, or by some equivalent procedure.) One of Mr. Haavelmo's laws is, from our point of view, the result of a confluence of unknown stability of unknown laws and observations, and is therefore an assumption.

General Comments on Econometric Models

The following comments are meant to apply only to econometric models in the form in which they have been developed so far as indicated by the last four examples, not to econometric models as such.

(1) The type of variable used for model-construction, and the type of relationship used to connect the variables to each other, are such that *no "informational" (nonassumptive) equations can possibly be arrived at.* The equations will always be of very doubtful reliability — always subject to violation by the actual phenomena. They are not dependable "laws of nature," and cannot therefore serve as reliable bases for predictions. As has been pointed out, it is not primarily the probabilistic nature of the equations that produces the difficulty, but rather the fact that sudden and unannounced shifts in these probability relationships are always possible.

(a) Technological equations — "transformation functions" — are not dependable because there is no necessity of the system to "adhere" to these equations. It is always possible, for example, for the volume of output, in relation to the input, to be reduced below the amount called for in the equation, by accidents, misplanning, labor disputes, acts of God, and other interferences. It is also possible for the output to exceed the computed amount as a result of better managerial methods, technological innovations, etc. In practice, of course, most of these deflections can be subsumed under the random disturbance, but basic changes always are possible and occasionally occur.

(b) Economic behavior equations are generally by far the weakest component of an econometric model. There just is no necessity for historical behavior patterns, of the type measured by econometricians, to continue into the future. There is no necessity for business firms to maximize profits. There is no necessity for investors to continue to respond, in the same way as in the past, to the rate of interest or the level of consumption. And there is no necessity for consumers to adhere to their previous total and specific expenditure patterns. The assumption of invariance in any of the aggregate behavior patterns is only an assumption — and one that is by no means binding upon the population at large. The fiasco of the 1945 postwar forecasts, which will be described below, bears eloquent testimony to this fact.

It seems unlikely that the difficulty can ever be fully overcome by the addition of more and more variables to the system. The actions of each individual in the group are governed by a very large number of variables specific to himself, and it seems entirely hopeless ever to take account in an aggregative model of all these variables. And besides, there is also the far more important general truth that, no matter how many variables are included in a model, there are always further exterior ones which may cause unanticipated reactions within the system. It may often be true that the "random disturbance" handles the effects of the non-considered variables quite satisfactorily, especially of the factors specific to the individual persons; but it is the danger of pervasive "systematic" effects that is responsible for the difficulty.

(c) Legal rules do not present dependable constraints upon the behavior of the system. First, the application of a law to specific circumstances is not something that is clearly and unambiguously predetermined; the law is, in general, a very flexible type of constraint. Second, laws always have been, are now, and probably always will be, violated in practice. These violations are frequently very widespread and general, and no random disturbance is likely to cover these deviations. Examples of generally violated laws: The 18th Amendment, the Internal Revenue Code, traffic rules, the Sherman Act, credit controls, foreign exchange controls, etc.

(d) Definitions are, of course, absolutely dependable constraints on the movement of the system, but this is a case of trivial dependability.

All these disturbing factors can be summarized as being the result of the internal volatility of the socio-economic system. Situations seldom remain constant for long, and even when they do there is always the possibility of change. There generally are a multitude of factors actively transforming the physical, institutional, and social structure of the system. Propositions which were true today are not (or need not be) true tomorrow; and propositions which will be true tomorrow are not true today, and generally are not even known today. This continuing turbulence makes the task of the economic forecaster considerably more difficult than that of, say, the doctor. The human body is also in a constant state of flux, but there is still, undoubtedly, much more stability in its anatomical structure and in the various interrelationship patterns. Doctors can make good (though by no means infallible) predictions about the macro-behavior of their object of study; the social scientist, trying to apply analogous logical tools to his more volatile object of study, unfortunately does not meet with the same degree of success.

It would be foolhardy to attempt a final judgment on the future prospects of econometric models. It is my guess, however, that econometric forecasting attempts, of the type considered here, constitute a dead end in the search for a foolproof method. A good deal of improvement in model-construction techniques may still be in the offing, but, in view of the various weaknesses pointed out so far, it seems impossible for such models ever to get out of the stage of artificial closure or artificial semiclosure. As long as they continue to build upon relationships which do not have, and cannot attain, the status of "invariant laws of nature" (as have, for example, chemical formulae), they will not be able to free themselves from the constant danger of suddenly, and without notice, becoming obsolete.

(2) Oskar Morgenstern [9] has pointed out an entirely different region of weakness in econometric models. We have taken it for granted so far that the state of the economic system at any given time and the values of specific variables at any given time can be accurately observed. Our entire concern has been (and will be) with the methodology of analysis, interpretation, and use of knowledge, not with the problems of original observation. Morgenstern, in contrast, shows very convincingly that original economic data are so full of inaccuracies that all model-building which proceeds from these data is on extremely weak ground to begin with. Not that this must necessarily be so, but the type of data we have available today must be used with great caution. As a practical matter, therefore, in current model-building activities, we must continually be conscious of two sources of error.

So long as no specific assumptions are made about the degree of error in the observation of economic phenomena, it is not easy to make useful statements about the randomness of the information given as due to the alleged presence of other factors hitherto neglected in the formulation of the model. To the extent that stochastic theory is at all possible, it must be designed so as to allow us to distinguish and to decide between the two sources: firstly, errors of observation and secondly, failure to account for disturbing factors that ought to form part of the theory and enter into a more adequate set of equations. In a strict sense, these neglected factors too become known only through information *also* beset with errors of observation. Hence, there is never a possibility of completely transforming the *observed* parameters into *true* parameters by accounting fully for excluded factors. "True" parameters can, on principle, only be theoretically determined.

Economic theory of various types is sometimes used to make *predictions*. Input-output studies in particular are designed with this purpose in mind. It must be understood that any such process — whatever its ultimate merits — involves four steps: (1) the initial data, (2) the model, (3) the computations and (4) the comparison of the numerical result with reality. Each one of them has its own

[9] *On the Accuracy of Economic Observations* (Princeton, N. J.: Princeton University Press, 1950).

errors: the initial data are known only with a certain degree of accuracy, the model is an idealization of reality, the computations produce errors that are added to those existing at the start and the numerical result with all its cumulative errors will be compared and "checked" with a reality that is again only revealed up to an unknown error factor [p. 35].

We shall not be further concerned with the problem of errors of observation. We mention it here only as a reference to a related area of inquiry.

(3) We come now to yet another, and very serious, drawback of econometric models. These models, and, for that matter, all the other forecasting methods discussed in this chapter, are *inherently unsuitable as guides to economic policy*. It is impossible to tell, from an inspection and analysis of the type of data incorporated into such models, whether a given state of the system is "desirable" or "undesirable," or whether the consequences of a given action are "good" or "bad." This is a consequence of the fact that the models (and also the accessory data) take into account only one (or a few) of the "dimensions" of the elements with which they deal. The labor force, for example, is taken into account only with respect to a few measurements (employment, unemployment, etc.); all other dimensions of the labor force, such as its happiness, its sociological structure, the personality characteristics of its members, their cultural attainments, their degree of capacity-realization, etc., are entirely ignored. The rate of consumption, also, is considered only in terms of some over-all quantitative measure (possibly broken down into a few major classes); and ignored are the physical, detailed characteristics of the goods and services consumed, their effect on the state of mental and physical health, on the degree of satisfaction attained, on the state of morality, on interpersonal relationships, on productive capacity and energy, on military strength, on the political line-up, on the accident rate, and on very many other nontrivial phenomena. It is as impossible to arrive at a sensible evaluation of the state of a system on the basis of such very incomplete observations as it is to judge the value of a house from a knowledge of its cubic

content alone, to form a judgment of a man from a knowledge of the color of his hair alone, to govern one's food intake on the basis of weight alone, or to choose a job merely according to the pay involved.

It is impossible to formulate and to carry out intelligent policies with only a partial one-sided knowledge of the state of the world, because we are not indifferent to the various non-considered aspects of the world. These other aspects are as much "charged with the social interest" as the dimensions which were incorporated into the model. And it is impossible to separate some of the aspects of phenomena out of their context and to operate with them independently of the rest of the world — an alteration of one of the aspects, as we have already noted, will necessarily alter most of the others as well. In changing the value of a particular variable, we change also the other aspects of that variable, and furthermore, the conditions of many other variables which are not directly connected with the model at all.

One cannot manipulate, say, the quantity of consumption without also manipulating its physical composition, its distribution among individuals, and the secondary consequences mentioned above. In order to arrive at and conduct intelligent policy, therefore, one must consider, simultaneously, all of the characteristics of the elements of the system which have a value-significance to us. In view of the tight interconnectedness of the system, the requirement of simultaneous consideration is indispensable.[10]

Even if we were concerned only with the quantities incorporated into the model, as has also been noted, we still could not freely manipulate these quantities without worrying about the rest of the universe. We still would have to consider the various "feedback" effects. The fate of all other aspects of the world might well be a matter of indifference to us, but we cannot ignore the way in which the rest of the world, as codetermined by our own actions, will influence the future course of the variables in which we *are* interested.

---

[10] See, in this connection, our discussion in Chapter 3 of artificial isolation.

Before turning to a methodological examination of some actual attempts at predicting the economic future by the aid of econometric models, let us look at one more set of ideas on the theory of such models. Professor Goodwin, the author of these ideas, is very much concerned with the problem of taking some cognizance, in constructing a model, of the rest of the world. The approach is quite sophisticated.

Example D–5. R. M. Goodwin: "The Nonlinear Accelerator and the Persistence of Business Cycles" [11]

Professor Goodwin's article is a very valuable contribution to business-cycle theory. It is an example of what is probably closed-system theory at its best. But it is still closed-system theory, and, try as it may, it cannot really overcome the inherent limitations of this kind of thinking.

Goodwin is concerned with one of the knottier problems of business-cycle theory: the attempt to explain the persistence of cycles over time. Most of the economists who so far have constructed models of the cycle have aimed for closure; they wanted models which would yield a fully determinate course of events for the entire cycle. In their attempts to attain this goal they were forced, for reasons of mathematical practicability, to resort to linear models. This was clearly recognized to be an expedient, but one which, it was hoped, would not cause major difficulties. This hope, unfortunately, proved unjustified: it was soon discovered that linear models yield some very awkward results with respect to the problem of persistence of the cycle. The oscillations produced by a linear model are such that they either explode or die out; [12] the intermediate case, an unchanging cycle, presupposes a set of such unrealistic conditions that it can safely be ignored.

Goodwin is not very happy with some of the alternative models that have been suggested. He rejects Frisch's model, for example — a damped model with frequent injections of re-

[11] *Econometrica* XIX (January 1951), 1–17.
[12] To be quite rigorous, they never *die*; they just fade away.

juvenating energy by outside random "shocks" — on the characteristic ground that, because "the source of maintenance lies
outside the theory," it is not a complete theory.

Instead, Goodwin proposes a modification of business-cycle
theory which, he believes, will bring the theory into closer
accord with the form of the observed sequence of cycles than
any of the other proposals. He suggests that we depart from the
assumption of linearity, specifically, by introducing a nonlinear
accelerator into the model of the cycle.

Without describing Goodwin's model in detail — it is a fairly
complicated mathematical affair — let us take a look at its most
important distinguishing characteristic. The customary accelerator is derived from model equations which show a linear
relation between the stock of capital goods and the national
income (or production). The accelerator is equal to the factor
of proportionality between the stock of capital and the national
income. As such the accelerator is independent of the absolute
amount of capital or income and, for that matter, of any other
variable or relation in the model. It is primarily because of this
fixity of the accelerator that linear models, depending upon the
particular value of the accelerator, either explode or dampen
down to an equilibrium position. Goodwin, in contrast, employs
an accelerator which changes in value, the variation depending
upon the state of the model otherwise. In regions of low oscillation, the accelerator is such that the oscillations tend to explode; but as soon as the system enters a region of wide oscillation, the value of the accelerator shifts, so as to dampen these
oscillations more and more strongly. The result of such a variable accelerator is, then, that the system tends to settle down
to a stable oscillatory motion. If now a number of realistic
assumptions concerning technological progress and population
growth are added to the model, and if "reasonable" values are
given to multipliers and production lags, etc., the motion of the
model produces a reasonably good replica of the actual course
of events.

A remarkable property of Goodwin's model is that the final
equilibrium motion is independent of any "initial position" of

the system, that the result is the same no matter what the starting point may have been. If any outside shock upon the system should ever cause a displacement in the path, the system would, after a time, again return to its equilibrium motion. The persistence of the cycle is thus explained even under "disturbing" external circumstances. And also, "the oscillation maintains itself without the need of any outside 'factors' to help in the explanation. In this sense it is a complete, self-contained theory."

In order to avoid unnecessary repetition of substantially the same points, we will, in our comments on Goodwin's model, ignore most of the elements of artificiality. But we do have something to say about artificial closure.

From one point of view, Goodwin's model does involve a certain amount of non-closed-system thinking. A considerable amount of "freedom" is given to initial positions and displacements. Goodwin believes that it is important to do so, because "otherwise we are involved in believing that the magnitude and turning points, for example, of a cycle now are completely determined by events which took place many years ago. The absurdity of such an assumption is obvious [p. 3]." We agree, of course, that such an assumption, being equivalent to a closed-system assumption, is absurd, and that some alternate kind of model is preferable. But Goodwin did not really escape this absurdity — he only disguised it by pushing it back one step. *His model presupposes a structure of the system which is fully determined in the objectionable way,*[13] and which is, moreover, determined so that it remains invariant over some given time period. The assumption of such a structure is as absurd as the assumption which Goodwin scorns.

Goodwin clearly is a closed-system theorist and, as a matter of fact, explicitly declares his goal to be the construction of "a complete theory." His constructs, therefore, are unavoidably vulnerable to the many pitfalls of closed conceptual systems

---

[13] It might be protested here that the structure could also be fixed by the same kind of equi-final process. This would, however, only push the objectionable determinacy even further back. Ultimately, the problem has to be faced.

that we have described heretofore. The model is artificially isolated from reality and cannot, therefore, be a constituent of a useful predictive model. At best, it can serve in the derivation of some dynamic economic laws in the same way as the previously discussed model of Somers. If it can show that, under almost any realistic conditions, oscillations of some sort will occur, it will have accomplished a great deal.

Example D–6. The 1945–1946 Postwar Forecasts

Our final example is taken from the history of actual forecasting experience. Probably no discussion of economic forecasting today can be complete without some mention of the disastrous and rather astounding performances of a whole flock of government and private forecasters in attempting to anticipate the course of the system during the postwar transition period. The most notable aspect of almost all of these forecasts was that they were so very wide of the mark. A considerable number of different approaches were employed (most of them in the form of econometric models), but they all yielded wildly inaccurate results. This experience served, apparently more than any other single factor, to bring a great deal of discredit on the very endeavor to foretell the economic future.

A considerable number of articles and monographs have been written on the subject, analyzing, first, what actually happened and, second, why it happened. The most complete and thorough of these studies is probably the one by Leo Barnes.[14] All of the following factual material will be taken from that excellent monograph.[15]

Our consideration here of these forecasts will not yield any

[14] "An Experiment That Failed; An Analysis of Economic Forecasting in American Reconversion, 1945–46" (unpublished Ph.D. dissertation, Graduate Faculty of Political and Social Science, New School for Social Research, May 1948).

[15] Another thorough and painstaking analysis of these forecasts is Michael Sapir's *Review of Economic Forecasts for the Transition Period*, Studies in Income and Wealth, XI (New York: National Bureau of Economic Research, 1949).

new principles. All of the relevant points have already been covered in the discussion of the previous examples. The present exhibit is to be understood as illustrative material for the methodological discussion above.

The postwar forecasters were faced with a rather formidable problem. The economy had just come through a period of considerable upheaval and was facing another period of very drastic and large structural changes. The precise nature of these changes was conjectural — there were no reliable indications anywhere of the developments ahead. Under these circumstances the forecasters had to take rather bold action. Most of them attacked their job, first, by making a number of necessarily heroic assumptions concerning the movements of the exogenous factors (political, military, etc.) which influence economic activity; second, by assuming the prewar relationships among the major variables of the system to reassert themselves; and third, by making a number of "corrections" in the prewar relationships in order to reflect the various special circumstances of the current scene. This cavalier treatment of economic reality enabled them to produce some definite forecasts; but the contrary events that actually occurred were what should have been expected in the first place.

Several different basic approaches were employed by the various forecasters. We shall take a look, first, at the method which puts primary emphasis on the determination of the Gross National Product and which then derives the other important magnitudes (consumption, employment, etc.) from the GNP forecast.

As always, all forecasting activity of this type must proceed from a set of basic assumptions. The details of these assumptions varied somewhat among different forecasters, but the main features were reasonably similar. One example of such a basis is that of the Office of War Mobilization and Reconversion. Their economic projections were conditional upon the following five assumptions:

    1. "War expenditures are reduced as rapidly as is feasible."

2. "Production reconversion is efficiently handled."
3. "Moderate tax cuts are enacted."
4. "No serious labor disturbances develop."
5. "No other measures are adopted by the Federal Government specifically directed at affecting the level of output, income and employment [pp. 9–10]."

The typical procedure for arriving at a GNP-centered economic forecast was as follows:

. . . to estimate the gross national product of the United States for any period, one must add together the dollar volume of spending for finished goods and services by all individual consumers, by all business enterprises, including farms, and by all local, state and federal government units. To that total must then be added or subtracted the net change in business inventories, exports, and other foreign investment. That will yield the total value of all goods and services produced or provided in the United States in the period covered.

The technique used to forecast this complex can be broken down into a number of steps:

Step 1: Distinguishing between autonomous and induced components of the gross national product.

[The former are determined by political, sociological, technological and other extra-economic factors, and must be forecast independently. Often, only a "well-informed guess" can be made about the future movements of autonomous variables.] [16]

Step 2: Determining which components are to be taken as autonomous.

[This varies with the circumstances. In situations, for example, where the demand clearly exceeds any possible supply, the capacities of the relevant industries set the limit to the volume of production and thereby to the contribution of those industries to the GNP.]

In most reconversion forecasts employing the GNP method, the following components of GNP were taken as autonomous.

1. Federal, state and local government expenditures (determined largely by fixed budgetary commitments).

[16] For the sake of brevity, the material in brackets is paraphrased from Barnes.

2. Private gross capital formation, including business purchases of producers' durable goods, private construction and housing, and net growth in business inventories and exports (all presumably determined by supply limitations).

3. Consumer expenditures for durable goods (primarily determined by supply limitations).

4. Consumer expenditures for rent (basically fixed by OPA).

There are left, accordingly, only consumer expenditures for nondurable goods and for services other than rent to be treated as induced components [p. 113].

Step 3: First estimate of the total gross national product.

A preliminary approximation of total GNP is now obtained from the autonomous variables on the basis of past relationships of GNP to these autonomous components of it. In most cases, the historical period used as a basis for multiple correlation is 1929–1940 [p. 113].

Step 4: Derivation of disposable income from the first approximation of GNP.

[This procedure is quite complicated. It involves large amounts of data and a large number of assumptions concerning the various kinds of taxes, transfer payments, business reserves, etc. In order to assure maximum accuracy, many other federal agencies are called upon for estimates on the items within their jurisdiction.]

Step 5: Derivation of induced expenditures from disposable income.

[This amounts to the application of the multiple correlation equations obtained from an analysis of prewar data.]

Step 6: Second approximation of total gross national product.

Adding the estimate of induced expenditures to the previous total of autonomous expenditures (Step 2) yields a second estimate of GNP [p. 115].

Step 7: Elimination of disparities and check for internal consistency.

[Verify, for example, that *total* consumer expenditures bear a sensible relation to disposable income.] (pp. 112–116)

The forecast of GNP obtained by this method is then translated into "reasonable" equivalents in terms of employment, unemployment, wage payments, personal saving, etc. These derivations are based on prewar relationships among the variables involved, corrected for current estimates and assumptions on worker productivity, average hours worked, and other relevant factors.

One of the other approaches to the problem centered around a forecast of industrial production rather than of GNP. The technique of Mordecai Ezekiel and Virginia Duncan of the Bureau of Agricultural Economics is a good illustration of this type of approach. Their procedure involves the following four steps:

1. Projecting *potential* industrial output in terms of the potential availability of the factors of production.

2. Incorporating this estimate into one of *potential* gross national product on the basis of historical correlations between GNP and industrial production.

3. Determining the extent to which this potential GNP will not be realized because of inadequacies in demand for different types of goods and services.

4. Translating the resulting estimate of *actual* GNP into one or more of the other customary measures of economic performance, such as national income, employment and unemployment, and, if desired, *actual* industrial production [p. 117].

The actual procedure implied by this technique requires large amounts of detailed and complex analysis. Each component of the aggregate of production must be treated separately. Most of the relationships used, however, are derived from prewar experience and many others are supplied by "reasonable estimates," so that the assumptive element is nevertheless quite predominant.

As stated before, both types of forecasts, as well as the various other ones, failed to come within hailing distance of the actual course of events. Some of the techniques yielded less bad results than others, but the differences appear to have been very largely a matter of chance. The most serious errors, percentagewise, occurred in the unfortunately well-publicized unemployment estimates. It was predicted by some that unemployment would exceed 8 million persons when, as a matter of fact, it never even reached 3 million.[17] The GNP projections and those of its components were also much too pessimistic, although, of course, the percentage error was not nearly as large. In this respect,

OWMR's most disastrous forecasting error occurred in the projection of consumer expenditures for non-durables. Percentagewise, its minimum error is 13.6 per cent for the third quarter of 1946, and its maximum 19.3 per cent for the first quarter. Errors of this magnitude occurred despite the fact that OWMR's estimate of consumer expenditures presumably "makes allowance for the effect of deferred demand and of the wartime accumulation of liquid assets [p. 19]."

If it were not for the fact that some of the errors offset each other, the forecasts for the aggregates would have been even further off than they actually were.

Not only did the Washington forecasts give incorrect values for the various economic magnitudes, but they misjudged the entire temper and spirit of the economy in the immediate postwar period. They predicted a sharply reduced demand, falling prices, pessimistic expectations, and rampant unemployment; the true picture was almost exactly the reverse of that. Spending was high, prices were driven upward, an optimistic mood pervaded the system, and unemployment never exceeded the "normal" level.

To explain these very dramatic failures, Barnes gives an impressive and lengthy list of specific procedural errors of which the forecasters were guilty. The most important failings, however, Barnes believes, stem from a single source:

Continued reflection upon the etiology of the forecasting errors leads the writer to the conclusion that the underlying cause of the errors was *psychological,* — not theoretical, statistical or methodological.

The originating cause of most of the reconversion forecasting errors was the prevailing psychological "mind-set toward depression"

[17] The Ezekiel-Duncan estimate was, in this case, much closer to the truth.

among the forecasters. Most of the forecasters had an unmistakable predilection to look at the economy through the dark glasses of the 1930's. This predilection had profound consequences for economic forecasting of postwar conditions. Almost inevitably, it led to an acceptance of the stagnation of the '30's as the economic norm for the American economy of the twentieth century. Given this bias, it was natural to regard *re*-conversion as a return to basic prewar conditions and to minimize the continuing economic consequences of the war [p. 161].

The *status quo ante* was an economy which had achieved record peacetime production in 1941 with 7 to 8 million workers still looking for jobs. Now, the discontinuance of war production and the demobilization of the armed forces would throw a total of at least 16 million persons back into the labor market. For economists conditioned to chronic peacetime underemployment it became next to impossible to understand how so many additional workers could be absorbed without serious unemployment and dislocation [pp. 162–163].

The following list gives most, but not all, of the errors found by Barnes.[18] These errors are, to some extent, self-offsetting; most tend to underestimate economic activity, but some tend to overestimate. We present this list here mainly to show, as graphically as possible, just how many things can go wrong with forecasts of this type.

Factual Errors Resulting From the Depression Mind-Set:

1. Industrial reconversion tempo underestimated.
   Partly this was due to the unfamiliarity of the forecasters with the speed with which businessmen could move when spurred by unprecedented demand for their goods; partly to the expectation that demand would not be unprecedented [p. 167].

2. Construction revival misjudged.
   [The cause of this underestimate is the same as above.]

3. Reduction of munitions employment after V-E Day overlooked.
   [Since substantial cut-backs occurred already before V-J Day, the shock of the later full demobilization was considerably reduced.]

---

[18] Chapters 15 and 16 of his book.

4. Quick retirement of emergency workers after V-J Day.
   [Withdrawal of school-age workers and women from the labor market substantially reduced unemployment.]
5. Undermanning of non-war activities overlooked.
   [Industries had been functioning with skeleton staffs; they now built up their personnel again.]
6. Factor of voluntary "non-employment."
   [Many people went to school; many took vacations. Barnes estimates that 2 million people were thus "non-employed" rather than "unemployed."]
7. Effect of post–V-J Day wage increase.
   [Because of their pessimistic estimates, forecasters regarded wage raises as unlikely; therefore ignored this source of demand.]
8. Psychological effects of release from war tensions.
   [Gave rise to a buying spree.]
9. Rush to build up inventories underestimated.
10. Industrial bottlenecks.
    [This retarding factor was underestimated.]
11. Labor disputes.
    [The possibility of these was discounted.]
12. Reduction in overtime work.
    [Not eliminated, as forecasters had anticipated.]

Other Factual Errors in the Reconversion Forecasts:

13. Employment-sustaining effect of the excess profits tax.
    [When the cost of retaining employees is so low, employers are reluctant to reduce their staffs.]
14. Overestimate of worker productivity.
    [Expected increases did not materialize; any given GNP therefore required a larger labor force.]
15. Underestimate of effective foreign demand.
16. Postponement of income tax payment.
17. Repeal of excess profits tax.
    [This caused errors only in the 1946 forecasts.]
18. Corporate saving and dividend policy.
    [Dividends were underestimated, and depreciation charges were overestimated.]

19. Rapid demobilization.
    [Proceeded faster than assumed.]

Errors in the Construction of Autonomous Variables and Intermediate Projections:

1. Errors in the estimation of autonomous variables.
2. Derivation of intermediate projections from GNP.
   For example: "Sapir correctly estimates that anywhere from one-third to one-half of the deviation in the typical OWMR projection of gross national product was the result of an underestimate of the amount of disposable income consumers would possess in the transition period at any given level of GNP [p. 182]."

Errors in Economic and Econometric Theory:

1. Use of prewar correlations as postwar norms.
   [The artificiality of this procedure is clear. There was no very good reason to suppose the prewar relationships to be reëstablished; and there was certainly no guarantee that this would take place.]

   The correlations used to build up gross national product from component expenditures were particularly open to question when applied to the reconversion period. To be sure, all the forecasters went through the motions of making allowances for special distorting factors. But the latter might well loom so large and important that, for all practical purposes, it would have been better to start from scratch. A discriminating qualitative rather than mechanically quantitative approach might have focused attention on factors that would otherwise be overlooked. The resulting forecast, while less precise, would have been more accurate. The ideal technique would undoubtedly have been a combination of both methods [p. 189].

   [Among the government forecasters, Ezekiel and Duncan came closest to this ideal, and they had the best forecast. The most mechanistic forecast, that of Jacob L. Mosak of OPA, was the one widest of the mark.]

2. Derivation of employment and unemployment from output or income.
   [This depends on too many intermediate assumptions, like the average length of the work-week, labor productivity, etc.]

3. Minimizing the role of price expectations.
   [This results from the use of constant dollars.]
4. Distinction between autonomous and induced variables.
   [Variables should have been regarded, more realistically, as being partly autonomous and partly induced.]
5. Divergent multiplier effects of different types of investment.
6. The consumption-saving function.
   [Usually unrealistic, particularly in the relations among the partial consumption functions.]

Comment: The forecasting experiences just described constitute an excellent illustration of one of the main points of this chapter, one that has been made several times before: that forecasts based on assumptions, *no matter how well-founded these may seem at the time*, are quite undependable. The transition forecasts were based on the best information available at the time, and were produced by well-trained and experienced economists; yet, they were disastrously wrong. While it is undoubtedly true that various improvements in technique were possible and would have resulted in closer estimates, it is the basic approach itself that is the most fertile source of difficulty and error. Relationships, no matter how carefully established, cannot be counted upon to continue into the future; they do break down. Structural parameters, likewise, cannot be assumed to remain constant; they do undergo change. And even statistical universes cannot be assumed to remain unchanged and thereby to yield a predictable error term for forecasts; they also change in response to surrounding circumstances. All of the comments made previously on econometric models per se apply here as well.

One of Barnes' conclusions is that the prevailing depression mind-set was responsible, more than any other single factor, for the poor showing of the forecasters. This points to another serious drawback of assumptive propositions as bases for forecasts. It is inevitable that the forecaster have some mind-set or other — no economist is completely unaffected by the economic climate in which he has been "raised" and in which he lives. Peoples' minds are necessarily shaped by their previous experiences. To the extent that this is true, errors in estimates and judgments will not occur at random (random with respect to the subject matter of the forecast), but will have a *systematic bias*. The process of formulating an assumptive proposition, which is a central part of the type of forecast we are considering, not only leaves room for this bias to creep in, but it virtually *guarantees* that the bias become part of the forecast.

Charitable-minded writers sometimes defend the Washington forecasters on the ground that their method had not really received a fair test. The events of the reconversion period were quite chaotic and entirely unprecedented — the forecasters had no previous experience under analogous circumstances on which they could draw for guidance in the present situation. Their task was unusually difficult. If their techniques had been applied during a more settled period in history, the performance would have been incomparably better. And, little doubt, these statements are true. But while these facts may be an adequate and justified personal vindication of the various forecasters, they do not by any means protect the forecasting methods from criticism. A forecasting method, to be worthy of respect, must be able to handle all eventualities, not just a "normal" course of events. Inasmuch as, at any given time, the continuance of a "normal" period cannot justifiably be assumed, the forecasts based upon such an assumption are clearly untrustworthy. And it is, after all, in times of actual or possible change that we need the forecasts most. There is no great benefit in having a forecasting method which works only if nothing happens.

The Washington transition-forecasting experience illustrates, first, how assumptive econometric forecasting is actually carried on, and second, what can happen to such forecasts. We are not saying that it was the subsequent errors that proved the techniques to be weak. Even if the various techniques had yielded perfect forecasts, the lack of what we have called "information" in their bases would still have made the results undependable *in advance*. The success would have been due to a stroke of luck, and not to any merit in the method. Our criticism rests on methodological ground alone.

E. STORY-TELLING

We conclude our survey of economic analysis with the least rigorous but most common form of reasoning employed in economic-forecasting attempts. It is comparatively simple to use and simple to understand. Moreover, the results are usually quite convincing (in the psychological sense). We have named it "story-telling," because its logical structure is the same as that of a story. The economist (or any other type of analyst) who uses this form of reasoning is operating on the same *logical* plane (though not, of course, the same *factual* plane) as the novelist or the dramatist. He presents, like the story-teller, a sequence of events, each event leading to the next; and, like the story-teller again, he presents the story in terms of the behavior of a few major "characters." The succession of events is made to appear to be caused, at each step, by the actions of the characters; and the entire story is made to unfold according to some "inner" necessity. Moreover, the action is of such a nature that we can usually "understand" (in the Max Weber sense of the word) what "caused" each of the constituent events.

Illustrations of this reasoning pattern are so plentiful and so commonplace that we do not need to analyze any one example in detail. Almost the entire school of historical analysis is a case in point. More generally, virtually all attempts at explanations of past events use the story-telling pattern. It appears in such cases to be the "natural" way of approaching the task. After a "story" has occurred, it is relatively easy to point out a number of "factors" which quite plausibly can be regarded as "the main causes" of the unfolding of the story. As long as such explanations are psychologically convincing — as long as they correspond to the individual's conception of cause and effect — they are generally accepted as valid. We all carry within us, as an enduring imprint of past experiences, a set of ideas as to what events are apt to follow what other events, and how some things typically come to be. When an explanation is developed in terms of these familiar patterns, we quite easily "see" it, no

matter how incomplete or fallacious it may really be in its
logic. And since, furthermore, these *ex post* explanations are very
seldom contradicted by the evidence — both the "causes" and
the story to be explained are known to have occurred before
the attempt at analysis is even begun — the established method
of explanation is seldom challenged, and very few doubts are
ever raised concerning its validity. It is however a safe generalization to make that all *verbal* explanations of past events
are inadequate (from our point of view). *The list of indicated
causes and structural elements is never such that, from the
knowledge of that list alone, the "explained" event could have
been predicted.* There are always many other possibilities which
could also have followed the set of indicated "causes." And as
long as there are *any* other possibilities which are not inconsistent with the stated "causes," the actual event is not fully explained.

Some typical examples of explanatory reasoning after the
event are not difficult to find. Explanations of the occurrence of
a war, the outcome of an election, the happening of an accident,
the development of organized crime, the current world tension,
the disappearance of a biological species, etc., are all of this
nature and are all inadequate (from our standpoint). None
point uniquely to the event they "explain." It is probably
another safe generalization to say that these "explanations"
show, if they are not counterfactual or fallacious, how an event
was facilitated by the "causes" — they do not prove the necessity of its occurrence.

There is, moreover, no hope that this characteristic type of
reasoning will ever provide adequate explanations of natural
phenomena. The reason is simple. Any interrelated set of phenomena of the real world, as long as they do not include the
entire space-time universe, constitutes, as we have seen, an
open system, one that is constantly subject to outside influence.
No amount of information about events within the system is
therefore adequate to "explain" later events in that system. The
later events are determined by both intrasystemic prior events
and outside influences; and any constellation of intrasystemic

events therefore can, depending upon the specific nature of the outside influences, "give rise" to *many* different patterns of later events. We may know, afterwards, that during a given time interval no outside influences "interfered" with the system and that therefore an intrasystemic calculation would have given us the actual later values of the variables within that system; but we can never *foretell* that such a convenient state of affairs will in fact obtain. At no stage in the story can we *predict* what the next stage will be.

It is only recently that attention is beginning to be paid to questions of adequacy of explanatory reasoning,[19] but for most of us the old habits of thought continue to prevail. It is generally only when these habits are transferred from the "explanation" of past events to the attempted forecasting of the future that their weakness becomes more clearly apparent to us. But even there our habits of thought still often operate to make a projected future story, if it is "reasonably" constructed, convincing to us.

The story-telling pattern of reasoning is quite frequently employed in economic forecasting attempts — almost invariably when a policy recommendation is being made. Such a recommendation is usually supported by a prediction of how the story will "naturally" unfold in the future when the policy is adopted. For an excellent example of this sort of thing, and at its best, the reader need only turn to one of the Annual Economic Reviews of the Council of Economic Advisors. Thus, the January 1951 report consists principally of a statement of the main problems confronting the American economy in 1951, and of a series of recommendations designed to deal with the situation in the most satisfactory possible fashion (as seen by the CEA). The report is full of assumptive informal predictions of what the consequences of given governmental policies will be.

Another excellent illustration of story-telling in economic prediction is provided by F. A. Hayek's famous essay, *The*

---

[19] For a recent outstanding example, see C. Hempel and P. Oppenheim, "Studies in the Logic of Explanation," *Philosophy of Science* (April 1948), pp. 135–175.

Road to Serfdom. This book is full of "dramatic" forecasts, mostly of the dire-forecast variety. And, interestingly enough, so is Herman Finer's hot-tempered reply to Hayek, the book, *Road to Reaction.* He "demolishes" Hayek's many unwarranted assumptions and finds holes in his informal chains of logic; but then proceeds to put forth unwarranted assumptions of his own and, by another story-type chain of logic, to arrive at entirely different but equally dubious forecasts. This debate as a whole is quite typical of almost all similar discussion. There is much heat and emotion and rhetoric and "fact" on both sides; and yet, because of the utter unreliability of their expressed and implied forecasts, both sides completely fail to support their contentions. It is sad indeed that policy is so often born in this sort of intellectual chaos.

We conclude that verbal forecasts, even if they are psychologically satisfactory, are generally untrustworthy. And this is true despite the fact that they often turn out to be successful. It is the ever present possibility of "interferences" that is the critical factor here. We can go on to say that forecasts based on habits of thought or on empirical knowledge of "typical" sequences of events are also undependable (except when the typical sequence or the habit of thought corresponds accidentally to a scientifically established law). Examples of such forecasts are farmers' or fishermen's weather forecasts, housewives' forecasts of cooking results, forecasts of political developments by "experienced observers," or judgment of "experienced" men in any field of activity. The logical structure of such forecasts is also of the story-telling variety; and the weaknesses described above apply in full force. It is not proposed here, of course, that these types of forecasts be abandoned — they are of very considerable practical usefulness. We could not conduct our day-by-day existence without them. We should, however, recognize them for what they are: makeshifts and expedients; we rely upon them only because, in our normal routine activity, we have no better method. It is primarily in unusual and/or important decision-situations that the weaknesses become dangerous.

CHAPTER 7: CONCLUSIONS

. . . I have been gradually coming under the conviction, disturbing for a professional theorist, that there is no such thing as economics — there is only social science applied to economic problems. Indeed, there may not even be such a thing as social science — there may only be general science applied to the problems of society. — Kenneth E. Boulding, *A Reconstruction of Economics*, p. vii.

A. ECONOMICS AS AN ART

In considering the various case studies of the preceding chapters jointly, one peculiarity of modern economics appears to stand out. It seems that "economic science" has the rather strange characteristic that whenever it is "economic" it is not "science," whenever it is "science" it is not "economic," and quite frequently it is neither.

This statement requires some explanation. If we confine the meaning of the word "science" to its most popular sense — that is, to denote a *nomothetic* science — and if by "economic" we refer to the familiar class of phenomena in the *real* world, then (and, to be fair, only then) the statement becomes true. As we saw in the preceding case studies, and as any reader can verify further by analyzing almost any other effort in the entire field, whenever an economist is thoroughgoingly empirical — that is, "economic" — he does not arrive at the knowledge of either static or dynamic laws of the world; and whenever the economist does deal with static and/or dynamic "laws," these are merely arbitrary assumptions akin to those of mathematics and not empirical generalizations, and hence not "economic."

Some examples of what we have in mind here are the following:

1. "Economic," but not "science." All of the empirical sta-

tistical investigations cited in Chapter 5 fall into this category. They all deal with economic reality, but they did not and will not lead to the discovery of valid general laws. Their findings invariably were temporary and perishable relationships and facts, always subject to sudden obsolescence without notice.

2. "Science," but not "economic." The theory of the firm and similar types of model have this characteristic. The theory of the firm, as we saw, studies the consequences of certain given assumptions — that is, it is concerned with the logical derivation of theorems from a given set of postulates. There is nothing empirical about the entire procedure. No new information about the real world is uncovered. As is well known, a theorem contains no information that is not already entailed in the postulates from which it is derived — it merely presents the information in a different way.

The theory is scientific in the same sense that mathematics is scientific: it proceeds in accordance with a method that is generally regarded as being scientific. But it makes no contribution to our stock of information about the real economic world.

3. Neither "economic" nor "science." To this class belong all those many studies that neither yield new empirical economic information nor follow any recognized scientific method. As examples we may think of most of the "verbal" attempts to analyze the consequences of certain assumptions (they usually fall far short of adequate logical rigor), of the various kinds of commentary writing, and of the studies that analyze the influence of a given factor X or another given factor Y (they usually are guilty of artificial isolation, at least).

Another way of expressing these general conclusions is to say that *economics is not a nomothetic, empirical science.* Moreover, this is not only true of economics as it has been practiced so far, but it appears to be true as well of whatever can be done along economic lines in the future.

We already came to that conclusion at the end of Chapter 4 when we said then that all of the "customary" economic systems are essentially open systems. *It is this essential openness that prevents us from discovering empirical laws within the system itself.* Most of the difficulties that economists have fallen into can be traced to their failure to recognize that the system they study is essentially open, that is, that economics is not a science in the sense stated. When economists proceed on their endeavors as if economics were a science like physics or psychology, they are inevitably forced into the many artificialities that we discussed before, and consequently become quite impotent insofar as successful prediction and policy-making is concerned.

If economics is not a science (in the nomothetic, empirical sense), what *is* it?

First, as we have seen, some parts of it are idiographic, descriptive science — something like geography or descriptive paleontology. It undoubtedly serves an important and very useful purpose in this role. It is interesting for us to know, for example, how the different systems of economic organization tend to function, or how widespread hedging operations are, or what the trend of the Gross National Product in the United States has been during, say, the last fifty years. Perhaps it would be correct to say that descriptive economics is properly a branch of *history*, inasmuch as the facts it describes are not relatively fixed, as in geography, but are quite volatile and ever changing.

Second, as we have also noted, other parts of economics are deductive science, like mathematics. There is considerable value in this kind of economics, too. Inasmuch as the human mind is a very imperfect logical instrument it cannot always detect at once what the logical consequences of a given set of postulates are. Anything that helps to derive such consequences, and to make them explicit, is therefore of great help in guiding those of our actions that depend on the information contained in the postulates.

But most important by far, *economics is an art.* The *College Standard Dictionary* gives the following definitions for art (among others): "(1) The skilful and systematic arrangement or adaptation of means for the attainment of some end. (2)

The practical application of knowledge or natural ability; skill; dexterity; facility; power. (3) A system of rules devised for procuring some scientific, esthetic, or practical result . . ." The art of economics is a policy-making one; it involves the skillful and systematic arrangement or adaptation of means (information) for the attainment of an end ("economic policy," private or governmental). Economics is, and should be, concerned with techniques of solving problems such as how to control inflation, how to maximize private profits, how to maintain full employment, how to forecast future prices, or how to conduct governmental finances, and with the formulation of proper policies to achieve such economic purposes. It does and should look into such questions as the following: Assume, say, I wish to forecast next month's gross national product. (1) What information do I need? (2) Where and how can the information be obtained? (3) How is the available information to be utilized in the derivation of the forecast? Or assume I am a government official wishing to stabilize the price level. (1) How can I forecast what would happen without any action on my part? (2) What possible courses of action are open to me? (3) What would be the effect of each of these courses of action? etc.

Note that the practice of the art of economics involves the collection and processing of many different kinds of information about the real world. But note also that this process is not that of empirical nomothetic science. Science uses the method of induction in the *derivation* of laws of nature that were not formerly known; the art of economics, as just described, *utilizes* laws *already established by other sciences* for some further purpose. The only new information-gathering that is involved in the procedure consists of observations of the details in the case. The art of economics is more like chemical engineering than like chemistry, more like animal husbandry than like zoology, and more like medicine than like physiology. It cannot be otherwise — as we have seen, it is incapable of deriving laws of its own.

Where can economists get knowledge of the laws of nature

they need in the solution of their problems? Information about human behavior patterns, motivations, and modes of response to environmental stimuli are supplied by psychology, social psychology, and, perhaps, sociology. The physical sciences can tell us about production functions and the possibilities of change in them. Geology, demography, and geography can supply us with information about natural and human resources and their location and other characteristics. And we can get information about the particulars of the present situation from law, political "science," meteorology, other "idiographic" sciences, including parts of economics, and from direct observation. The art of economics comes in at the beginning and at the end: in the decision of what information is to be selected and in the final analysis of that information.

When we say that economics is an art, that does not mean that it is self-consciously an art. Indeed, the very opposite is true. Many, perhaps most, of the practitioners of this art are under the impression that they are doing something different altogether, such as engaging in scientific endeavors or in statecraft. That is one of the reasons why so many economists practice their art so poorly when "the chips are down," when it comes to prediction and control. As long as they devote so much time, resources, and energy to the pursuit of the ever elusive empirical laws of economics, they cannot pay adequate attention to their proper tasks: the collection and analysis of otherwise ascertained information. So they continue to go along with preposterously unrealistic assumptions concerning matters on which much reliable information is already at hand; and they persist in their attempts to transfer to a "Euclidean" world the conclusions of their entirely "non-Euclidean" mathematics. Small wonder then that their endeavors so often end in the familiar futility.

Precisely what is it that economists *are* equipped to do, and equipped to do well? Clearly there is a great need for the services of economists — the economic problems of business, of labor unions, and of government are perennial and insistent. In what way can professional economists be most helpful?

It seems to me that there are really two separate branches of the art of economics, rather different from each other, but both very important. To use the most descriptive terms we might call them (a) general decision theory and (b) economic policy-making. The first is perhaps not, properly speaking, an art; it is more like a branch of applied mathematics. But the second does clearly fall into the category of an art.

General decision theory is concerned with the solution of the basic problem of how to decide upon the best course of action in any given set of specific circumstances. As is slowly becoming recognized, there is a real field of analysis there and a rather large one at that. The difficulties of rational decision-making stem from a variety of sources, such as (1) the great number of alternatives of action that may be available at any one time, (2) the ever-present uncertainty about the outcomes of any of these actions, (3) the conflict among the different value-criteria that may be relevant, and (4) the problem of how much information to collect, at what cost in resources and time, before deciding upon a policy; and many others. So far, comparatively little has been done in the field of general decision-making. There was a slow start in the seventeenth and eighteenth centuries, when the theory of probability began to be created, but most of whatever work has been done in this field took place in the last fifty years, and especially in the last twenty. We are referring now to such developments as the theories of statistical decision pioneered by Neyman, Pearson, and Wald, the theory of games pioneered by von Neumann, the entire "new" welfare economics, the modern techniques of "programming" and operations research, and the entire school of modern logic.

Very little of the general theory of decision-making, even to the extent that it does exist, has so far percolated down to the level of actual practice. It is a rather remarkable fact that the principles of decision-making that are in fact employed by most people today are virtually the same as they were 2000 years ago. Thus a United States senator today, in considering the enactment of a new piece of legislation, employs much the same pattern of analysis as his Roman counterpart did in his time for a similar purpose. He also employs the same thought-patterns as the Roman did in deciding what to eat for lunch, in choosing a wife, or in formulating a personal philosophy of life. The concrete alternatives, of course, are not the same today as they were then, but the process of choosing among the alternatives, whatever they happen to be, has not changed. At both times the decision-process is (or was) apt to be characterized by much the same degree [1] of (a) incomplete consideration of alternatives; (b) incomplete awareness of the many possible outcomes of any given choice among the alternatives; (c) cliché-thinking or habit-thinking in estimating the probable outcome of a given choice; (d) primitiveness of the probability analysis involved; (e) prevalence of simple logical error (*non sequiturs* being the favorite type of error); and (f) blind-hunch decision-making, or stab-in-the-dark decision-making. The fact that the typical man today, in whatever capacity he may be functioning, is likely to be more effective and more productive than his ancestors were is due to the availability to him of better instruments (the most powerful instrument being "knowledge of scientific laws"), not to his greater skill in using the instruments for the attainment of given purposes. The typical man today, as compared to his forebears, is, in this respect, something like an ape who has been moved from his native jungle into a modern house equipped with push-buttons and all kinds of appliances, and has been trained to use these push-buttons and appliances. He is now able to do many things that would have been utterly impossible for him before, but he is, nevertheless, despite his immeasurably greater accomplishments, still an ape. Today doctors and engineers can do many things their earlier counterparts could not, but they very likely are no better in their general skill of adapting means to ends, that is, in decision-making.

It appears, then, that the decision-making branch of the art of economics has a rather sizable task ahead of it; and it may well occupy the energies of a large number of capable men for a long time to come.[2]

[1] I cannot, of course, prove this contention here. But a little introspection on the part of the reader should make the point at least plausible.

[2] Appendix A at the end of this book gives an example of the author's idea of the direction such work might take.

But it should be clearly realized, and realized early, that there is nothing peculiarly "economic" about the art of decision-making — "economic" being understood here in its traditional sense. It applies as well to medicine, engineering, statecraft, military strategy, politics, wife-choosing, diet-choosing, and almost any other field one can imagine. However, the principles of decision-making should not be applied within any narrowly defined area, or its application would involve the error of artificial isolation. Thus, the Point-Four people soon learned that technical improvements in an underdeveloped area cannot be undertaken independently of any consideration of social structure and ideology; and doctors are beginning to discover that physical ills cannot always be treated effectively without attention being given to psychological and sociological factors.

The second branch of the art of economics, which I have called *economic policy-making*, is concerned with a more concrete and specific matter than is general decision-making. It would work on appropriate methods of solution of what are customarily called "economic problems," governmental or private. It is thus closely akin to *medicine* in its approach and method, differing from the older discipline only in its concrete field of application.

The economist specializing in economic policy-making could be an "economic doctor" in the literal sense of the term. He could well render all the different functions a medical doctor renders to his patients. He could perform a diagnostic service, analyzing the present state and the presently existing trends and tendencies in the "patient" — the national economy, a particular industry, a firm, or whatever other analogous entity the "patient" may be; he could perform a prescriptive service, advising the guardians of the patient on what actions are appropriate to change the state of the patient from its present position to whatever other position is considered desirable; and he could even perform a pharmacological service, fashioning the instrumentalities — laws, institutions, modes of organization, etc. — through which the "cure" might be facilitated.

The "economic doctor," in going about his duties, can employ tools of thought and of analysis very similar, again, to those of the medical doctor. His skills would be acquired in the same way. He would learn, by experience and by textbook, how to recognize "danger signs" and characteristic symptoms, where to find relevant information, what the standard cures are for the various possible ailments, what are the characteristics and effects of the various available "medicines," and how to treat patients with different "personalities" and with different surrounding environments. His skills and abilities would consist of being able to apply the general principles of rational decision-making to one particular problem area through being familiar with the many kinds of information that are relevant to that specific problem area, and through having developed the personal characteristics and the manipulative skills required for effective action in that area.

B.   GENERAL RECOMMENDATIONS

In the light of the entire preceding discussion it appears that it was an altogether first-rate mistake for the field of economics ever to develop the way it did. The history of economic thought, at least in the development of its main line of theory, constitutes a gigantic blind alley, against the end of which economists have been bashing their heads for decades. Economics is not an autonomous, self-sufficient discipline except by sheer custom, and it certainly is not and never can be an empirical nomothetic science.

The road to progress in economics seems to be blocked, at the present time, by a great deficiency in necessary methodological analysis. Before economists are able to accomplish very much they need to be clear in what they *can* do and what they *cannot* do, and then concentrate their attention, of course, on the solvable problems. The following suggestions are offered for a general, broad orientation toward further work in economics:

a. Those economists interested in general decision theory should come to regard their field as an independent area of specialization, and combine their efforts with similarly interested people in statistics, philosophy, medicine, engineering, and other disciplines concerned with rationality of action.

b. Economists whose primary interests lie in the field of economic policy-making should self-consciously adopt the attitude of doctors and begin to learn the things they should know to do their job well. They should become acquainted with the findings of general decision theory and should get to know the results of social psychology, sociology, jurisprudence, technology, demography, geology, and other disciplines relevant to their tasks. Further, they should become familiar with the concrete environment surrounding their "patients," the characteristics of these "patients," and the relevant findings of the idiographic economists. They should develop the manipulative skills required for putting policies into effect smoothly and expeditiously, these skills referring to methods of dealing with legislative bodies, of designing institutions, of persuasion, and, if necessary, of economic "surgery." But most of all, they should overcome their conscious or unconscious pretense of being scientists engaged in the discovery of laws, and try to become adept at the art of economic "healing."

c. Economists interested in institutional analysis, national-income accounting, labor, and the various other idiographic fields should frankly acknowledge themselves to be historians, join ranks with the avowed economic historians in the interest of a more complete and thoroughgoing study of the passing economic scene, and also give up the idea of being engaged in a search for universal principles.

d. A very much larger number of economists than at present should concentrate on the methodology of economics. They should become familiar with the philosophy of science, with epistemology, with the methodologies of other disciplines, with axiology, with mathematics, and above all with modern logic and its related fields. From the vantage-point of this foundation they should make a study of each of the many typical procedures and methods of economists (and of the workers in other fields) and determine the range of proper applicability for each such procedure and method. They should set themselves to a ruthless cleaning-out of the Augean stables of current practices of economic analysis and then begin to fill the void by designing and constructing new and effective conceptual frameworks and analytic procedures.

C. APPENDIX

One of the more dramatic, and more vexing, consequences of the widespread misapprehensions among economists concerning the nature of their field of study is the sequence of methodological controversies that has enlivened economics for the past 60 to 80 years. Though the characteristics and the doctrines of the combatants keep changing from time to time, the conflict is basically between the "empiricists" on the one side and the "theorists" on the other. On the "empirical" side there have been fighting such types of men as historicists, institutionalists, statistics-gatherers (the National Bureau of Economic Research, for example), and economic anthropologists; on the other side there are arrayed the neoclassicists, the mathematical economists, and the model-builders and theory-constructors in general. Both sides devote considerable energy and enthusiasm to the deprecation of the efforts and results of their opponents. The "empiricists" like to charge the "theorists" with the sterile manipulation of empty concepts and symbols, with otherworldliness, and with the willful or ignorant failure to look at the actual world. And the "theorists" are fond of replying by accusing their "empiricist" critics of blind statistics-grubbing, of practically useless historical reporting, and of the futile accumulation of mountains of undigested, and indeed indigestible brute facts.

The sad truth of the matter apparently is that both sides of the controversy are perfectly correct in their appraisal of the accomplishments of their opponents. But it is even sadder to observe how these various schools of thought have traditionally reacted to the criticisms of their basic presuppositions. To the extent that they paid serious attention to these criticisms at all, they usually responded with only some relatively slight changes in their original methods of approach. The adjustments were usually kept as small and as quiet and as undisturbing to ingrained habits of thought as was at all possible. The theorists, for example, acknowledged the institutionalist position only to the extent of making slight modifications in the postulates of their theories but leaving their basic deductive methods fully intact. This is even true for some of the few real changes in techniques of theory construction that did take place. The development of stochastical models, as we have seen, proceeded largely along the structural lines of the earlier types of model. The "empiricists" were usually equally conservative in their adaptations to warranted criticism. They began, instead of just gathering facts, to compute averages, to analyze historical time series, to classify and to categorize, and to perform other presumably interpretive operations upon their data; but they left their basic approach entirely unchanged. Economists of all schools have always shied away as if from the plague from the conclusion that there is something faulty in their basic approach; and they have always held fast to the belief that a few minor changes here and there would straighten everything out.

We have already seen why neither the "empiricists" nor the "theorists" forsook their respective approaches in favor of a more useful scientific method — in view of the fact that economics is not a science, that would have been quite impossible. But it should cause more than a little wonder that both schools of thought have remained so well satisfied with their traditional procedures, and that this satisfaction persisted in the face of an apparently never ending series of reverses and failures in the attempted application of their results. Why is it, when the traditional methodologies are so obviously inadequate and impotent, that economists have so staunchly maintained their loyalty to them?

An interesting and, quite possibly, a correct theory of the mechanisms underlying this state of mind is given by Walter A. Weisskopf in his article "Psychological Aspects of Economic Thought." [3] He observes:

[3] *Journal of Political Economy*, LVII (1949), 304–314. (Published by the University of Chicago Press.)

One gains the impression that these ideas and methods [unrealistic concepts and analytic tools in economics], somehow, fulfil certain psychological requirements and that possibly on this account they are retained in spite of their insufficiency on purely scientific grounds [p. 305].

Of course, it is not only economists that fall prey to these psychological weaknesses. Rather it is a general trait of human beings that their thought-processes tend to play tricks with reality if inner satisfaction is achieved thereby.

One of its functions [of thought] is to ward off anxieties caused by conflict, separation, and helplessness. For this purpose reality is often interpreted in such a way that conflicts are settled by intellectual compromise. Unbearable facts are eliminated and desires are satisfied by imagery so that man can live in harmony with himself and with his environment. Intellectual concepts, unintelligible from the point of view of logic and factual observation, become meaningful if interpreted in the light of the anxiety-avoiding function of thought [p. 305].

The most important of the psychological mechanisms involved in this "creative" way of looking at reality are, in Mr. Weisskopf's opinion, isolation, projection, repression, and compensation.

Isolation is a mechanism used by the ego as a protection against unwelcome impulses and ideas. In order to avoid anxiety, unwelcome thoughts are mentally separated from other, permissible ones, although the two may be logically and factually interconnected [p. 306].

Values are externalized and objectified for the sake of avoiding anxiety-creating internal conflicts. Here, the mechanism of projection is in operation . . . Whenever value judgments are presented in the form of statements of fact, the mechanism of projection is at work [p. 308].

The concept of man becomes identical with the normative concept of 'economic man.' An ideal is converted into a fact in order to make it palatable.

Repression consists in the elimination of impulses from consciousness. . . In compensation actual gratification is replaced by wishfulfilling intellectual imagery. Fantasy is substituted for real satisfaction. . . Compensatory intellectual fantasy gratification cannot be created without some misrepresentation of reality. Something is added to the picture of reality which really is not there; or parts of reality may be denied and repressed by means of intellectual phantasy. Both processes, repression and compensation, perform an anxiety-avoiding function. . . [p. 309].

These mechanisms play a wide variety of roles in the shaping of economic thought. For example:

The interrelated ideas of harmony, equilibrium, omniscience, and perfect rationality, so prominent in pure theory, may be cases in point. The concepts of economic harmony and equilibrium tend to repress the idea that our social and economic system is but a sequence of unpredictable and haphazard fluctuations. The idea of an automatic market mechanism leading to a beneficial harmony or, at least, to an equilibrium helps to repress this anxiety-creating thought of chaos [p. 309].

Also, the many elements of what we have previously called artificial mechanization, artificial generalization, artificial closure, artificial isolation, etc., can easily be seen to follow from the operation of the stated psychological mechanisms. The reader might amuse himself by explaining to himself the various theories and analytical techniques of economics in terms of Mr. Weisskopf's (and Freud's) theories. The results should be interesting, if not necessarily fruitful.

Another, but closely related, explanation of the astonishing loyalty of economists to nonproductive methods of analysis is given by Dr. Lawrence S. Kubie of the Yale Medical School.[4]

One of the world's outstanding economists has taught in the academic world, has organized and led his own university department, has done pure research in fundamental economic theory, and has held government posts of great practical and diplomatic importance during

---

[4] "Some Unsolved Problems of the Scientific Career," Part II, *American Scientist*, Vol. 42 (January 1954), 104–112.

times of war and peace, and during economic crisis. . . From his years of varied, successful, and useful experience this economist now views with concern the processes of higher education in his own field. He finds among his purely academic colleagues an almost total lack of something which is equivalent to what in medicine is called clinical maturity. They seem to him neither to derive their problems from the world's needs nor to test their hypotheses against such realities. He points out that this condition is in part due to the fact that all higher education now takes so long that among those who succeed in attaining the higher ranks there will automatically be a large proportion of individuals who harbor a secret inclination to retreat from life, and who are relatively deficient in aggressive, outgoing, reality-oriented impulses.

Furthermore, if the young scholar is to remain in academic work he has to teach; and our economist agrees with me that teaching is a dangerous sport for the young. Teaching makes it easy to appear scholarly and to sound profound; and gradually to believe that one really has these qualities. The young teacher usually has too great an edge on his young audience for his own good; students have no way of gauging the adequacy of the experience which lies behind the teacher's words. Anyone who lives in an atmosphere where nobody can answer back, soon begins to feel omniscient, with the result that effective self-criticism is almost as rare among young teachers as it is among dictators and generals. The fall is painful when those hard realities which have no respect for the pedagogue's fantasies of omniscience are encountered [pp. 104–105].

While fully agreeing with Kubie's remarks, we might question if it is necessary to restrict the comments about teachers to only young teachers, or, indeed, to teachers at all. The same basic situation — in which effective criticism of their actions is lacking — exists for most scholars, policy-advisers, and even executives. Even the supposedly acid test of experience is of little help in the frequent case in which there is no way of tracing consequences directly to one's own actions. In the typical event, a happening is the consequence not only of one's own policy but also of a large number of other factors, usually well beyond our control. It is always possible, in such a case, to attribute a failure to the actions of these noncontrollable factors, and to maintain our self-respect and our confidence in our methods perfectly intact. As an example we might think of the witch doctors in many primitive tribes, who, even with considerable "clinical experience" and, we suppose, a considerable number of failures, are able to maintain for hundreds of years their self-confidence and their social acceptance. The illustration is, of course, far fetched, but the socio-psychological mechanism is familiar.

CHAPTER 8: PREDICTION IN ECONOMICS

The foundation for our suggested redirection of the efforts of economists is already being constructed. There is a great deal of work currently being carried on by economists, logicians, mathematicians, statisticians and philosophers that promises to bear important methodological fruit in the not-too-distant future. One of these fruits will be, it appears, a useful and relevant conception of "prediction" for the "social sciences," and another should be the proper formulation of the related conception of rational decision-making. Many of the methodological errors that characterized so much of the work of economists in the past were made in the belief that they were unavoidable. The work to be cited shows that this belief is unfounded, and this fact promises much for the future of economics and "social science."

Economists worth their salt always wanted their work to be useful (in a policy-making or in an explanatory sense), and usefulness seemed to demand that economic theories be cast in the same mold as the theories of the natural sciences, and that the empirical research in economics follow the patterns set by these more successful and more prosperous sister disciplines. Artificial mechanization, artificial isolation, artificial generalization, and most of the other artificialities discussed before can all be traced to an attempt (sometimes deliberate, sometimes unconscious) to take over the procedures of the natural sciences and thus to equal, or at least to approach, the success of these disciplines at their own game. We have already mentioned the basic misconceptions that led to this futile quest; economists accepted uncritically and almost completely the notion of "prediction" that was and is current in physical science, and combined this acceptance with a closed-system view of their domain of study. Most economists like to visualize themselves, in unguarded moments, as rising to the same sort of role as the astronomer who can predict a solar eclipse with dismaying accuracy and dependability, or the physiologist who can do almost as well in forecasting, say, the effects of drugs on the human body. The extreme view of prediction as unconditional prophecy did not do much harm in natural science; the natural scientists, through no particular merit of theirs, were quite lucky in that their subject matter did lend itself to this kind of analysis and interpretation. The economist, being confronted with essentially open systems, was less fortunate — and hence his frustratingly ineffective and failure-studded academic history.[1]

Modern research in logic and in related fields has shown that the extreme view of prediction and the derivative artificialities in economic analysis are all unnecessary for the useful and successful practice of economics. There is a great hope, therefore, that, when this work becomes more widely known and appreciated, it will lead to a fruitful reorientation of scholarly effort. Economists and other "social scientists" would do well to pay far more attention to the writings of modern logicians than they customarily do.

A. A MODEL OF PREDICTION

We can formulate a concept of prediction suitable for economic analysis, and for essentially open systems in general, by elaborating further the terminology described in Chapter 4. The originators of these concepts are discussed in the appendix to this chapter.

One fundamental statement can be made at the outset. The operation of predicting is a logical operation. A prediction is the assertion of information about the future. Inasmuch as we do not and cannot have direct knowledge of the future, any

[1] Natural sciences who are as ill-favored by the fates as economics with respect to the structure of their field of inquiry have had as depressing a record as economics. Outstanding example: meteorology.

information about the future must inevitably be a logical consequence of information available in the present. In other words, we can assert about the future only those bits of information that are entailed, according to an accepted set of postulates of logic, in the body of information about the "present" and about the "past" that we have available at the time we wish to make a prediction. This is, of course, a fairly obvious point, but it is nevertheless frequently ignored under the pressure of actual practice. And, as long as the belief continues that a prediction to be worthwhile must be of the solar-eclipse type, it will continue to be ignored. As we have seen, it is impossible to make such a prediction in an essentially open system without overreaching our available information or without committing unwarranted artificialities upon our data.

Our task, therefore, is to specify a rigorous logical procedure that will lead to predictions which are solidly grounded in the available information and which also are dependable and usable. Such predictions will not and cannot be of the solar-eclipse type, but will always contain some lesser quantity of information about the future.

It is necessary now to continue the construction of concepts begun in Chapter 4. Inasmuch as a great deal of information comes to us, the forecasters, in probabilistic form, we must design our concepts so as to be able to "digest" efficiently that kind of information. This makes our concepts more unwieldy and more difficult than they otherwise would be, but there is unfortunately no known escape from these difficulties.

The reader should keep in mind here the distinction between the relative-frequency concept and the logical concept of probability which has become fairly customary and which we find it useful to accept, (in a somewhat modified way).[2] We regard all of our starting empirical information as coming to us in the form of relative-frequency propositions which have been, in some fashion that we shall take for granted, fully confirmed.

---

[2] For an excellent discussion of the various conceptions of probability as applied to economics, see Edward Ames, "Induction and Probability Theories in Economics." Ph.D. dissertation, Harvard University, 1952.

(The ensuing discussion, therefore, will not at all consider the weaknesses of predictions that may stem from an uncertain confirmation of empirical laws.) All laws, static or dynamic, are viewed as assigning such probabilities to empirical events (and thereby to states or histories of our conceptual systems). The second type of probability, the logical "inductive" type, is represented in our model in the logical operations of deriving conclusions from that information. This kind of probability is involved in the measures, defined below, of degree of openness of a system, strength of a prediction, and especially, degree of confirmation of a prediction. (Whenever, in the following discussion of concepts, we explicitly use the term "probability," we shall mean the relative-frequency concept.)

Class of states of a system: This class contains the totality of all logically possible states (ignoring time) of the system under consideration.

Probability distribution of states: Each such probability distribution is an assignment of probability to every member of the class of states of a system such that (1) each member has a probability between "zero" and "one," inclusive; and (2) the sum of all the probabilities equals "one."

Class of state probabilities of a system: This class consists of the totality of all logically possible probability distributions of states of a given system.

We may, for practical reasons, make a simplifying assumption here. Since probabilities can vary continuously from zero to one, and since some of the variables of the system may have continuous ranges of variation, the class of state probabilities has, of course, a nondenumerable infinite number of elements. We can avoid some of the analytical difficulties deriving from this infinity by assuming that all of our variables have a finite number of possible values, and that probabilities, also, can assume only a finite number of possible values between zero and one. By making our finite numbers large enough we can keep the errors resulting from these assumptions as small as we please. We shall therefore assume, from now on, that classes of state probabilities have finite (though possibly very large) numbers of elements.

Probability history of a system: A probability history is any logically possible sequence of probability distributions of states of a system, such that there is one such distribution, and one only, for each point of time.

Probability range of system: This is the entire set of logically possible probability histories of the system. It comprises the totality of different a priori possible patterns of events, and of probability distributions of occurrences, that could conceivably come about in the system.[3]

Probability space of a system: The probability space of a

---

[3] The relationships among these various concepts may become clearer by considering the relationships among the numbers of elements contained in classes of states, classes of state probabilities, probability ranges, etc.

Consider a system S in which:

(1) the number of variables (excluding time) $= v$

(2) the number of possible values that the variables can assume $=$

$$r_1, r_2, r_3, \ldots, r_v$$

(3) the number of values that probabilities may assume $= p$, where the lowest element is zero, the highest one, and the $(p - 2)$ other elements are spaced equally in the interval. The distance between successive probabilities is therefore $1/(p - 1)$.

(4) the number of time points in the time interval considered $= t$.

All numbers are assumed to be finite.
Then:

(a) the number of elements in the class of states of S,

$$N_s = r_1 \, r_2 \, r_3 \, \ldots \, r_v$$

(b) the number of elements in the class of state probabilities of S,

$$N_{sp} = \frac{(p + N_s - 2)!}{(p - 1)! \, (N_s - 1)!}$$

(c) the number of elements in the probability range of S

$$N(PR) = (N_{sp})^t$$

I am indebted to Professor Robert W. Wagner of the mathematics department of the University of Massachusetts for advice and assistance on this section.

system, relative to a given body of information, is what is left of the probability range after the removals [4] for all the available information have been made. It consists of all the patterns of events and of probability distributions of occurrences that, in the light of the available information, are possible of occurrence.

These concepts and constructions can be used for the derivation of predictions in roughly the following way:

First, assemble all [5] the information currently available and relevant to the problem under study. Make certain that all the information is information in the sense discussed in Chapter 4.

Second, construct a system S consisting of all the variables that are of interest, or that are necessary to take account of the available information. (A variable A may be included because we are interested in its course of behavior over time; and a variable B may be included solely because it is linked, directly or indirectly, to A by static or dynamic laws, and thus permits us to take account of the restrictive effect of these laws in making a prediction for A.)

Third, construct the probability range of S. This, as we have seen, is a rather elaborate task in itself, and very likely would require a great deal of computing machinery and other aids to human reasoning and remembering capacity. Prior to the use of information, each and every element of the probability range should be regarded as a possible occurrence.

Fourth, using the assembled available information, derive the probability space of S from the probability range of S. Each item of information, if it is not entirely vacuous, tells us that one or several of the elements of the probability range of S are in fact impossible of occurrence, and hence need not be considered further. That item of information, therefore, authorizes us to *remove* from the probability range of S all the elements incompatible with it. An observation, for example, permits us

---

[4] This term is defined below.

[5] For the moment, we are ignoring the problem of the cost and the time-element of information gathering. We are also ignoring all costs of deriving our predictions.

to remove every probability history that contains even a single state-probability distribution which conflicts with that observation.[6]

A static law authorizes the removal of every probability history containing a state probability which assigns a nonzero probability to at least one state with an "impossible" combination of values of the variables, or which assigns a probability to a state (or disjunction of states) which differs from that specified in the law by more than a predetermined "small" amount.[7]

A dynamic law, finally, justifies the removal of every probability history in which successive [8] state-probabilities assign nonzero probabilities to both of two states in a way that conflicts with the law (to within a "small" amount).

After all the removals have been made, the remaining elements in the probability range of S constitute its probability space. Each element in that space represents a chain of occurrences, which, in the light of all the available information, must be regarded as "possible." The probability space of an open system will always contain *many* elements, and, in making our attempts at prediction, we have no right to prefer any one of these elements over any other, but must pay equal attention to all.

Fifth, read off all predictions about S from its probability space. The procedure of doing that is discussed below.

---

[6] In the case in which a given observation is free of error, a particular probability distribution of states "conflicts" with that observation if it assigns a nonzero probability to any state (or disjunction of states) which is inconsistent with the observation. In the case in which errors of observation must be considered, the "conflict" occurs if the particular probability distribution of states assigns, to any state, a probability which differs by more than a predetermined small amount from the probability that, in the light of the observation, the state actually occurred.

[7] To take a simple example of the first case, consider a system S' containing as three of its variables the volume, temperature, and pressure of a given body of gas. The gas law, a static law, then permits the removal of every probability history containing one or more state-probabilities which assign a nonzero probability to at least one state of S' in which these three variables violate the gas law.

[8] Not necessarily immediately successive.

We can easily obtain a measure of the *degree of openness* of a system, relative to a given body of information, in the following way. Let $N(PR)$ equal the number of elements in the probability range of S, and let $N(PS)$ equal the number of elements in the probability space. Then the degree of openness of S, relative to body of information I,

$$DO-I = \frac{N(PS) - \mathrm{I}}{N(PR) - \mathrm{I}}.$$

As can be seen the degree of openness ranges from a minimum of zero to a maximum of one. The value of zero occurs in the extreme case of a closed system (where only a single probability history remains), and the value of one occurs in the other extreme case, where we have no information at all (have made no removals).

By using counts of elements of the probability space we can also obtain measures pertaining to predictions. We shall define now two important concepts: the measures of the "strength" and the "degree of confirmation" of a prediction.

Strength of a prediction (pertaining to a given time point or interval): Let P be a certain proposition asserting information about a future time interval (or a past interval, or a combination of past, present, and future) of the system S; and let $N(P)$ be the number of elements in the probability range of S consistent with P. Then the strength of P can be measured by

$$St_P = \mathrm{I} - \left(\frac{N(P) - \mathrm{I}}{N(PR) - \mathrm{I}} \right).$$

The strength of a given P can range from a minimum of zero (for a proposition asserting nothing) to a maximum of one (for an absolute, unqualified, fully detailed prophecy — one that is consistent with only a single probability history).

Degree of confirmation of a prediction: The information I incorporated in the probability space of a system S may fully confirm, partly confirm, or refute a given proposition P. Full confirmation occurs if P is logically entailed in I; partial confirmation occurs if P is consistent with I but not fully deducible from it; and refutation occurs if P conflicts with I. It seems desirable to define degree of confirmation so that a full confirmation will yield a value of one, a refutation a value of zero, and a partial confirmation some intermediate value. The following definition has these properties:

$$DC_P = \frac{N(P \cap PS)}{N(PS)},$$

where $(P \cap PS)$ refers to the set of elements of the probability range which are contained in the probability space *and* are consistent with P.

As can be seen by an inspection of the two formulas, generally speaking, (1) an increase in the strength of P usually reduces its degree of confirmation, and vice versa, holding I constant; (2) an increase in I, and a consequent reduction in $N(PS)$, may increase, leave unaffected, or decrease DC_P, depending upon which probability histories are removed on the authority of the new information; (3) an increase in I leaves St_P unaffected.

B. COMMENTS ON THE MODEL OF PREDICTION

(1) The first, and the most emphatic, comment on the model of prediction should be that *it is not a finished product*. It is little more than a sketch of what a workable model should be like. The measures are quite rough, the details are inadequate, and some of the definitions are only provisional. The full elaboration and discussion of the model is a very large task indeed.[9] It is briefly considered here only because it does point out, at least approximately, how some of the recent work in

[9] The present author hopes, in a forthcoming book on prediction and decision theory, to be able to present more satisfactory formulations of the concepts mentioned here.

logic and in related fields can help solve the methodological problems of economics.

(2) It should also be acknowledged that there are enormous difficulties in performing the indicated manipulations on our model. These difficulties are not fundamental in the sense that they involve conceptual problems, but they are troublesome in the amount of logical labor that they entail. Presumably, however, it should be possible to design machinery to do most of the routine phases of the work.

(3) The model is efficient in its handling of information. It is able to "digest" every bit of available information in whatever form that information may be presented; and it always takes cognizance of the full import of the information. It can take account of, with equal facility, qualitative and quantitative information, probability statements, complete and incomplete observations, strong or weak laws, and the findings of any of the sciences.

(4) It is important to note that the model needs only information, in the rigorous sense in which we have been using the term. It does not require, or even suggest, that artificialities be imposed upon the data. Whatever logical deductions can be drawn from the model, therefore, carry with them the same authority as the original data. Consequently, any proposition P which has a degree of confirmation of "one" with respect to a given model is certainly a "true" one, and, if P is a prediction, it is a dependable prediction.

(5) The entire process of information-assembling and model-constructing constitutes the practice of the *art* of economics (as discussed in Chapter 7). It involves the *use* of the results of science for a presumably worth-while purpose, the results of science being merely the "raw material" upon which we perform our operations. An important part of our art is to be able to locate relevant information and, perhaps, to suggest to the "scientists" concerned the type of information that they could profitably be looking for in their research activities. We, as economists, would very likely have to depend for our nomothetic information on psychology, the technological sciences, geog-

raphy, and other natural sciences, and for our idiographic information, on economic historians (in the widest sense), the various other so-called "social sciences," and, again, the appropriate natural sciences.

(6) It is a virtue of the model to be able to encompass probability information and probability logic of both the relative-frequency type and the "inductive" type.[10] The first type of probability (which is the foundation of most of modern statistics) is represented, as has been mentioned, in the original construction of the model and in the form of the probability information (presumably of statistical origin) incorporated into it. "Inductive" probability is represented in the evaluation of propositions P with reference to the model — in the concepts of "degree of confirmation" and "strength."

(7) We should pay special attention to those predictions that can be derived from the model with a degree of confirmation of "one." (These predictions will never have a *strength* of "one," our systems being open rather than closed). The probability space of the system, taken in its entirety, is such a prediction, and, moreover, the fully confirmed prediction of maximum strength.[11] The probability space consists of all those probability histories which, in the light of the totality of our available information, are "equally" possible of occurrence, and only those probability histories. It is to be interpreted as the statement that *one* of the constituent probability histories will definitely occur; it is, in other words, the logical disjunction of these probability histories. Any statement about the future, therefore, that is stronger than the probability space (and thereby ignores some of the elements of the probability space) overreaches the data (asserts more than is warranted by the information); hence it has a degree of confirmation of less than "one," and does not merit full confidence. Any fully confirmed

[10] For an authoritative discussion of these concepts see Rudolf Carnap, *Logical Foundations of Probability* (Chicago: University of Chicago Press, 1950).

[11] We might quite well confine our use of the term "prediction" to propositions with a degree of confirmation of "one." All other propositions can be termed "forecasts" with indicated degrees of confirmation.

statement, on the other hand, carries with it all the certainty that is attainable, insofar as we presently know, by human beings in this world. Such a statement will usually be far *weaker* than we would like it to be, but this weakness is the concession we have to make to the refractory and perverse nature of our subject matter. Weakness in a prediction is a reflection of weakness or inadequacy in the information available; and, in the interests of rigor, these weaknesses and inadequacies should not be suppressed or hidden.

(8) The final comment here is, I believe, an important one. The economist, if he is to play well his role as doctor to the economy, must be conversant with the principles of modern decision theory and with the methods of applying these principles to his subject matter. Our model of prediction can be of great help in this matter: it serves very well indeed as a foundation for the application of modern decision theory. The principal decision criteria,[12] such as the minimax solution, the Bayes solution, the Savage solution, and the others, all are designed to be applied to *sets* of possible occurrences, such as pay-off matrices or probability spaces.

An explicit tie-in between the present model and decision theory would, unfortunately, take us a little far afield here. Readers who are interested may refer to Appendix A for one set of views on this subject.

C. APPENDIX

Most of the principal ideas that went into the construction of our model of prediction have already been discussed, many quite intensively, by a variety of authors, largely logicians and mathematicians. All that has been done here is the adaptation of these ideas to the particular requirements of prediction in economics. Since the literature in this field is quite varied and extensive, it is not feasible to present a survey of it here. In-

[12] For a series of excellent summaries and discussions see "Decision Processes," edited by R. M. Thrall, C. H. Coombs, and R. L. Davis (New York: Wiley, 1954).

stead, I should like to make an acknowledgment of the writers whom I, personally, have found to be most helpful and instructive.

Willard Gibbs. It was Willard Gibbs, I am told, who first invented the concept of the "phase-space" of a mechanical system, the concept which we have generalized into the probability range of a system in general. In Gibbs' scheme, for exemple, an n-particle mechanical system is regarded as having a $6n$-dimensional phase-space, each particle being described by three coördinates of position and three of velocity. Items of information about the particles are interpreted as restrictions on the movement of the system in its phase-space. This method of representation has since been applied to different fields, notably statistics and econometrics. We have, in our model, taken over the phase-space concept, but enlarged it to include a wider class of variables, with more diverse ranges of variation, and probabilities.

Trygve Haavelmo. Professor Haavelmo's paper "The Probability Approach in Econometrics," [13] discussed in Chapter 6, has been a very suggestive one in several respects. It shows a way of applying the phase-space concept to the analysis of economic systems; it discusses clearly the logical import of items of information; and, perhaps most importantly, it presents a useful method of treating probability laws.

Rudolf Carnap. Professor Carnap, one of the foremost contemporary logicians and semanticists, has done a great deal of work on a number of logical problems which are closely analogous to the problems of prediction. In his article "On Inductive Logic," [14] he constructs a semantic analogue of our probability range. He builds up his system of ideas from the concept of a "formal language" L_N, which consists of a set of predicates

[13] See Example D–4 in Chapter 6.
[14] *Philosophy of Science*, XII (1945), 72–97. His book *Logical Foundations of Probability* elaborates his ideas more completely. We use the earlier reference here because it presents the essential ideas in a beautifully compact and accessible form.

and a set of N "individual constants" to which the predicates refer.[15]

A sentence consisting of a predicate of degree n with n individual constants is called an *atomic sentence* (e.g. 'Pa_1', i.e. 'a_1 has the property P', or 'Ra_3a_5', i.e. "the relation R holds between a_3 and a_5"). The conjunction of all atomic sentences in a finite language L_N describes one of the possible states of the domain of the N individuals with respect to the properties and relations expressible in the language L_N. If we replace in this conjunction some of the atomic sentences by their negations, we obtain the description of another possible state. All the conjunctions which we can form in this way, including the original one, are called *state descriptions* in L_N [p. 73].

This state description is evidently the analogue of a state in our model, although we have used only one-place predicates for the definition of states. (It seems more convenient to regard predicates with more places as configurations in space, rather than "dimensions.") In Carnap's subsequent discussion of reasoning within these language systems, he uses, among others, the following concepts: "The class of those state-descriptions in a language system L (either one of the systems L_N or L_∞) in which [a given proposition] j holds is called the *range* of j in L [p. 73]." (In our model, the range of a proposition is the set of those points which are not inconsistent with the proposition. In other words, it consists of all the probability histories which are not removed by authority of that proposition.)

If the range of a sentence j in the language system L is universal, i.e. if j holds in every state-description (in L), j must necessarily be true independently of the facts; therefore we call j (in L) in this case *L-true* (logically true, analytic) . . . Analogously, if the range of j is null, we call j *L-false* (logically false, self-contradictory). If j is neither L-true nor L-false, we call it *factual* (synthetic, contingent). Suppose that the range of e is included in that of h. Then in every possible case in which e would be true, h would likewise be true. Therefore we say in this case that e *L-implies* (logically implies,

[15] What Carnap calls a predicate is, in our language, a variable (specifically, a 2-valued variable).

entails) *h*. If two sentences have the same range, we call them *L-equivalent*; in this case, they are merely different formulations for the same content [p. 74].

We have, in our model, not made explicit use of the concepts of L-truth and L-falsity. All of our information consists of factual statements in the above meaning of the word. However, we have artificially made these items L-true with respect to the probability space of our model, by having removed those elements of the probability range with respect to which the law does not hold. A removal covers, in Carnap's terminology, those points which are L-implied by the negation of the item of information, the entire removal being L-equivalent to this negation.

To illustrate further the extent of our debt to Professor Carnap, we now quote from his discussion of the concept of the "degree of confirmation" of one proposition by a set of others. We have, in our model, taken over this concept almost literally.

A numerical function $\mathfrak{m}$ ascribing real numbers of the interval o to 1 to the sentences of a finite language L_N is called a regular $\mathfrak{m}$-function if it is constructed according to the following rules.
(1) We assign to the state-descriptions in L_N, as values of $\mathfrak{m}$ any positive real numbers whose sum is 1.
(2) For every other sentence *j* in L_N, the value $\mathfrak{m}(j)$ is determined as follows:
    (a) If *j* is not L-false, $\mathfrak{m}(j)$ is the sum of the $\mathfrak{m}$-values of those state-descriptions which belong to the range of *j*.
    (b) If *j* is L-false and hence its range is null, $\mathfrak{m}(j) = $ o.
(The choice of the rule (2)(a) is motivated by the fact that *j* is L-equivalent to the disjunction of those state-descriptions which belong to the range of *j* and that these state-descriptions logically exclude each other.)
If any regular $\mathfrak{m}$-function $\mathfrak{m}$ is given, we define a corresponding function $\mathfrak{c}$ as follows:
(3) For any pair of sentences *e*, *h* in L_N, where *e* is not L-false,

$$\mathfrak{c}(h,e) = \frac{\mathfrak{m}(e \cdot h)}{\mathfrak{m}(e)}.$$

$\mathfrak{m}(j)$ may be regarded as a measure ascribed to the range of *j*; thus the function m constitutes a metric for the ranges. Since the range of the conjunction $e \cdot h$ is the common part of the ranges of e and of h, the quotient in (3) indicates, so to speak, how large a part of the range of e is included in the range of h. The numerical value of this ratio, however, depends on what particular m-function has been chosen. We saw earlier that a statement in deductive logic of the form "e L-implies h" says that the range of e is entirely included in that of h. Now we see that a statement in inductive logic of the form "$c(h,e) = \frac{3}{4}$" says that a certain part — in the example, three fourths — of the range of e is included in the range of h. Here, in order to express the partial inclusion numerically, it is necessary to choose a regular m-function for measuring the ranges. Any m chosen leads to a particular c as defined above. All functions c obtained in this way are called *regular* c-*functions*.[16]

The c-function of which Carnap speaks represents the degree of confirmation of the hypothesis h on the basis of the evidence e.[17] The entire system of concepts was easily adapted to our predictive model — only minor modifications were necessary. The body of information constitutes the evidence e, and the un-removed point set — the probability space — is the range of e.

Most importantly of all, we owe to Professor Carnap a clear notion of the relationship between relative-frequency probabilities and inductive probabilities.

Carl G. Hempel and Paul Oppenheim. A set of closely allied logical ideas are set forth in an excellently lucid and stimulating article by Carl G. Hempel and Paul Oppenheim.[18] The article points out, first, the logical equivalence of explanation and

[16] "On Inductive Logic," pp. 74–75.

[17] This is not quite true. Carnap first imposes a restriction upon the form of the m-function before defining the degree of confirmation; namely, that the m-functions must give equal values to isomorphic state descriptions (two or more state descriptions being isomorphic if they differ only in the individual constants involved). This restriction is not important for us, however; the feasible applications of Carnap's concepts to our predictive models involve situations in which there is only *one* individual constant, the "state of the world" at the time considered. All the variables represent predicates applying to that constant.

[18] "Studies in the Logic of Explanation," *Philosophy of Science*, XV (1948), 135–175.

prediction. A phenomenon is said to be explained by certain other facts if the sentence embodying it is logically deducible from the sentences embodying these other facts. The latter group of sentences must include sentences of two types: statements of antecedent conditions, and general laws. In the case of explanation, the statement of the phenomenon is usually given before the explaining sentences are at hand; in the case of prediction, we have the explaining sentences first and from them deduce the occurrence of a phenomenon before it actually occurs. The article then proceeds to a development of the logical principles involved, but inasmuch as it deals only with causal explanation in a closed system, it is not, in its details, too closely connected with our topic. The item of main interest for us in this discussion deals with a measure of the amount of information contained in a sentence and with the relation of this amount to the range of that sentence.[19]

If, as will be assumed here, the vocabulary of L contains fixed finite numbers of individual constants and of predicate constants, then only a certain finite number, say n, of different atomic sentences can be formulated in L. By a minimal sentence in L, we will understand a disjunction of any number k ($o \leq k \leq n$) of different atomic sentences and the denials of the $n-k$ remaining ones. Clearly, n atomic sentences determine 2^n minimal sentences. Thus, if a language L_1 contains exactly one individual constant, 'a', and exactly two primitive predicates, 'P' and 'Q', both of degree 1, then L_1 contains two atomic sentences '$P(a)$' and '$Q(a)$', and four minimal sentences, namely '$P(a) \lor Q(a)$', '$P(a) \lor \sim Q(a)$', '$\sim P(a) \lor Q(a)$', '$\sim P(a) \lor \sim Q(a)$' . . . The term 'minimal sentence' is to indicate that the statements in question are the singular sentences of smallest non-zero content in L, . . . By virtue of the principles of the sentential calculus, every singular sentence which is not formally true in L can be transformed into a conjunction of uniquely determined minimal sentences; this conjunction will be called the minimal normal form of the sentence. Thus, e.g. in the language L_1 referred to above, the sentences '$P(a)$' and '$Q(a)$' have the minimal normal forms

---

[19] To repeat: A "sentence" is any assertion concerning the system. The range of the sentence is the set of points not removed by it. The relationship to be discussed is therefore of importance to our concept of "strength."

'$(P(a) \lor Q(a)) \cdot (P(a) \lor \sim Q(a))$', and '$(P(a) \lor Q(a)) \cdot (\sim P(a) \lor Q(a))$', respectively . . . [pp. 165–166]. A maximal sentence is the dual of a minimal sentence in L; it is a conjunction of k ($0 \leq k \leq n$) different atomic sentences and of the denials of the remaining $n - k$ atomic sentences. In a language with n atomic sentences, there exist 2^n state descriptions. Thus, e.g., the language L_1 . . . contains the following four maximal sentences: '$P(a) \cdot Q(a)$', '$P(a) \cdot \sim Q(a)$', '$\sim P(a) \cdot Q(a)$', '$\sim P(a) \cdot \sim Q(a)$' . . . As we saw, every singular sentence can be represented in a conjunctive, or minimal, normal form, i.e., as a conjunction of certain uniquely determined minimal sentences; similarly, every singular sentence can be expressed also in a disjunctive, or maximal, normal form, i.e., as a disjunction of certain uniquely determined maximal sentences. In the language L_1, for example, '$P(a)$' has the minimal normal form '$(P(a) \lor Q(a)) \cdot (P(a) \lor \sim Q(a))$' and the maximal normal form '$(P(a) \cdot Q(a)) \lor (P(a) \cdot \sim Q(a))$'; the sentence '$P(a) \supset Q(a)$' has the minimal normal form '$\sim P(a) \lor Q(a)$' and the maximal normal form '$(P(a) \cdot Q(a)) \lor (\sim P(a) \cdot Q(a)) \lor (\sim P(a) \cdot \sim Q(a))$' . . . The minimal normal form of a singular sentence is well suited as an indicator of its content, for it represents the sentence as a conjunction of standard components whose contents are minimal and mutually exclusive. The maximal normal form of a sentence is suited as an indicator of its range, that is, intuitively speaking, of the variety of its different possible realizations, or the variety of those possible states of the world which, if realized, would make the statement true. . . Range and content of a sentence vary inversely. The more a sentence asserts, the smaller the variety of its possible realizations, and conversely. This relationship is reflected in the fact that the larger the number of constituents in the minimal normal form of a singular sentence, the smaller the number of constituents in its maximal normal form, and conversely [pp. 168–169].

We have, as is quite obvious, used these ideas in our model, but in a somewhat less sophisticated form. The range of a law is, in our scheme, represented by the complement of its exclusion, and the content is measured simply by the size of the exclusion, which, of course, varies inversely with the range. As can easily be seen, the "content" of a prediction is analogous to its "strength" (as we have defined it).

John von Neumann and Oskar Morgenstern. Von Neumann

188   Failures of Economics

and Morgenstern's great book *The Theory of Games and Economic Behavior* was an important stimulus to our ideas here, as it has been in so many other contexts. The concept of the "rules of a game" is analogous to what we have called "information"; and the "pay-off matrix" is analogous, even though it may not seem that way at first sight, to our construct of the probability space. (Strictly speaking, the probability space is a row in a pay-off matrix, the row corresponding to the strategy "stand back and watch.") The most important single idea originating from game theory, to my mind, pertains to the relationship between information ("rules") and rational action ("strategy").

APPENDIX A

TOWARD A GENERAL DEFINITION OF RATIONAL ACTION [1]

The article reproduced here describes one set of views on how information can be used as a basis for rational decision-making without enlisting the "aid" of the various artificialities. The basic notions are simpler here than in Chapter 8, and, furthermore, there are a few errors in details. But perhaps the disadvantages resulting from these shortcomings are adequately offset by the resulting greater clarity.

There is some repetition here of material already covered in Chapters 4 and 8. In the interests of greater clarity and easier readability, again, it seemed wise to leave it that way.

INTRODUCTION

One of the most prominent developments in current economic analysis is the renewed interest in the principles of "rational" behavior and choice. And the new interest has a focus somewhat different from that of the traditional point of view. Historically, modern economic analysis began with the *assumption* that human beings do behave "rationally" — whether as producers, traders, gamblers, or consumers — and proceeded to deduce and analyze the consequences of this assumed universal mode of action. The theories of the firm and of the consumer, for example, were regarded as *descriptive* of actual behavior, at least in the sense of being a good first approximation, and were used primarily as instruments in the study of the more complicated social phenomena. Economists, both the neoclassicists and their critics, the institutionalists, spent comparatively little thought

[1] Reprinted by permission from *Kyklos*, Vol. VII (1954), No. 3, pp. 245–271, with minor changes. The author wishes to acknowledge gratefully the help and advice rendered by his colleagues Professors William Haller, Jr., James B. Ludtke, Clarence Shute, and, especially, Jerome Rothenberg. Professor Rudolf Carnap of U.C.L.A. has made several valuable suggestions. Of course, responsibility for the faults remaining in this article rests solely with the author.

on the problem of analyzing just what "rationality" means; they merely defined it as the maximization of a fully known utility function or profit function, and proceeded on to the more "interesting" questions.

Modern economic analysis has at the present time by no means fully abandoned this aproach to "rationality"; but there has occurred a strong shift of emphasis toward a *normative* approach. It is being more and more widely recognized that in this complex world of ours it is not as easy to behave "rationally" as was formerly assumed, that businessmen as a group are far from knowing the secret, and that economists might make an important contribution by telling the men of affairs *how* to conduct their affairs rationally — after, of course, first figuring it out themselves. Concurrently with this shift in point of view among economists, workers in other fields of study are beginning to pay an increasing amount of attention to the problem of rationality of behavior, usually when confronted with a situation in which they themselves are required to act rationally. The following list, a very incomplete one, indicates some of the fields of study in which the problem of rationality, in various guises, is currently very important. (The reference in each case is to a single one of the leading works in this field.)

The theory of the firm: Many economists today are engaged in the process of enlarging the theory of the firm to include not only considerations of current profit but also of future profits, composition of assets, financial strength and liquidity, public policy, flexibility, safety, peace of mind of stockholders, and many others. Several economists are under the impression that this is an effort at better *description* of the behavior of firms, but, while this may often be true, it also has great *prescriptive* importance.[2]

Programming: Programming is concerned with the efficient, or rational, scheduling and planning of *interdependent* activities. Under the leadership of the Cowles Commission for Research in Economics a great deal of work is being done, much of it with

[2] See K. E. Boulding: *A Reconstruction of Economics* (New York: Wiley, 1950).

government support, in developing procedures for the rational conduct of complex economic, military, and government affairs.[3]

Operations research is a somewhat more general concept than programming. First intensively developed during the second world war, it applies probability theory and other analytical methods to the rational solution of practical problems.[4] Its current applications are primarily, but not exclusively, in the various types of engineering.

The theory of games: This, the most dramatic of the recent innovations in the theory of rational behavior, treats of situations in which an "actor" has to contend with opponents or, more generally, with uncertainty in given situations. The principles of the theory are today yielding many norms of action in economics, politics, military strategy, and even in such fields as statistics. The theory of games is currently probably the most intensively cultivated field, and deservedly so, in the study of rationality.[5]

Statistical inference: Statisticians have long faced the difficult problem of estimating unknown probability distributions from relatively scanty observations. It is a problem of choice from among a set of possible probability distributions, each of the possible choices involving dangers of error. The names of J. Neyman, E. S. Pearson, and A. Wald are most prominently associated with the development of principles of rationality in that choice.[6]

The theory of probability: The entire theory of probability can be interpreted as a study of the principles of rational conduct in situations in which a certain definite type of uncertainty exists. This is true for both the mathematical and the philosophical branches of the theory. The origins of the theory are quite venerable (in age, if not in motive), but we see today

[3] See *Activity Analysis of Production and Allocation*, edited by Tjalling C. Koopmans (Cowles Commission Monograph 13, New York: Wiley, 1951).

[4] See P. M. Morse and G. E. Kimball: *Methods of Operations Research* (Cambridge: Technology Press and Wiley, 1951).

[5] See J. von Neumann's and O. Morgenstern's: *Theory of Games and Economic Behavior*, 2nd ed. (Princeton: Princeton University Press, 1947).

[6] See A. Wald: *Statistical Decision Functions* (New York: Wiley, 1950).

somewhat of a renaissance in the intensity with which it is being studied.[7]

Philosophy: A great deal of modern philosophical analysis studies the problems of rational behavior in various situations. The theory of induction, for example, is concerned with rational scientific conclusions; modern logic looks for "good" definitions of rationality of thought; and a few philosophers study rationality in general.[8]

All of the listed approaches to rationality have it in common that they define it rather *narrowly*; they prescribe a course of behavior for only stated (and limited) circumstances, and they usually pay attention to only a few of the consequences of the actions studied. But, on the other hand, they all contain important and useful ideas and concepts.[9] *This article will seek to draw from the best elements of all of these approaches to rationality in an attempt to arrive at a general definition of rationality, one that is applicable in all possible circumstances.*

Somewhat surprisingly, and for reasons that will soon become clear, it is extraordinarily difficult to arrive at such a definition. This article, as the title connotes, makes no pretense whatever of reaching even a provisionally satisfactory result. The definition that follows should be regarded as no more than a working approximation — a guide to future investigation and research. (At least, it is the author's hope that it will be useful in this way.)

It should be made quite explicit at the very outset what our general orientation shall be. First, to repeat what was stated above, our approach is purely *prescriptive*. The definition should *not* be interpreted as in any way attempting to *describe* the decision procedures that are actually being carried on in the

[7] See W. Feller: *An Introduction to Probability Theory and Its Applications*, Vol. 1 (New York: Wiley, 1950). R. Carnap: *Logical Foundations of Probability* (Chicago: University of Chicago Press, 1950).

[8] For example: F. E. Oppenheim: "Rational Choice," *Journal of Philosophy*, Vol. L, 1953, No. 12 (June 4, 1953), 341–350. – I. J. Good: "Rational Decisions," *Journal of the Royal Statistical Society*, Series B, Vol. XIV (1952), 107–114.

[9] It is assumed that the reader has at least a vague familiarity with the various listed approaches to rationality. Because of space limitations they cannot be described or discussed here.

real world today. Second, we shall *assume the existence of an adequate method of scientific induction.* In other words, we shall *not* be concerned with the problems of rationally inducing general laws from a set of available observations. Instead, we shall suppose that the induction problem has been solved in some fashion and go on to the question of how to utilize the knowledge so obtained (together with other knowledge) in the formulation of rational actions of the "applied" type. This is not to assert that the problems of scientific induction and of the rational application of knowledge are in any real sense distinct; it does mean that we believe that a more-or-less artificial separation of the problems does facilitate their analysis. Third, we wish our definition of rationality to be sufficiently general to serve as a guide to action in almost any set of circumstances. For example, we wish it to apply to the situation of a private individual in his personal actions, to the manager of a business firm, to the commander of an armed force, to a government official, to a union leader, or to anyone else at all in a decision-making situation.[10]

REQUIREMENTS OF A SATISFACTORY DEFINITION OF RATIONAL ACTION

Let us start our search for a definition by mentioning the *properties* that we wish the definition to have. This involves a specification of the "errors" we wish it to avoid, of the "facts of the world" that we wish the definition to take into account, and of the situations we wish it to be able to encompass.

I. *Actions to be designated as "nonrational"*

First, let us enumerate the types of action that we wish the definition to label as being *nonrational:*

   1. *Ignorant action,* which is defined as being action that is

---

[10] We have used the word "rational" quite a bit up until now, with the intention that the reader should understand it in its customary vague sense. From this point on it will be regarded as a technical term whose precise meaning is to be defined.

decided upon on the basis of either (a) mistakes in the facts considered, or (b) the omission of available relevant [11] facts.

An example of action based on a mistake in fact is one that assumes that black cats bring bad luck, or that a more northern locality is always colder than a more southern one, or that war inevitably produces inflation. Ignorant action based on the omission of available relevant facts is exemplified by a statesman who adopts a policy without considering the findings of social science bearing upon the consequences of that policy.

2. *Illogical action.* This is defined as action that is based on either (a) erroneous deductions or predictions from the facts considered, or (b) erroneous application of normative criteria.

Some typical examples of erroneous deductions or predictions are:

(1) Simple mistakes in reasoning.

(2) The wishful (or fearful) thinking of a strongly motivated person who overreaches the available facts, i.e., who jumps to conclusions that cannot be logically deduced from the available information.

(3) The confusion by a reformer or innovator between a *possible* consequence of his plan and a *necessary* consequence. For example, on the basis of available knowledge it is possible that the adoption of "socialized medicine" will increase human wellbeing, but it is by no means proven that this will necessarily follow.

Typical examples of erroneous application of normative criteria are:

(1) The adoption of an action "because it is right," or because of something that happened in the past, without considering its future effects. (It is assumed that future happenings are not a matter of indifference to the "actor.") Many of our penal practices are based on this type of error.

(2) The confusions that may accompany the attempted applica-

---

[11] "Relevance" is given an explicit definition below.

tion of unclear or partially self-contradictory criteria. People who seek to promote "the greatest good for the greatest number" are quite familiar with these confusions, as are other people who seek to attain incompatible ends.

(3) The failure to consider *all* relevant value criteria.

3. *Blind action* is that action which ignores at least some of the value-affected [12] consequences of the action. It can safely be asserted that most actions of men, in whatever capacity they may be functioning, are blind in this sense. An actor usually confines his attention to a few "intended" consequences of the action and ignores its manifold "unintended" ones. Whenever an act is being judged within a frame of reference that is narrower than the total range of interest of the actor, his action is blind. What is "good" in a narrow context is very often "bad" in a wider one. Typical examples of blind actions are:

(1) The abolition of a tariff on strictly economic grounds, without considering the effect on national security, on the sociological values of a diversified industry, on the educational standards of the country, etc.

(2) The adoption of a balanced budget policy by a government on grounds of financial prudence, without considering *all* the direct and indirect consequences of the appropriate tax and expenditure policies, economically, sociologically, psychologically, esthetically, morally, medically, etc., both in the present and in the future.

(3) Profit-maximization by a firm, where all considerations other than profit are ignored.

(4) Food consumption by an individual on the bases of taste and cost alone.

4. *Rash action,* which is defined as being action that is adopted after an incomplete consideration of the various *alternatives* of action that may be present. Commitment to one form of economic organization, for example, without a careful study

[12] An event is said to be "value-affected," relative to a given "actor," if its occurrence is *not* a matter of indifference to the "actor."

of the actually existing or possible other forms, is rash. So is, to take another instance, the purchase by a customer of the first item the salesman shows him.

As has been said, we want our definition of rationality to be such that any person acting in accordance with it will not be acting ignorantly, illogically, blindly, or rashly. It seems quite reasonable, at least to the author, to make this one of the basic requirements of "rationality."

II. Important facts to be considered

Next, let us look at a number of important characteristics of the world in which we live and act that must be taken into account by our definition. It is the following facts, primarily, that make the problem of satisfactorily defining rationality so very difficult and complicated. Every existing definition of rationality known to the author ignores at least some of these facts.[13]

1. *Action, in general, is not a "one-shot" affair but rather stretches over time.* We should really speak of *courses of action*, not of actions.[14] Accordingly, we want our definition of rationality to be able to specify the correct courses of action over time.

2. *The effects of an action radiate out in many directions*, and infringe upon an enormous number of value-affected and other aspects of the world. It is quite possible that a given action will affect, directly or indirectly, every variable of the world discernible to the actor. Of course, a great many of these influences will be quite small, but nonetheless they will be present. And, since the number of possible variables that can be discerned in the world is infinite, it may be said that an action may have in infinite number of consequences.

3. The results of an action not only involve a huge number of variables but *affect these variables over a period of time.*

[13] None of these points will be *proven* to be true here. Most of them are well-known. As for the others, the reader probably will, after a little reflection, be willing to accept them as true and valid.

[14] But we shall (as a short-cut device) continue to use the word "action."

Strictly speaking, the effects of an action stretch from the moment the action is inaugurated on to *infinity*. Even a simple action like the adoption of a given strategy in a game of chess has effects that extend past the end of the game to infinity and that may well be of far greater importance than the outcome of the game.[15] The same holds true for all other actions even though they may have only limited intended objectives and only immediate visible outcomes.

4. *The state of information of the "actor" must inevitably be taken into account* in determining what is rational for him. For an omniscient being the problem of rational behavior is much easier than for a mere human. The human being, always being in partial ignorance of the world around him, can not do anything better than just to get the most out of the information he has or can obtain. What is a warranted action in accordance with a given body of information may be a quite foolish one when more, or different, information is available. We want our definition to take cognizance of the ever present deficiency of knowledge of human beings, and of the inevitable relation between information and rationality. We have reference here to two types of information, both having to do with the characteristics of the world in which we do our acting: (a) that pertaining to the number and character of the alternatives of action and (b) that pertaining to the multitudinous effects of each of the various alternatives.

Ordinarily the state of information of an actor will be far short of completeness in *both* respects.

5. *The accumulation of further information is difficult and costly.* This cost must be taken into account, because it may often be the case that it is "not worth it" to collect further information before acting. The process of information-gathering is a potentially endless one, and its cost therefore tends to infinity. Also, the process takes time, and action frequently cannot wait. The world does not stand still while the actor makes

---

[15] As an example the reader need think only of a game in which the opponent is one's boss, or one's spouse.

up his mind. It is therefore not usually a good idea to seek an absolute maximum of information before deciding upon a course of action, but to settle for some lesser amount. The definition of rationality should recognize this point.

6. *The outcome of an action is, in general, not controllable by the actor*.[16] The outcome of a given action may be visualized as being a function of two variables: (a) the action itself, and (b) the behavior of the rest of the universe. Since the actor can control only (a), and since (b) is only incompletely known and poorly predictable by him, the result of the joint action of both these variables cannot be known to the actor with any degree of assurance. In other words, the actor, at the time he chooses an action, does so without controlling, or even knowing, its outcome.

There are basically *three* levels of the uncertainty of an actor with respect to the outcome of his actions.

(1) He may be able to discover the set of possible values of (b), and thereby the set of all the possible outcomes of his action. Further, he may also be able to discover the *probabilities* of the various possible outcomes. ("Probability" here means an empirically ascertained relative frequency.)

(2) He may be able to discover the set of all possible outcomes, but not the respective probabilities.

(3) He may not even know the various possible outcomes of his action. (Except, perhaps, that "anything might happen.")

The definition of rationality should be able to cope with any of these levels of uncertainty on the part of the actor.

7. *The value criteria of different actors differ.* It is a commonplace that there exists a tremendous diversity in the value criteria — the motives, tastes, goals, opinions, and esthetic and moral ideas — by means of which different individuals appraise

[16] The "outcome" of an action here means the entire set of effects of the action.

the various outcomes of their possible actions. We want our definition of rationality to be able to specify a "correct" course of action for *any* set of value criteria, i.e., to be usable by *all* actors to maximize the satisfaction of their "tastes," *whatever these may be.* We want this to be true for actors who subscribe to inconsistent criteria or who are motivated by unconscious drives as well as for those who behave in a more calculating fashion.

8. *The value criteria of a given actor tend to change over time.* An action which is "satisfactory" at the time it is first adopted may therefore become quite "unsatisfactory" as the tastes and ideas of the actor change. The available evidence indicates that such changes are often the normal rather than the exceptional thing, and our definition of rationality must therefore be sufficiently flexible to take these possibilities into account.[17]

9. One of the main reasons why the value criteria of individuals change so often is that *a person's memories of the past and expectations of the future influence the criteria with which he judges the world today.* And, since both memories and expectations are constantly changing, the value criteria through which presently available alternatives are evaluated change as well.

10. In view of points 2, 3, and 8 above, *the process of judging the outcome of a given action may potentially be infinitely long.* We must consider a possibly infinite number of variables, over a possibly infinite stretch of time, in the light of a possibly infinite diversity of value criteria. (Obviously this is a rather difficult situation to contend with, and the definition of rationality should therefore contain a stop-rule for the process of judging.) The customary analytic methods of finding a maxi-

---

[17] For example, we want to call it "irrational" to take an action that, even while being "satisfactory" today, may make it impossible for us to satisfy the value criteria we may have tomorrow. To take a simple example, assume an actor is quite fond of milk today. He should not commit himself to large future purchases of milk if it is possible that his tastes may shift to beer tomorrow.

mum (in a finite number of steps) do not, in most cases, apply here. The available information will not generally be in the form of well-behaved, manageable mathematical functions.

11. The difficulty of potential infinity is even aggravated by the fact that *there may be an infinity of possible actions among which an actor has to choose.* (This may, at first, be a startling assertion, but the reader will probably see the truth of it if he tries to enumerate merely all the physical movements he can make in the next month.[18]) As was seen above, each of the possibly infinite number of actions should be judged by a possibly infinitely long process.

12. *The process of judging the various possible actions — of making all the required calculations and logical deductions — is difficult, time-consuming, and costly.* Also, the actor may have value criteria bearing upon the various types of calculation. And further, during the time the judging takes place the world does not stand still. The definition of rationality must fully consider these inevitable facts.

13. *The actor usually has value criteria bearing upon the necessity of choosing an action without having complete knowledge of the various possibilities of action and their outcomes.* He may dislike acting on very little information because it is "foolhardy," or "dangerous," or "morally wrong"; or, on the other hand, he may like it because it is "thrilling" or "comfortable" or "easy." Such criteria are equally important with the ones mentioned under 7 above, and should therefore be considered fully. (The insurance principle and the pleasures of gambling are involved here.)

The ideal definition of rational action — one which we will not be able to formulate satisfactorily here — would specify how, in view of the 13 points just mentioned, we can adopt a course of action without committing one or more of the four irrationalities discussed before.

---

[18] As a matter of fact, there is a non-denumerably infinite number of ways in which the reader can put down this journal.

TERMINOLOGY

Before proceeding further, it is necessary for us to develop a somewhat more precise terminology than we have been using up until now. Here, like in so many other instances, clarity of concept is indispensible for clarity of thought.[19]

Variable: A variable is anything whatsoever that continues through time and that assumes, at each instant of time, one of the set of mutually exclusive values [20] in its characteristic range of variation. (One of these values will usually be "zero," "none," or some equivalent.) We place no limitation at all on the type of entity that can be considered to be a variable other than that it must have the defining properties. It may in fact vary, or it may remain constant; it may take on quantitative or qualitative values; it may vary over a continuum or it may have a denumerable or finite number of values; and it may be directly observable or not. If an object has two or more ranges of variation that interest us, it is considered to constitute as many variables as it has such ranges of variation. A given person, for example, might be regarded as being the following six variables: John Doe (weight), John Doe (age), John Doe (religion), John Doe (social status), John Doe (wealth), and John Doe (occupation).

Value-affected variable: This is a variable whose behavior is not a matter of indifference to a given actor. It is one to which at least one of the value-criteria of the actor refer, *or* one describing the value-criteria themselves.

World: The world is the infinite set of variables that we can perceive or conceive of. In other words, it is the raw material in which we can discern as many variables as we choose and study their behavior. It is the inexhaustible "grab-bag" of vari-

[19] We shall assign a technical meaning to a number of familiar terms, and the technical meaning may diverge a little from the familiar meaning. I hope that no undue confusion will result.

[20] It is hoped that our double use of the word "value," as a point in the range of variation of a variable and as an axiological entity, will not prove confusing. The context will indicate what meaning is intended.

ables and their values that constitute all our experiences.

System: Any set whatsoever of jointly considered variables, including the "world" or any lesser set, is a system. For the purpose of this paper, we shall always regard *time* to be one of the variables of a system.

Value-set: This is the set of all value-affected variables of a given actor.

State of a system: A state is any logically possible combination of values of the variables of the system. In an n-variable system, a state is always a set of n values, one value of each of the n variables.

History of a system: This is one of our key concepts, and a somewhat tricky one. It denotes a set of states of the system such that there is one state, and one only, for each point of time (in the time interval considered). It is, in other words, a time-sequence of states stretching over any given finite or infinite period of time. *Any* logically possible sequence of this sort shall be called a history of the system.

A priori range of a system: The entire set of logically possible histories of a system shall be called the a priori range of that system.[21] It is the totality of different courses of events that could conceivably transpire in the system.

Event: An event is the alternation of a set of histories that have some property in common.[22] That property may be a given value at a given moment of one of the variables of the system, a certain relation among some of the variables, an equal

[21] Consider, for example, a system of 4 variables: A, B, C, and time. Assume that A can assume 10 values, B 3 values, C 5 values, and time 100 values. At each point in time this system can assume one of $10 \times 3 \times 5$ or 150 different states. Since there are 100 points of time to be considered, the system has 150^{100} possible histories. (Of course, if any of the variables had an infinite number of possible values, the number of histories also would have been infinite.) That set of 150^{100} histories is the a priori range of the system.

[22] An alternation of a set of histories is described by the proposition that one of these histories is the "true" one. It is the proposition in which the various histories are joined by the logical connective "or."

degree of satisfactoriness, or anything else at all. Each single history is an event, as is the alternation of all histories in the a priori range of the system, and as is any other set of histories.

Information: Information, in relation to a given system, is knowledge concerning the behavior of the variables that constitute the system. An item of knowledge is information in this sense if, and only if,

(a) it is *valid,* i.e., established as being true. We are assuming now that we have available appropriate methods for distinguishing between true and false propositions, and that, in general, our methodology of science is capable of coping with questions of this sort. A proposition whose validity is neither established nor disproven is *not* information;

(b) it assigns probabilities [23] to at least one event of the system. It may declare an event to be impossible (probability of zero), or to be necessary (probability of one), or to be probable in some intermediate way;

(c) its validity conditions are fully stated, i.e., it holds true, as it stands, under all possible surrounding circumstances. There should be no unstated validity conditions a change in which could, without previous notice, make the statement untrue. (But reasonable allowance should be made here for the "finitude" of the human mind in conceiving of validity conditions.)

Information consists of definitional identities and of synthetic propositions; and synthetic propositions, in turn, consist of observations, static laws, and dynamic laws.

Space of a system: The space of a system, relative to a given body of information, is what becomes of the a priori range of the system after the information is applied to it. It is the set of all possible histories *together with* the known probabilities of

[23] "Probability" should here be understood in the sense of a *relative frequency.*

the various histories and events. A typical space will contain histories with each of the following types of probability:

(a) Many histories will have a probability of zero; they are unconditionally "ruled out" by the available information.

(b) Others will have definite non-zero probabilities — those concerning which we have explicit information.

(c) For many we will know a *range* of possible probability but not the specific probability. These may be the histories that are component parts of events of which we do know the probability. Assume, for example, that we know a certain event, consisting of n histories, to have a probability of p. Then, in the absence of further relevant information, each of the n histories can have a probability between zero and p. Other histories, not part of such events, and concerning which we have no explicit information, can have probabilities between (zero) and ($1 -$ the sum of the known probabilities of other events). In all cases the probability of an event equals the *sum* of the probabilities of the component histories.

In the case of a system for which the available information is of the "yes-or-no" rather than of the probability type, the space will consist of histories with either zero or entirely unknown probability.

Action: An action of a given actor is a course of behavior of that actor which specifies, for each moment of time, a fixed mode of response to the information available at that time, whatever that information may be.[24] It prescribes his pattern of response, over time, to the unfolding flux of events, insofar as it is known to him.

Not all actions will *explicitly* prescribe a mode of behavior for all conceivable contingiencies. Some "degenerate" types of action are:

[24] It is analogous to what von Neumann and Morgenstern call a "strategy."

(a) A predetermined course of behavior that will ignore new information entirely and proceed rigidly according to a preconceived fixed plan.

(b) An action in which the mode of response to some contingencies is unstated; i. e., left to hunch or to chance (with unspecified probabilities).

An action specifies, among the other kinds of behavior, when and to what extent the actor will engage in additional *information-gathering*, with respect to both (a) additional possible actions, and (b) the behavior of the rest of the universe.

It also specifies when and how a system under consideration is to be enlarged by the addition of new variables, usually in order to be able to "digest" new information.

Outcome of an action: The outcome of an action, relative to a given system, is what becomes of the space of that system when the action is assumed to be adopted. (In practice the outcome of an action will never be known to within a single non-zero-probable history.)

THE DEFINITION OF RATIONAL ACTION

We are now ready to formulate our tentative general definition of rational action. *We shall do so by describing a "rational" procedure for selecting an action from among the set of all possible actions.* Because of the complexity of the problem we shall proceed in two steps: first by making a few unrealistic assumptions and then by removing them.

Step 1:

Assume that:

(a) we are, at the present time, choosing an action once and for all;

(b) there is no cost or effort in calculation and judging, and no value criteria bearing upon the procedures involved;

206 Appendix A

   (c) all calculations can be made now; i.e., calculation is not time-consuming;

   (d) the number of possible actions is finite; and

   (e) the system to be considered consists of a finite number of variables, and every variable, including time, has a finite number of possible values.

Under these assumptions, the following method of choosing an action is "rational": [25]

1. Consider a system that contains

   (a) the entire value-set;

   (b) all other variables that are needed to take account of the available information bearing upon the behavior of the value-set;

   (c) time.

2. Applying all the available relevant information, construct the space of the system. This information normally should include knowledge referring to all of the following:

   (a) the behavior of the "outside world";

   (b) the effects of further information-gathering by the actor on the value-set;

   (c) the possible changes in the value-criteria of the actor as a result of his experiences, or any other source.

3. Determine the set of all possible actions.

4. Compute the outcome of *each* of these actions.

5. Judge each of these outcomes, in the following way:

   (a) Evaluate the "satisfactoriness" [26] of *each* non-zero-probable history in the outcome by

     i) evaluating each time-point in that history (using

---

[25] The procedure to be described is illustrated in the appendix to this article.

[26] The reader may think of "satisfactoriness" as a numerical utility. I am avoiding the more familiar term in order not to become involved in the as-yet-not-fully settled controversy on the cardinality of utility.

the value-criteria contained in its description to judge the other values of the variables);

ii) aggregating the "satisfactorinesses" of the various time points to arrive at a "satisfactoriness" of the history as a whole. This aggregation requires the use of a *secondary value-criterion relating to time-preference* in weighting the "satisfactorinesses" of the various time-points. Different actors will, of course, have differing patterns of time preference. The time-preference criterion will ordinarily set a "horizon," a time-point beyond which all states of the system are weighted at zero.

(b) Using *another secondary value-criterion*, one pertaining to *risk-taking preferences*, determine the *"significant worth"* of the outcome. The significant worth is that "satisfactoriness" of an outcome that the actor chooses to use in comparing the outcomes of different actions. If the actor is the cautious, conservative type, he may adopt the minimax risk-taking criterion, and the significant worth of the outcome of a given action is the "satisfactoriness" of the *worst* non-zero-probable history in that outcome. An optimistic gambler may choose the worth of the *best* such history. In some cases, when the probabilities are sufficiently well-known, the significant worth will be the mathematical *expectation* of "satisfactoriness." Other actors may choose to disregard the very improbable histories and minimax the rest, or they may choose to minimax what has been called "regret," or they may adopt any other risk-taking criterion at all. There is no way in which we can say, in general, what risk-taking criterion an actor "should" adopt — that is in most cases purely a matter of taste, as were his criteria in judging the different histories themselves.

6. Adopt the action whose outcome has the greatest significant worth.

Step 2:

Let us now abandon the stated assumptions we have made in Step 1 and attempt to set forth a rational method of choosing an action in general, considering all of the 13 complicating factors previously enumerated.

As might be expected, the main difficulty arises from the before-mentioned fact that the process of calculation and judging is potentially infinitely long. Also, it may be desirable from time to time, as more information and evaluations become available, or as the time-preference and risk-taking criteria change,[27] to abandon a present action and to adopt another one.

Under these circumstances, the procedure of rational action assumes a somewhat different character than in Step 1. No longer can we do our computations and judging first, decide upon a course of action, and then proceed to carry it out. Now, the calculation and judging and the acting must proceed *concurrently*. Furthermore, our decision to adopt an action will always be based on an *incomplete* calculation, and will usually turn out to be "mistaken" as the calculation proceeds.

The process of calculation and judging, as has been seen, is potentially infinitely long in *several* directions:

(a) in the number of possible actions to be considered;

(b) in the quantity of information to be used in computing the outcome of a given action;

(c) in the length of the time period for which a given outcome is to be computed;

(d) in the number of value-affected and other variables of the world to be considered;

(e) in the number of different "primary" value criteria that might have to be considered;

(f) in the number of different "secondary" value-criteria — time-preference and risk-taking — that might become relevant.

[27] We have, in Step 1, silently assumed the actor's tastes with respect to these two "secondary" criteria to remain constant.

At any given moment of time, the calculations will inevitably be incomplete with respect to at least the first *four* directions. We shall denote the sum total of all the calculations and judgments made up to a given point of time (and not forgotten) the *inventory of knowledge* at that point. This inventory should be visualized as an ever-increasing one, the rate of increase at any given time being the rate of calculation at that time.

There is another important factor to be considered here: the "cost" of calculation and judging is largely an *opportunity cost*. Since there is a basic limitation on available resources (including time) there exists a relationship of complementarity between action and calculation. The more we calculate, the smaller is the number of possible actions open to us; and the more resource-consumingly we act, the less we can calculate. Similarly, some types of action preclude some types of calculation, and vice versa. The opportunity cost of a given calculation, therefore, is the difference between the significant worth [28] of the best action [28] that could have been taken if we did not engage in this calculation and the significant worth of the best action [28] available now.

Keeping these various facts in mind, we define the rational procedure for choosing actions to be the following:

1. *At each moment of time [or at periodic intervals]* consider the set of all the possible *combined actions* that are given in the inventory of knowledge at that moment, where a combined action is an action as previously defined *plus* a given *rate* and *type* of further calculation and judging.

2. Evaluate *each* combined action in the following way:
   (a) Using only the present inventory of knowledge, and proceeding as in Step 1, determine the significant worth of the outcome of the "regular" part of the combined action.
   (b) Determine the "worth" of the further calculation and judging specified in the combined action. This *cannot*

[28] To the extent known to the actor.

be done by referring to the results of these efforts — the results are by their very nature unknowable, and we cannot have information bearing upon them. Instead, we must have recourse to two further secondary value-criteria, (i) a *computation criterion*, dealing with the "pain" or "pleasure" of the various types and quantities of calculation and judging, and (ii) an *uncertainty criterion*, dealing with the "pain" or "pleasure" of acting on the basis of incomplete knowledge. Ordinarily, the computation criterion will be such that the "pain" of computation, past a certain point, varies *directly* with the rate of calculation and judging, and *inversely* with the skill of calculation and judging of the actor. (The availability and competence of computing machinery, etc., is reflected in the "skill" of the actor.) As for the uncertainty criterion, there is a wide variety of patterns possible. The typical actor will probably have a "pain" of acting on the basis of incomplete computation that varies *inversely* with both the size of the inventory of knowledge and the significant worth of the outcomes considered so far. The actor's hopes of improving his choice of action by doing additional calculation and judging will normally fade as the amount of calculation already done increases and as the significant worth of the already considered actions increases. In addition, this "pain" will probably vary *directly* with the number of alternative actions in the inventory of knowledge in relation to the amount of computation in that inventory. (Ignorance may be bliss.)

(c) Add (a) and (b) to obtain the combined significant worth of the combined action.

3. Adopt, at the present moment of time, that combined action which has presently the greatest combined significant worth.

4. Repeat the process periodically.

EVALUATION OF THE DEFINITION

It is necessary at this point to ask ourselves whether or not the definition just stated satisfies the requirements we had originally set up for a satisfactory definition of rational action. The reader can verify for himself that it *does* take account of all the various relevant characteristics of the world listed above. But he will also note that a person proceeding in accordance with the definition may quite well commit some of the four acts that we have designated as being nonrational. For example, because of the inevitable incompleteness of the inventory of knowledge, that person will probably be acting blindly and rashly, at least. Does this mean that either our definition or our requirements for the definition are unsatisfactory, or that the two are inconsistent?

The difficulty here arises from the fact that a complete and perfect satisfaction of our stated requirements necessitates, as we have seen, an infinitely long computation process. And the best that can ever be done about an infinitely distant goal is to *proceed in its direction* — it can never actually be attained. Will a person acting in accordance with our definition of rationality approach progressively closer to the perfect rationality? This is a question that is quite difficult to answer, with certainty, one way or the other. But intuitively it seems clear that that *will* be the case. Assuming that no information or calculations or judgings are forgotten or otherwise lost, the ever expanding inventory of knowledge will make possible an ever continuing correction of error, and thus a progressively closer approach to the satisfaction of our requirements for rationality. It may well be true that our errors are so numerous and so serious that the continuing correction process is only a small thing in relation to the magnitude of the problem, but then even a slow approach to an ideal is nevertheless an approach. If our requirements for rationality are understood as defining the *ideal*, and our definition as a method of *approaching* the ideal, the inconsistency between the two disappears.

SOME UNSOLVED PROBLEMS

The most serious [29] shortcoming of the present definition is its incompleteness. It presumes to tell a person what he should do in order to be acting rationally, but it does not indicate at all *how* these things can be done. Perhaps, however, this is not really a shortcoming — it was, after all, the main purpose of this tentative definition to suggest areas of useful study. The following list enumerates some of the problems that must be solved before action can become much more rational than it generally is today.

1. We need a method of assigning numbers, preferably cardinal numbers, to the "satisfactoriness" of given histories. The method should be sufficiently flexible to be able to apply *any* set of value criteria to the judgment of *any* history whatever. (The famous problem of the measurability of utility is only a small part of the general problem.)

2. We need a scientific language capable of expressing, in a way suitable for further calculation, all kinds of knowledge.

3. We require an efficient technique of specifying sets of histories and their probabilities. The space of a system may often consist of a several-dimensional continuum of possible histories. We need to develop, as the mathematicians have done, practical methods of dealing with infinity (or, at least, with very large numbers of items).

4. We must discover, if possible, a way of determining in what order the various possible actions should be investigated. The rapidity of our aproach to perfect rationality depends on this order.

5. We need to discover a good way of determining the "best" frequency of making the computation described in Step 2 in the formulation of our definition.

6. We need a method of calculating the mathematical expecta-

---

[29] Insofar as the author is presently aware.

tion of satisfactoriness of an action where some or all of the probabilities of the various histories in the outcome of the action are known only to within a range of values.

7. We need methods of determining whether a given variable is of "small" or of "great" importance to a given actor. The problem is that the behavior of a non-value-affected variable can always, in the absence of knowledge to the contrary, have repercussions on other variables that *are* of great concern to the person.

8. We should investigate whether it is sometimes "good" to forget or destroy information and computations. Would that make possible additional actions that have a high significant worth?

9. We need to analyze the whole problem of the relation between rational methods of scientific induction and rational ways of using the information so obtained. (An adaptation of the Neyman-Pearson-Wald method would probably be of use here.)

APPENDIX

The rational procedure of choosing an action is, as has been seen, a quite complicated one; and for that reason we cannot go into a realistic example of it here. But it might promote a clearer understanding of the concepts involved if we examine a simplified illustration of the process.

Let us consider a grossly simplified system S consisting of five variables: A, B, C, D, and *Time*. Each of these variables can assume only a finite number of values. A can assume 9 values, B 4 values, C 5 values, D 5 values and *Time* 10 values. We shall denote the values of A by

$$a_1, a_2, \ldots, a_i, \ldots, a_9;$$
the values of B by
$$b_1, \ldots, b_j, \ldots, b_4;$$
the values of C by
$$c_1, \ldots, c_k, \ldots, c_5;$$

the values of D by
$$d_1, \ldots, d_l, \ldots, d_5;$$
and the values of *Time* by
$$t_1, \ldots, t_m, \ldots, t_{10}.$$

At each point of time m the system S can assume, as far as we know a priori, any one of $9 \times 4 \times 5 \times 5$ or 900 states, the "general" state to be denoted by $(a_i\ b_j\ c_k\ d_l\ t_m)$.

Since there are 900 possible states of S, and since there are 10 points of time to be considered at each of which S can assume any one of these 900 states, the a priori range of S consists of 900^{10} possible histories. (A history of S, as should be recalled, is a sequence of 10 states of S, one for each point of time.)

We shall take the variable C as being the only one of the system which can be directly manipulated by the actor. An action, therefore, involves the choice of a sequence of 10 values for C, one value for each point of time. Since at each time point the actor might choose any one of 5 values of C, the total set of possible choices consists, a priori, of 5^{10} different sequences. The number of possible "actions" is much larger than 5^{10}, but several such actions may lead to the same sequence of choices for C.

Assume that the actor has available to him the following information pertaining to the behavior of the variables of S:

Static laws ("Laws of coexistence"):

(1) [30] $i = j + k - 1$
(2) $\quad |j - k| \le 2$

Dynamic laws ("Laws of succession"):

(3) $\quad$ i cannot change by more than 3 between successive time points.
(4) $\quad \sim([k]_m \cdot [(l + 1) \vee (l + 3)]_{m+1})$
(5) $\quad$ At any given point of time the actor is familiar with the course of the system only up to the *preceding* time point.

[30] The letters i, j, k, l and m are the *indices* of the values of variables A, B, C, D, and *Time*, respectively.

Observation:

(6)   At t_1, the state of the system is $(a_1\ b_1\ c_1\ d_1\ t_1)$.

The variable B, we further assume, describes the *value criteria* by which the actor might judge the various possible states of S. We assume that there are just 4 such criteria:

b_1: the higher the sum of i, k, and l, the "better" the state is;
b_2: the lower the sum of i, k, and l, the "better" the state is;
b_3: the higher the value of i, the better it is;
b_4: the lower the value of k, the better it is.

At any given time point, of course, the actor subscribes to one (and only one) of these criteria. As is true in the real world, he does not consciously and voluntarily choose that criterion; and, as is also true, the behavior of the rest of the world influences his ideals and ideas.[31]

In order to keep the present illustrative case as simple as possible, we shall assume the situation of Step 1 of our definition of rationality with the additional assumptions that the volume of information is fixed and that that information, as was seen above, just assigns probabilities of zero to some of the a priori possibilities, and no other probabilities. Further, the time-preference value criterion is taken to be unchangeable, and it assigns an *equal* weight to the "satisfactoriness" of each time point. The risk-taking criterion, also unchangeable, is the *minimax* criterion.

The space of the system S should be ascertained in the following way. Taking each of the six items of information in turn, we *eliminate* from the a priori range of S all those histories that are inconsistent with that item. Item (1), for example, by assigning a probability of zero to all the a priori possible states of the system that violate the given relation among the variables

---

[31] In every more realistic case, the actor would hold *several* value criteria simultaneously, some of them perhaps even inconsistent with each other. In such instances we need to find a common denominator for the entire set of evaluations at each moment and to convert that set into a single number. (Obviously, some rather thorny problems are involved here.)

A, B, and C, justifies the elimination of all those histories of which *at least one* component state violates that relation. Any history containing the state, say, $(a_3\ b_3\ c_2\ d_4\ t_m)$ is now known to be impossible of occurrence (to have a probability of zero) and can therefore be eliminated from further consideration. Item (6), as another example, warrants the elimination of all histories whose first state is different from the given one. The elimination procedure for the other items of information follows the same pattern. After the entire process is completed, and all the histories of zero probability eliminated from the a priori range, the remaining set of possible histories of S is the *space* of S.

Inasmuch as we have (by assumption) no further information relevant to S, there is nothing we can say about the probabilities of the various histories remaining in the space of S. All we can say is that any given such history is, as far as we know, "possible" of occurrence. Its "true" probability might be anything from zero to one, inclusive.

Let us now consider the following one of the many actions available to the actor: [32] At each point of time he will choose the value for C which, in the light of the value of B prevailing at the preceding [33] time point, contributes the maximum possible amount to the "satisfactoriness" of the present. Accordingly, if the relevant value criterion is

b_1, he will choose the highest possible k;
b_2, he will choose the lowest possible k;
b_3, he will choose the highest possible k;
b_4, he will choose the lowest possible k.

The highest or lowest possible k is, in each case, the highest or lowest one, respectively, permitted by the present value of B and the last previous value of A, the relationship being given by items of information (1), (2) and (3).

The following are two of the many histories of S that might

[32] Let us call this action $\mathfrak{A}$.
[33] We are here taking account of the time-lag given by item of information (5).

follow, insofar as we "presently" know, the adoption of action $\mathfrak{A}$. (Ignore for the moment the numbers to the right.)

History $\mathfrak{A}_1$					Relevant Criterion	Raw Score	Standard Score
$(a_1$	b_1	c_1	d_1	$t_1)$	b_1	3	3
$(a_4$	b_2	c_3	d_3	$t_2)$	b_2	10	12
$(a_2$	b_2	c_1	d_5	$t_3)$	b_2	8	14
$(a_3$	b_3	c_1	d_5	$t_4)$	b_3	3	7
$(a_5$	b_2	c_4	d_3	$t_5)$	b_2	12	10
$(a_3$	b_3	c_1	d_4	$t_6)$	b_3	3	7
$(a_6$	b_3	c_4	d_1	$t_7)$	b_3	6	13
$(a_8$	b_4	c_5	d_3	$t_8)$	b_4	5	3
$(a_5$	b_4	c_2	d_3	$t_9)$	b_4	2	15
$(a_2$	b_1	c_2	d_1	$t_{10})$	b_1	5	5
						Total:	89

History $\mathfrak{A}_2$					Relevant Criterion	Raw Score	Standard Score
$(a_1$	b_1	c_1	d_1	$t_1)$	b_1	3	3
$(a_4$	b_2	c_3	d_5	$t_2)$	b_2	12	10
$(a_3$	b_3	c_1	d_3	$t_3)$	b_3	3	7
$(a_6$	b_3	c_4	d_3	$t_4)$	b_3	6	13
$(a_8$	b_4	c_5	d_1	$t_5)$	b_4	5	3
$(a_5$	b_4	c_2	d_1	$t_6)$	b_4	2	15
$(a_3$	b_3	c_1	d_4	$t_7)$	b_3	3	7
$(a_3$	b_1	c_3	d_5	$t_8)$	b_1	11	11
$(a_6$	b_3	c_4	d_5	$t_9)$	b_3	6	13
$(a_3$	b_1	c_3	d_4	$t_{10})$	b_1	10	10
						Total:	92

Note that both of these histories are consistent with all of our available information and hence are included in the space of S. Note also that, in both cases, the value of C is always either the highest or the lowest [34] consistent with the values of B and A and laws (1), (2) and (3).

The figures given to the right of the two histories represent the computations involved in the *judging* of these histories. The following procedure was used:

(a) We adopted, first, a system of assigning numbers to the

---

[34] Depending on the value criterion applicable in the case.

"satisfactorinesses" of the various states. In the case of criterion b_1 the problem was relatively simple; we just let the sum $i + k + l$ represent the degree of satisfactoriness of a given state of S. The lowest degree of satisfactoriness, in this scheme, is 3, and the highest, 19.

It seemed convenient to adopt these numerical values as our *standard* scores, and to convert the scores of the various states according to the three other value criteria to the same numbers.

1. According to criterion b_2, the sum $i + k + l$ also represents the satisfactoriness of a state of S, but with 19 being the lowest value and 3 the highest. The translation to the standard score can therefore be the following:

Raw Score: 3 4 5 6 7 8 9 10 11 12 13 14
↓ ↓ ↓ ↓ ↓ ↓ ↓ ↓ ↓ ↓ ↓ ↓
Standard Score: 19 18 17 16 15 14 13 12 11 10 9 8

15 16 17 18 19
↓ ↓ ↓ ↓ ↓
7 6 5 4 3

2. According to criterion b_3 the value of i serves as a raw score, ranging from a low of 1 to a high of 9. The translations is:

Raw Score: 1 2 3 4 5 6 7 8 9
↓ ↓ ↓ ↓ ↓ ↓ ↓ ↓ ↓
Standard Score: 3 5 7 9 11 13 15 17 19

3. According to criterion b_4 the value of k serves as a raw score, ranging from a low of 5 to a high of 1. The translation is:

Raw Score: 1 2 3 4 5
↓ ↓ ↓ ↓ ↓
Standard Score: 19 15 11 7 3

(b) Next, we proceeded to judge each of the ten states in the respective histories separately. Consider, for example, history $\mathfrak{A}_2$. The criterion relevant for judging the *first* state is b_1. The raw score therefore is $1 + 1 + 1 = 3$, and this is also the standard score. For judging the *second* state, criterion b_2 becomes relevant. Here the raw score is $4 + 3 + 5 = 12$, which, according to the translation given above, is equivalent to a standard score of 10. To take another example, for the judging of the *sixth* state criterion b_4 is to be used. The value of k in that state is 2, making a standard score of 15. The other states in $\mathfrak{A}_2$ (and all the states in $\mathfrak{A}_1$) were judged by the same procedure.

(c) Since we had assumed a time-preference criterion assigning equal weights to the satisfactorinesses of all states, and since the adoption of standard scores made the satisfactorinesses comparable, we could determine the satisfactorinesses of the two histories as a whole by simply adding the standard scores of the component states. Accordingly, the score of history $\mathfrak{A}_1$ came out to 89, and of $\mathfrak{A}_2$ to 92.[35]

The *outcome* of action $\mathfrak{A}$ consists of histories $\mathfrak{A}_1$ and $\mathfrak{A}_2$, as well as of *all* the many other histories in the space of S consistent with $\mathfrak{A}$. In order to determine the significant worth of the action we should have to judge *all* the histories in its outcome in the same way as we judged $\mathfrak{A}_1$ and $\mathfrak{A}_2$. In the present case, since the actor subscribes to the *minimax* risk-taking criterion, the significant worth of $\mathfrak{A}$ would be the *lowest* of the scores of the histories in its outcome.

After having done all the above, we have ascertained the significant worth of only *one* of the many actions available to the actor. In order actually to choose an action, the actor needs first to determine the significant worths of all of the other possible actions as well. The actor is behaving rationally if he then chooses the action with the *highest* significant worth.

[35] We are *not* forgetting here that persons, in applying their value criteria to the evaluation of the world, usually judge an entire *sequence* of *events* as a *unit* rather than the individual states separately. In our terminology, the specification of each state includes the remembered past and the expected future at that time point. The value criterion subscribed to at a given moment is, therefore, applied to an entire profile of occurrences, as it exists in the actor's mind at that moment. Our example is so simplified that this fact is not apparent from it.

SUMMARY

In recent years there has been a great development of interest in the principles and the problems of rational decision-
making and rational action. Economists, mathematicians, statisticians, logicians, engineers, and philosophers have all addressed their efforts to various phases of the general problem
of rationality. This paper attempts a provisional synthesis of
their basic results so far, in the form of a suggested preliminary
definition of rationality that is sufficiently general to be applicable in all circumstances.

The general definition of rationality, to be usable for "practical" decision-making, must take full cognizance of each of the
following characteristics, at least, of the "real" world: the time-
dimension of action and of the consequences of the action; the
multitudinous side-effects of an action; the inevitable uncertainty of the "actor" in connection with the alternatives of action open to him and the consequences of each of these; the
costs of information-gathering; the costs of performing logical
operations; the variety of the value-criteria of different actors;
the changes in the value-criteria of any given actor over time;
and the "tastes" of the actor in relation to time-preference,
risk-taking, logical processes, and the facing of uncertainty.
The definition of rationality should specify the course of action
which, in the light of all these factors, is the "best" one.

The present suggested definition outlines a "rational" procedure for choosing one from among the set of all known possible actions, where the word "action" refers to a particular
time-sequence of (a) acting (in the usual sense), (b) information-gathering, and (c) logical analysis. The procedure consists,
roughly, of these four steps: (1) the specification of the set of
known possible action; (2) the determination, for *each* of the
actions, and using all available relevant information, of the set
of all possible consequences of that action and their respective
probabilities; (3) the evaluation, in the light of the relevant
value-criteria, of each of the possible consequences of each of
the possible actions; and (4) the derivation from (3) of the

"correct" action to be adopted. In carrying out these steps we employ a logical construction patterned after those of Carnap, Hempel and Oppenheim.

For the sake of greater understandability, the definition is presented in two stages. The appendix to this paper contains a (grossly oversimplified) illustration of the application of the definition.

APPENDIX B

ADOLPH LOWE ON THE ROLE OF ECONOMIC THEORY

The present writer hereby acknowledges a debt to his teacher, Professor Adolph Lowe, for, among a great number of other insights, a clear conception of the relationships between economic theory and the "data" which it assumes, and also for the related understanding of the connections between the actual economic process and the physical and social setting which contains it. Clearness in this respect is an indispensable prerequisite for an evaluation of the role of economic theory in any attempt at economic prediction. The following quotations provide the best expression of Professor Lowe's views on this subject which could be found in print. Unfortunately, they do not nearly adequately reflect the full range of his ideas as they were expounded in classes and seminars. Unfortunately, also, this is not the place to reproduce the application of these views to the field of study in which they have yielded the most impressive results — the investigation of the cyclical-evolutionary process of capitalist development.

Economic theory is first of all based on a *deductive* method. We draw conclusions from a given set of assumptions. The assumptions are concerned with the material substrata of economic activity such as factors of production, technique, organisation, etc., and with active forces such as human tastes, working incentives, etc., dominating the concrete extent and direction of economic activity. From what sources the assumptions or "data" are to be obtained in any particular case of theoretical analysis, is a problem in itself.[1]

The choice of the set of assumptions upon which a structure

[1] Adolph Lowe: "Economic Analysis and Social Structure," *The Manchester School*, VII (1936), 18–19.

of theory is to be built is entirely arbitrary from the point of view of the logical validity of the theory; but the matter is not arbitrary from a pragmatic point of view. "Once we disregard logical errors in reasoning, obviously the concrete value of knowledge or the realistic bearing of theoretical deduction, apart from the abstract values of logical conclusiveness, simply depends on how accurately the assumptions have been selected [pp. 18–19]." This implies the following lesson for the forecaster, who is necessarily concerned with an actual, not an assumptive, world.

The value of economics as an empirical science ultimately depends on how accurately the natural and social background of economic activity is depicted in the assumptions of any deductive analysis. Here the autonomy of economics comes to an end . . . as soon as the economist sets to work with any realistic problem, no one can relieve him of the responsibility, not only of assuming his data but of answering for their occurrence, structural order and evolutionary tendencies in space and time [p. 21].

It is probably not too much to say that this entire essay constitutes an attempt to contribute to the solution of the problem suggested by the last sentence.

The most disconcerting thing about the "data" for economic analysis is their volatility; change, evolutionary or otherwise, is taking place almost continually. The applicability of the various economic theories must necessarily be equally volatile. Economic analysis, therefore, should not be viewed as yielding us absolutely invariant relationships.

Therefore the exact laws of the market have no deductive self-evidence at all but the mere probability which marks every empirical law. The degree of probability of their realization depends upon how probable it is that the basic social conditions will themselves materialize, that is to say, on the historical fact whether and to what extent liberal society exists.[2]

[2] Adolf Löwe, *Economics and Sociology* (London: Geo. Allen and Unwin, Ltd., 1935), p. 73. Our judgment would be that the probability of realization of the conditions presupposed by most of modern economic theory is close to zero; but that does not affect this principle.

The following quotation gives a somewhat more precise statement of the idea.

Any realistic theory of the modern economic system must start from the general premise that it can no longer deal with a constant structure and with homogeneous processes, but that the economic order under consideration is subject to an evolutionary transformation. Therefore any deductive operation with invariable data is defective from the very outset. Long period analysis cannot dispense with a previous examination of the tendencies of the data themselves, that is to say, the corresponding sociological constellation and its regular changes, and moreover with the examination of the mutual relations of the variations on both sides. Above all this dynamic chain of reciprocal causation between the economic process and its social environment calls for a theoretical system of co-ordinates which is on the one hand determinate enough to define the course of individual movements, and on the other hand elastic enough to reproduce the regular transformation of the system as a whole.[3]

A realistic theory of the capitalist process, one which is useful for prediction and policy matters, should, therefore, include a theory of data changes as well as a sufficiently flexible system of economic analysis. Economic theory is concerned with the typical consequences of normally occurring economic phenomena in the various probable constellations of the data.[4]

Speaking more technically than before, Professor Lowe states the following kinds of assumption [5] which must be made for any specific economic theory:

There are at the one end of the scale of abstraction the fundamental data or "categories" which constitute the necessary substratum of economic activity generally. Social grouping, natural and technical order of means, social regulation of the power of disposal,

---

[3] Page 138. This quotation shows quite well both the strength and the weakness, from the view of prediction, of the general ideas referred to here. The strong point is the stress on the interrelatedness between economic and noneconomic phenomena; the weak point, the concern with the precise determination of individual movements. The latter presupposes a closed system.

[4] This conception is, for the purpose of prediction, too loose. We should pay attention not to typical consequences, but to necessary consequences.

[5] In "Economic Analysis and Social Structure."

psychology of human wants and working incentives, these and other institutions and attitudes form the indispensable background for any materialisation of economic behaviour [p. 22].

(2) At the other end of the scale of abstraction we find the specific data which adapt the generalisations of economic theory to the particular conditions of an individual phenomenon, such as e.g. the granting of a tariff to the British Iron and Steel Industry in 1932 [p. 23].

Less obvious, but equally important, is the (usually implicit) assumption that we are dealing with a type of actual system which permits, in its conceptual replica, the kinds of reasoning processes in which economists customarily indulge. The following remark applies, for example, to economic micro-analysis.

As long as we keep the individual economic action isolated, the natural, psychological and institutional data may be arbitrarily selected and substituted for another. In such an analysis the individual action is cut off from the main structure of the social process, and is examined as a unique phenomenon "ceteris paribus." The far reaching significance of this famous working hypothesis has, however, not always been realised. In every isolating analysis it tacitly implies a structure of the system as a whole which makes it possible, that, during the particular process under consideration, other things in fact remain equal. In other words, it assumes such general conditions as secure the permanent working of the system.

If we now make these working conditions themselves the subject of research, we recognize at once that not every arbitrary combination of data fulfils these conditions. Every economic system is obviously based on certain *natural, psychological and institutional constants* which constitute the meta-economic framework of the individual economic transactions [p. 24].

Professor Lowe then proceeds to judge modern economic theory by the criteria he has developed. Not unexpectedly, the verdict is unfavorable.

It [economic theory] picks out imaginable constellations of data and deduces therefrom movements and states of rest under varying hypotheses. Any such constellation implies a set of sociological premises. But the conditions of the origin and persistence of these con-

226 Appendix B

stellations are intentionally disregarded, and equally their connection
with the system as a whole and any influences which might arise from
outside the particular set of data under consideration. For the sake
of argument the isolation and continuance of the initial constellation
simply are assumed. . . We must know beforehand what constellation of the real market process as a whole is typical, if our instru-
mentalistic deductions are to have any chance of being applicable.[6]

In summary form, the connection between economics and
other sciences, sociology in particular, can be expressed in this
way:

Now we are able to ascertain the basic relations between sociology
and modern realistic theory. Formally they are very similar to the
relation between sociology and classical economics. In both cases
determinateness of reasoning is secured by inserting some middle principles into the categories of a pure theory of exchange, and in both
cases the purport of these principles is a sociological one, pointing to
certain objective institutions and subjective rules of conduct which
prevail in the society under consideration. What makes the difference
is the substance of the respective middle principles, and with that
the resulting form of the circular flow [p. 98].

It is, to my mind, an important insight that various noneconomic facts (or assumptions) are necessary for "determinateness of reasoning" in economics. And it is clear, I hope, that
this paper has taken over the sum and substance of these ideas.
We have, however, attempted to eliminate the "looseness" in
the theory — the lack of absolute invariance in the principles
of economic theory — which is due to the volatility of the
underlying data, by a two-fold generalization of the ideas. First,
we do not assume, for purposes of theory construction, a constellation of the data which is "typical" for the society under
study; we would attempt to have a theory for each possible
data constellation and to supplement that with a set of dynamic
laws of change. Second, we would not introduce a uniform set
of "middle principles" into the entire system under study. Codes
of behavior, institutions, etc., do not vary only from historical

[6] *Economics and Sociology*, pp. 139–140.

period to historical period, and from society to society, but among individuals and firms in a given society as well. Our illustrative model of Chapter 8 has demonstrated how this diversity can be recognized in the construction of a predictive model. (Of course, this program would entail a rather extensive amount of work.)

BIBLIOGRAPHY

Books

Ackoff, Russell L. *The Design of Social Research*. Chicago: University of Chicago Press, 1953.

Arrow, Kenneth J. *Social Choice and Individual Values*. Cowles Commission Monograph No. 12. New York: Wiley, 1951.

Baumol, W. J. *Economic Dynamics — An Introduction*. New York: Macmillan, 1951.

Blackwell, David, and M. A. Girshick. *Theory of Games and Statistical Decisions*. New York: Wiley, 1954.

Boulding, Kenneth E. *A Reconstruction of Economics*. New York: Wiley, 1950.

Braithwaite, R. B. *Scientific Explanation*. London: Cambridge University Press, 1953.

Bratt, Elmer C. *Business Cycles and Forecasting*, 4th ed. Chicago: Irwin, 1953.

Brown, J. F. *Psychology and the Social Order*. New York: McGraw-Hill, 1936.

Burns, Arthur F. *The Frontiers of Economic Knowledge*. Princeton: Princeton University Press, 1954.

Burns, Arthur F., and Wesley C. Mitchell. *Measuring Business Cycles*. New York: National Bureau of Economic Research, 1946.

—— *Statistical Indicators of Cyclical Revivals*. Bulletin 69. New York: National Bureau of Economic Research, 1938.

Carnap, Rudolf. *The Continuum of Inductive Methods*. Chicago: University of Chicago Press, 1952.

—— *Logical Foundations of Probability*. Chicago: University of Chicago Press, 1950.

Carter, C. F., G. P. Meredith, and G. L. S. Shackle. *Uncertainty and Business Decisions — A Symposium*. Liverpool: University Press, 1954.

Charnes, A., W. W. Cooper, and A. Henderson. *An Introduction to Linear Programming*. New York: Wiley, 1953.

Churchman, C. West. *Theory of Experimental Inference*. New York: Macmillan, 1948.

229

Cowles Commission for Research in Economics. *Rational Decision-Making and Economic Behavior*, 19th Annual Report, 1950–1951.

Dahl, R. A., and C. E. Lindblom. *Politics, Economics and Welfare*. New York: Harper, 1953.

Dewey, Edward R., and E. F. Dakin. *Cycles: The Science of Prediction*. New York: Holt, 1949.

Dorfman, Robert. *Application of Linear Programming to the Theory of the Firm*. Berkeley: University of California Press, 1951.

Duesenberry, James S. *Income, Saving, and the Theory of Consumer Behavior*. Cambridge: Harvard University Press, 1949.

Eddington, A. S. *The Nature of the Physical World*. New York: Macmillan, 1928.

Eiteman, W. J. *Price Determination: Business Practice versus Economic Theory*. Ann Arbor: University of Michigan, School of Business Administration, 1949.

Feller, W. *An Introduction to Probability Theory and Its Applications*, Vol. I. New York: Wiley, 1950.

Ferber, R. A. *A Study of Aggregate Consumption Functions*. Technical Paper 8. New York: National Bureau of Economic Research, 1953.

Festinger, Leon, and Daniel Katz. *Research Methods in the Behavioral Sciences*. New York: Dryden, 1953.

Finer, Herman. *Road to Reaction*. Boston: Little Brown, 1946.

Fisher, R. A. *The Design of Experiments*. Edinburgh and London: Oliver and Boyd, 1935.

Friedman, Milton. *Essays in Positive Economics*. Chicago: University of Chicago Press, 1953.

Gee, Wilson. *Social Science Research Methods*. New York: Appleton-Century-Crofts, 1950.

Good, I. J. *Probability and the Weighing of Evidence*. New York: Hafner, 1950.

Goodman, Nelson. *Fact, Fiction, and Forecast*. Cambridge: Harvard University Press, 1954.

Haavelmo, Trygve. *A Study in the Theory of Economic Evolution*. Amsterdam: North-Holland Publishing Company, 1954.

Hagen, Everett E., and Nora Kirkpatrick. *Forecasting Gross National Product During the Transition Period: An Example of the Nation's Budget Method*. Studies in Income and Wealth,

Vol. X. New York: National Bureau of Economic Research, 1947. Pages 94–109.

Haley, B. F., editor. *A Survey of Contemporary Economics.* Homewood, Ill.: Irwin, 1953.

Haney, Lewis H. *Business Forecasting.* Boston: Ginn, 1931.

Hansen, Alvin H. *Business Cycles and National Income.* New York: Norton, 1951.

Hardy, Charles O., and Garfield V. Cox. *Forecasting Business Conditions.* New York: Macmillan, 1928.

Hart, A. G. *Anticipations, Uncertainty, and Dynamic Planning.* New York: Augustus M. Kelley, 1951.

Hayek, Friedrich A. *The Road to Serfdom.* Chicago: University of Chicago Press, 1944.

Hempel, Carl G. *Fundamentals of Concept Formation in Empirical Science.* International Encyclopedia of Unified Science, Vol. II, No. 7. University of Chicago Press, 1952.

Hicks, J. R. *A Contribution to the Theory of the Trade Cycle.* Oxford: Clarendon Press, 1950.

—————— *Value and Capital,* 2nd ed. Oxford: Clarendon Press, 1946.

Higgins, Benjamin. *What Do Economists Know?* New York: Cambridge University Press, 1952.

Hilbert, D., and W. Ackermann. *Grundzüge der Theoretischen Logik.* New York: Dover, 1946.

Hood, W. C., and T. C. Koopmans, eds. *Studies in Econometric Method.* New York: Wiley, 1953.

Horst, Paul, et al. *The Prediction of Personal Adjustment.* New York: Social Science Research Council, 1941.

Kalecki, M. *Theory of Economic Dynamics.* New York: Rinehart, 1954.

Kantor, J. R. *The Logic of Modern Science.* Bloomington: Principia Press, 1953.

Katona, George. *Psychological Analysis of Economic Behavior.* New York: McGraw-Hill, 1951.

Kaufmann, Felix. *Methodology of the Social Sciences.* New York: Oxford University Press, 1944.

Keirstead, B. S. *The Theory of Economic Change.* Toronto: Macmillan, 1948.

Keynes, John M. *A Treatise on Probability.* London: Macmillan, 1921.

Keynes, John N. *The Scope and Method of Political Economy.* London: Macmillan, 1891.

Klein, L. R. *Comment on Econometric Models.* Studies in Income and Wealth, Vol. XI, 352. New York: National Bureau of Economic Research, 1949.

———— *Economic Fluctuations in the United States, 1921–1941.* Cowles Commission Monograph No. 11. New York: Wiley, 1950.

Kneale, William. *Probability and Induction.* Oxford: Clarendon Press, 1949.

Koopmans, Tjalling C., ed. *Activity Analysis of Production and Allocation.* Cowles Commission Monograph No. 13. New York: Wiley, 1951.

———— *Statistical Inference in Dynamic Economic Models.* Cowles Commission Monograph No. 10. New York: Wiley, 1950.

Lazarsfeld, Paul F., ed. *Mathematical Thinking in the Social Sciences.* Glencoe: Free Press, 1954.

Leffler, George L. *The Stock Market.* New York: Ronald, 1951.

Leontief, Wassily. *The Structure of the American Economy, 1919–1939,* 2nd ed. New York: Oxford University Press, 1951.

Leontief, Wassily, et al. *Studies in the Structure of the American Economy.* New York: Oxford University Press, 1953.

Lerner, Abba P. *The Economics of Control.* New York: Macmillan, 1947.

Lerner, D., and H. D. Lasswell, eds. *The Policy Sciences — Recent Developments in Scope and Method.* Stanford: Stanford University Press, 1951.

Löwe, Adolf. *Economics and Sociology.* London: Allen and Unwin, 1935.

Lundberg, George. *Foundations of Sociology.* New York: Macmillan, 1939.

MacIver, R. M. *Social Causation.* Boston: Ginn, 1942.

Madge, J. *The Tools of Social Science.* London: Longmans, Green, 1953.

Mannheim, Karl. *Men and Society in an Age of Reconstruction.* London: Kegan Paul, Trench, Trubner, 1940.

Mathematics and the Social Sciences. International Social Science Bulletin, Vol. VI, No. 4. Unesco, 1954.

McDonald, John. *Strategy in Poker, Business and War.* New York: Norton, 1950.

McKinsey, J. C. C. *Introduction to the Theory of Games.* New York: McGraw-Hill, 1952.

von Mises, Richard. *Probability, Statistics and Truth.* New York: Macmillan, 1939.

Mitchell, Wesley C. *What Happens During Business Cycles?* New York: National Bureau of Economic Research, 1951.

Modigliani, Franco. *Fluctuations in the Saving-Income Ratio: A Problem in Economic Forecasting.* Studies in Income and Wealth, Vol. XI. New York: National Bureau of Economic Research, 1949.

Moore, Geoffrey H. *Statistical Indicators of Cyclical Revivals and Recessions.* Occasional Paper 31. New York: National Bureau of Economic Research, 1950.

Morgenstern, Oskar. *On the Accuracy of Economic Observations.* Princeton: Princeton University Press, 1950.

——— *Wirtschaftsprognose.* Wien: Julius Springer, 1928.

Morse, P. M., and G. E. Kimball. *Methods of Operations Research.* Cambridge: Technology Press and Wiley, 1951.

Mukerjee, Radhakamal. *The Institutional Theory of Economics.* London: Macmillan, 1942.

Myint, Hla. *Theories of Welfare Economics.* Cambridge: Harvard University Press, 1948.

Nagel, E. *Principles of the Theory of Probability.* International Encyclopedia of Unified Science, Vol. I, No. 6. Chicago: University of Chicago Press, 1939.

National Bureau of Economic Research. *Long-Range Economic Projection.* Studies in Income and Wealth, Vol. 16. Princeton: Princeton University Press, 1954.

von Neumann, John, and O. Morgenstern. *Theory of Games and Economic Behavior,* 2nd ed. Princeton: Princeton University Press, 1947.

Neurath, Otto. *Foundation of the Social Sciences.* International Encyclopedia of Unified Science, Vol. 2, No. 1. Chicago: University of Chicago Press, 1944.

Newbury, Frank D. *Business Forecasting: Principles and Practice.* New York: McGraw-Hill, 1952.

Neyman, J., ed. *Second Berkeley Symposium on Mathematical Statistics and Probability.* Berkeley: University of California Press, 1951.

Neyman, J., and E. S. Pearson. *Contributions to the Theory of Testing Statistical Hypotheses*. Statistical Research Memoirs, Parts I and II, 1936 and 1938.

Norris, R. T. *The Theory of Consumers' Demand*, Rev. Ed. New Haven: Yale University Press, 1952.

Northrop, F. S. C. *The Logic of the Sciences and the Humanities*. New York: Macmillan, 1948.

Noyes, C. Reinold. *Economic Man in Relation to His Natural Environment*. 2 vols. New York: Columbia University Press, 1948.

Quine, Willard V. *Mathematical Logic*. Cambridge: Harvard University Press, 1947.

Reder, Melvin W. *Studies in the Theory of Welfare Economics*. New York: Columbia University Press, 1947.

Redfield, Robert, ed. *Levels of Integration in Biological and Social Systems*. Biological Symposia, Vol. VIII. Lancaster, Pa.: The Jacques Cattell Press, 1942.

Reichenbach, Hans. *Experience and Prediction*. Chicago: University of Chicago Press, 1938.

——— *The Theory of Probability*. Berkeley and Los Angeles: University of California Press, 1949.

Robbins, Lionel. *An Essay on the Nature and Significance of Economic Science*, 2nd ed. London: Macmillan, 1935.

Rose, Arnold M. *Theory and Method in the Social Sciences*. Minneapolis: University of Minnesota Press, 1954.

Russell, Bertrand. *Human Knowledge, Its Scope and Limits*. New York: Simon and Schuster, 1948.

Samuelson, Paul A. *Dynamic Process Analysis*. A Survey of Contemporary Economics. Philadelphia: Blakiston, 1949. Pages 353–387.

——— *Foundations of Economic Analysis*. Cambridge: Harvard University Press, 1948.

Sanderson, Fred H. *Methods of Crop Forecasting*. Cambridge: Harvard University Press, 1954.

Sapir, Michael. *Review of Economic Forecasts for the Transition Period*. Studies in Income and Wealth, Vol. XI. New York: National Bureau of Economic Research, 1949.

Savage, Leonard J. *The Foundations of Statistics*. New York: Wiley, 1954.

Schumpeter, Joseph A. *Business Cycles*. 2 vols. New York: McGraw-Hill, 1939.

——— *Economic Doctrine and Method.* New York: Oxford University Press, 1954.

Shackle, G. L. S. *Expectation in Economics.* Cambridge: Cambridge University Press, 1949.

Social Science Research Council. *The Social Sciences in Historical Study.* Bulletin 64. New York, 1954.

Sorokin, P. A. *Society, Culture, and Personality.* New York: Harper, 1947.

Thrall, R. M., C. H. Coombs, and R. L. Davis, eds. *Decision Processes.* New York: Wiley, 1954.

Tinbergen, Jan. *On the Theory of Economic Policy.* Amsterdam: North-Holland Publishing Co., 1952.

——— *Statistical Testing of Business-Cycle Theories,* Business Cycles in the U.S.A., 1919–1932, Vol. II. Geneva: League of Nations, 1939.

Tinbergen, Jan, and J. J. Polak. *The Dynamics of Business Cycles.* Chicago: University of Chicago Press, 1950.

Toulmin, Stephen. *The Philosophy of Science.* New York: Longmans, Green, 1953.

Wald, Abraham. *Statistical Decision Functions.* New York: Wiley, 1950.

Weber, Max. *Objektive Möglichkeit und adäquate Verursachung in der historischen Kausalbetrachtung. Gesammelte Aufsätze zur Wissenschaftslehre.* Tübingen: J. C. B. Mohr (Paul Siebeck), 1922. Pages 266–290.

Whittaker, E. T. *A Treatise on the Analytical Dynamics of Particles and Rigid Bodies,* 4th ed. New York: Dover, 1944.

Woodger, J. M. *Biology and Language.* London: Cambridge University Press, 1953.

——— *The Technique of Theory Construction.* International Encyclopedia of Unified Science, Vol. II, No. 5. Chicago: University of Chicago Press, 1939.

Wootton, Barbara. *Lament for Economics.* London: Allen, 1938.

——— *Testament for Social Science — An Essay in the Application of Scientific Method to Human Problems.* New York: Norton, 1951.

Wright, Wilson. *Forecasting for Profit.* New York: Wiley, 1947.

Young, P. T. *Motivation of Behavior.* New York: Wiley, 1936.

Articles

Ablowitz, Reuben. "The Theory of Emergence," *Philosophy of Science*, VI (1939), 1–16.

Alchian, Armen A. "Uncertainty, Evolution, and Economic Theory," *Journal of Political Economy*, LVIII (1950), 111–121.

Allen, R. G. D. "The Mathematical Foundations of Economic Theory," *Quarterly Journal of Economics*, LXIII (1949), 111–127.

Alt, Franz L. "Distributed Lags," *Econometrica*, X (1942), 113–128.

Altschul, E., and E. Biser. "Probability Models in Modern Physics and Their Methodological Significance for Social Sciences," *Jahrbuch für Nationalök. und Stat.* (1954).

Andrews, P. W. S. "A Reconsideration of the Theory of the Individual Business," *Oxford Economic Papers*, New Series, I (1949), 54ff.

Armstrong, W. E. "Uncertainty and the Utility Function," *Economic Journal*, LVIII (1948), 1–10.

Arrow, Kenneth J. "Alternative Approaches to the Theory of Choice in Risk-Taking Situations," *Econometrica*, XIX (1951), 404–437.

Bar-Hillel, Yehoshua. "A Note on State Descriptions," *Philosophical Studies*, 2 (1951), 72–75.

Barbour, Justin F. "An Analysis of the Conclusions of the Cowles Studies with Respect to the Dow Theory," *Security Analysts Journal*, IV (1948), 11–20.

Barnes, Leo. "How Sound Were Private Postwar Forecasts?" *Journal of Political Economy*, LVI (1948), 161–165.

Bates, James. "A Model for the Science of Decision," *Philosophy of Science*, 21 (1954), 326–339.

Baylis, Charles A. "Are Some Propositions Neither True Nor False?" *Philosophy of Science*, III (1936), 156–166.

Beck, Lewis W. "The 'Natural Science Ideal' in the Social Sciences," *Scientific Monthly*, LXVIII (1949), 386–394.

Bernadelli, H. "What Has Philosophy to Contribute to the Social Sciences and to Economics in Particular?" *Economica*, New Series, III (1936), 443–459.

Birkhoff, G. D., and C. D. Lewis, Jr. "Stability in Causal Systems," *Philosophy of Science*, II (1935), 304–333.

Bode, Karl. "Plan Analysis and Process Analysis," *American Economic Review*, XXXIII (1943), 348–354.

Boulding, K. E. "Implications for General Economics of More Realistic Theories of the Firm," *American Economic Review,* XLII (1952), *Proceedings,* 35–44.

———— "Projection, Prediction, and Precariousness," *Review of Economics and Statistics,* XXXV (1953), 257–260.

———— "Samuelson's *Foundations:* The Role of Mathematics in Economics," *Journal of Political Economy,* LVI (1948), 187–199.

Bridge, Lawrence, and Bernard Beckler. "Capital Investment Programs and Sales Expectations in 1950," *Survey of Current Business,* XXX (April 1950), 6–10.

Bush, R. R., and F. A. Mosteller. "A Stochastic Model with Applications to Learning," *Annals of Mathematical Statistics,* 24 (1953), 559–585.

Carnap, Rudolf. "Application of Inductive Logic," *Philosophy and Phenomenological Research,* VIII (1947–48), 133–147.

———— "On Inductive Logic," *Philosophy of Science,* XII (1945), 72–97.

———— "The Problem of Relations in Inductive Logic," *Philosophical Studies,* 2 (1951), 75–80.

———— "Testability and Meaning," *Philosophy of Science,* III (1936), 419–471; IV (1937), 1–40.

———— "Theory and Prediction in Science," *Science,* New Series, CIV (1946), 520–521.

———— "The Two Concepts of Probability," *Philosophy and Phenomenological Research,* V (1944–45), 513–532.

Carnap, Rudolf, and Yehoshua Bar-Hillel. "An Outline of a Theory of Semantic Information," Technical Report No. 247, Research Laboratory of Electronics, Massachusetts Institute of Technology, 1952.

Chernoff, Herman. "Rational Selection of Decision Functions," *Econometrica,* 22 (1954), 422–443.

Christ, Carl F. "Discussion in Seminar on the Development of Economic Thought," *American Economic Review,* XLIII (1953), *Proceedings,* 271–274.

Churchman, C. West. "Statistics, Pragmatics, Induction," *Philosophy of Science,* XV (1948), 249–268.

Clark, Colin. "A System of Equations Explaining the United States Trade Cycle, 1921 to 1941," *Econometrica,* XVII (1949), 93–123.

Clark, John M. "Varieties of Economic Law, and Their Limiting Factors," *Proceedings of the American Philosophical Society,* XCIV (1950), 121–126.

Clower, R. W. "Professor Duesenberry and Traditional Theory," *Review of Economic Studies,* XIX (3), 165–178.

Colp, Ralph, Jr. "Ernest Starling," *Scientific American,* 185 (1951) No. 4, 56–61.

Cowles, Alfred, 3rd. "Can Stock Market Forecasters Forecast?" *Econometrica,* I (1933), 309–324.

———— "Stock Market Forecasting," *ibid.,* XII (1944), 206–214.

Dorfman, R. "The Nature and Significance of Input-Output," *Review of Economics and Statistics,* XXXVI (1954), 121–133.

Douglas, Paul H. "Are There Laws of Production?" *American Economic Review,* XXXVIII (1948), 1–41.

Ducasse, C. J. "Truth, Verifiability, and Propositions About the Future," *Philosophy of Science,* VIII (1941), 329–337.

Durbin, E. F. M. "Methods of Research — A Plea for Cooperation in the Social Sciences," *Economic Journal,* XLVIII (1938), 183–195.

Estes, W. K. "Toward a Statistical Theory of Learning," *Psychological Review,* 57 (1950), 94–107.

Farrell, M. J. "Deductive Systems and Empirical Generalizations in the Theory of the Firm," *Oxford Economic Papers,* 4 (1952), 45–49.

Ferber, R. "Measuring the Accuracy and Structure of Businessmen's Expectations," *Journal of the American Statistical Association,* 48 (1953), 385–413.

Firestone, O. J. "Government Economic Intelligence in Canada," *Public Affairs* (Spring 1949).

Frank, L. K. "Structure, Function and Growth," *Philosophy of Science,* II (1935), 210–235.

Friedman, Milton, and L. J. Savage. "The Utility Analysis of Choices Involving Risk," *Journal of Political Economy,* LVI (1948), 279–304.

Friend, Irwin, and Jean Bronfenbrenner. "Business Investment Programs and Their Realization," *Survey of Current Business,* XXX (June 1950), 11–22.

Frisch, Ragnar. "Repercussion Studies at Oslo," *American Economic Review,* XXXVIII (1948), 367–372.

Garfield, Frank R. "Measuring and Forecasting Consumption," *Journal of the American Statistical Association*, XLI (1946), 322–333.

—— "Transition Forecasts in Review," *American Economic Review*, XXXVII (1947), *Proceedings*, 71–80.

Georgescu-Roegen, N. "The Theory of Choice and the Constancy of Economic Laws," *Quarterly Journal of Economics*, LXIV (1950), 125–138.

Good, I. J. "Rational Decisions," *Journal of the Royal Statistical Society*, Series B, XIV (1952), 107–114.

Goodwin, Richard M. "The Non-Linear Accelerator and the Persistence of Business Cycles," *Econometrica*, XIX (1951), 1–17.

Gottlieb, M. "The Theory of an Economic System," *American Economic Review*, XLIII (1953), *Proceedings*, 350–363.

Grayson, Henry. "The Econometric Approach: A Critical Analysis," *Journal of Political Economy*, LVI (1948), 253–257.

Grelling, Kurt, and Paul Oppenheim. "Der Gestaltbegriff im Lichte der neuen Logik," *Erkenntnis*, VII (1937–38), 211–225.

Grunberg, E., and F. Modigliani. "The Predictability of Social Events," *Journal of Political Economy*, LXII (1954), 465–478.

Haavelmo, Trygve. "The Notion of Involuntary Economic Decisions," *Econometrica*, XVIII (1950), 1–8.

—— "The Probability Approach in Econometrics," *ibid.*, XII (July 1944), Supplement.

Hahn, L. A. "Über Wirtschaftsprognosen," *Schweiz Zeitschr. f. Volkswirtschaft und Stat.* (1953).

Hailperin, Theodore. "Foundations of Probability in Mathematical Logic," *Philosophy of Science*, IV (1937), 125–150.

Harberger, A. C. "Pitfalls in Mathematical Model-Building," *American Economic Review*, XLII (1952), 855–865.

Harwood, E. C. "What is Economic 'Knowledge'?" in *Reconstruction of Economics*. Great Barrington: American Institute for Economic Research, 1955.

Hayek, F. A. "The Use of Knowledge in Society," *American Economic Review*, XXXV (1945), 519–530.

Hays, Samuel P., Jr. "Some Psychological Problems of Economics," *Psychological Bulletin*, XLVII (1950), 289–330.

Hellman, Geoffrey T. "How Many Short Cuts Make a Maze?" *New Yorker* (June 9, 1951).

240   **Bibliography**

Helmer, O., and P. Oppenheim. "A Syntactical Definition of Probability and Degree of Confirmation," *Journal of Symbolic Logic,* X (1945), 25–60.

Hempel, Carl G. "The Function of General Laws in History," *Journal of Philosophy,* XXXIX (1942), 35–48.

Hempel, Carl G., and Paul Oppenheim. "A Definition of 'Degree of Confirmation,' " *Philosophy of Science,* XI (1945), 98–115.

———— "Studies in the Logic of Explanation," *Philosophy of Science,* XV (1948), 135–175.

Hitch, Charles. "Sub-Optimization in Operations Problems," *Journal of Operations Research Society of America,* I (1953), 87–99.

Hodges, J. L., Jr., and E. L. Lehman. "The Use of Previous Experience in Reaching Statistical Decisions," *Annals of Mathematical Statistics,* 23 (1952), 396–407.

Hood, William C. "Some Aspects of the Treatment of Time in Economic Theory," *Canadian Journal of Economics and Political Science,* XIV (1948), 453–468.

Hotelling, Harold. "Problems of Prediction," *American Journal of Sociology,* XLVIII (1942–43), 61–76.

Huntington, E. V. "The Method of Postulates," *Philosophy of Science,* IV (1937), 482–495.

Hurwicz, Leonid. "Stochastic Models of Economic Fluctuations," *Econometrica,* XII (1944), 114–124.

Hutchison, T. W. "The Significance and Basic Postulates of Economic Theory," *Journal of Political Economy,* IL (1941), 732–750.

Kaplan, Oscar. "Prediction in the Social Sciences," *Philosophy of Science,* VII (1940), 492–498.

Kemeny, John G. "Carnap on Probability," *The Review of Metaphysics,* 5 (1951), 145–156.

———— "Extension of the Methods of Inductive Logic," *Philosophical Studies,* 3 (1952), 38–42.

———— "A Logical Measure Function," *Journal of Symbolic Logic,* 18 (1953), 289–308.

Kemeny, John G., and Paul Oppenheim. "Systematic Power," *Philosophy of Science,* 22 (1955), 27–33.

Klein, Lawrence R. "Macro-Economics and the Theory of Rational Behavior," *Econometrica,* XIV (1946), 93ff.

———— "The Use of Econometric Models as Guide to Economic Policy," *ibid.,* XV (1947), 111–151.

Knight, Frank H. "Institutionalism and Empiricism in Economics," *American Economic Review*, XLII (1952), *Proceedings*, 45–55.

—— "Salvation by Science: The Gospel According to Professor Lundberg," *Journal of Political Economy*, LV (1947), 537–552.

—— "What is Truth in Economics?" *Journal of Political Economy*, XLVIII (1940), 1–32.

Koopmans, Tjalling C. "The Econometric Approach to Business Fluctuations," *American Economic Review*, XXXIX (1948), *Proceedings*, 64–72.

—— "The Logic of Econometric Business Cycle Research," *Journal of Political Economy*, IL (1941), 157–181.

—— "Measurement Without Theory," *Review of Economic Statistics*, XXIX (1947), 161–172.

Kubie, Lawrence S. "Some Unsolved Problems of the Scientific Career," *American Scientist*, 41 (1953), 596–613; 42 (1954), 104–112.

Lange, Oscar. "The Scope and Method of Economics," *Review of Economic Studies*, XIII (1945–46), 19ff.

Leibenstein, H. "Bandwagon, Snob, and Veblen Effects in the Theory of Consumers' Demand," *Quarterly Journal of Economics*, LXIV (1950), 183–207.

Leontief, Wassily. "Econometrics," in *A Survey of Contemporary Economics*. Philadelphia: Blakiston, 1949. Pages 388–411.

—— "Exports, Imports, Domestic Output, and Employment," *Quarterly Journal of Economics*, LX (1945–46), 171–191.

—— "Input-Output Economics," *Scientific American*, 185 (1951), No. 4, 15–21.

—— "Output, Employment, Consumption, and Investments," *Quarterly Journal of Economics*, LVIII (1943–44), 290–313.

—— "Mathematics in Economics," *Bulletin of the American Mathematical Society*, 60 (1954), 215–233.

—— "Recent Developments in the Study of Interindustrial Relationships," *American Economic Review*, XXXIX (1948), *Proceedings*, 211–225.

—— "Wages, Profits and Prices," *Quarterly Journal of Economics*, LXI (1946–47), 26–39.

Lillie, Ralph S. "Biological Causation," *Philosophy of Science*, VII (1940), 314–336.

—— "Some Aspects of Theoretical Biology," *ibid.*, XL (1948), 118–134.

Little, I. M. D. "The Foundation of Welfare Economics," *Oxford Economic Papers*, New Series, 1 (June 1949).

Lowe, Adolph. "Economic Analysis and Social Structure," *The Manchester School*, VII (1936).

—— "On the Mechanistic Approach in Economics," *Social Research*, 18 (1951), 403–434.

Lukasiewicz, Jan, and A. Tarski. "Untersuchungen über den Aussagenkalkül," *Comptes Rendus des séances de la Société des Sciences et des Lettres de Varsovie*, XXIII (1930), Classe 3, 1–21.

Lundberg, George A. "Alleged Obstacles to Social Science," *Scientific Monthly*, LXX (1951), 299–305.

—— "Operational Definitions in the Social Sciences," *American Journal of Sociology*, XLVII (1941–42), 727–743.

Machlup, Fritz. "Why Bother With Methodology?" *Economica*, New Series, III (1936), 39–45.

Malisoff, W. M. "Emergence Without Mystery," *Philosophy of Science*, VI (1939), 17–24.

Margenau, H. "Probability, Many-Valued Logics, and Physics," *Philosophy of Science*, VI (1939), 65–87.

Marschak, Jacob. "Economic Structure, Path, Policy, and Prediction," *American Economic Review*, XXXVII (1947), *Proceedings*, 81–84.

—— "Neumann's and Morgenstern's New Approach to Static Economics," *Journal of Political Economy*, LIV (1946), 97–115.

—— "Rational Behavior, Uncertain Prospects, and Measurable Utility," *Econometrica*, XVIII (1950), 111–141.

McCracken, H. L. "Discussion in Seminar on the Development of Economic Thought," *American Economic Review*, XLIII (1953), *Proceedings*, 274–278.

McDonald, John. "The War of Wits," *Fortune*, XLIII (March 1951).

von Mises, Richard. "On the Foundation of Probability and Statistics," *Annals of Mathematical Statistics*, XII (1941), 191–205.

Morgenstern, Oskar. "Perfect Foresight and Economic Equilibrium," *Zeitschrift für Nationalökonomie*, VI (1935), Part 3.

—— "When is a Problem of Economic Policy Solvable?" in *Wirtschaftstheorie und Wirtschaftspolitik*, Festschrift für Alfred Amonn. (Bern: Francke, 1953), 241–249.

Neisser, Hans. "The Strategy of Expecting the Worst," *Social Research*, 19 (1952), No. 3.

Neyman, Jerzy. "Outline of a Theory of Statistical Estimation Based on the Classical Theory of Probability," *Philosophical Transactions of the Royal Society*, Ser. A., 236 (1937), 333–380.

Northrop, F. S. C. "The Impossibility of a Theoretical Science of Economic Dynamics," *Quarterly Journal of Economics*, LVI (1941–42), 1–17.

Nichol, A. J. "Probability Analysis in the Theory of Demand, Net Revenue and Price," *Journal of Political Economy*, IL (1941), 637–661.

Novick, D. "Mathematics: Logic, Quantity, and Method," *Review of Economics and Statistics*, XXXVI (1954), 357–358. See also the excellent discussion on this article by Klein, Duesenberry, Chipman, Tinbergen, Champernowne, Solow, Dorfman, Koopmans, Samuelson, and Harris, pp. 359–386.

Novikoff, A. B. "The Concept of Integrative Levels and Biology," *Science*, New Series, CI (1945), 209–215.

Oppenheim, F. E. "Rational Choice," *Journal of Philosophy*, L (1953), 341–350.

Orcutt, G. H. "Actions, Consequences, and Causal Relations," *Review of Economics and Statistics*, XXXIV (1952), 305–313.

Papandreou, A. G. "Economics and the Social Sciences," *Economic Journal*, LX (1950), 715–723.

Park, R. E. "Human Ecology," *American Journal of Sociology*, XLII (1936–37), 1–15.

Popper, Karl. "The Poverty of Historicism," *Economica*, New Series, XI (1944), 86–103, 119–137; XII (1945), 69–89.

Prescott, C. H., Jr. "The Scientific Method and Its Extension to Systems of Many Degrees of Freedom," *Philosophy of Science*, V (1938), 237–266.

Pribram, Karl. "Patterns of Economic Reasoning," *American Economic Review*, XLIII (1953), *Proceedings*, 243–258.

Reiss, Albert J., Jr. "The Accuracy, Efficiency, and Validity of a Prediction Instrument," *American Journal of Sociology*, LVI (1950–51), 552–561.

Rothenberg, Jerome. "Welfare Comparisons and Changes in Tastes," *American Economic Review*, XLIII (1953), 885–890.

Rougier, Louis. "The Relativity of Logic," *Philosophy and Phenomenological Research*, II (1941–42), 137–157.

Rousseas, S. W., and A. G. Hart. "Experimental Verification of a Composite Indifference Map," *Journal of Political Economy,* LIX (1951), 288–318.

Samuelson, P. A. "Economic Theory and Mathematics — An Appraisal," *American Economic Review,* XLII (1952), *Proceedings,* 56–66.

Sarbin, Theodore R. "The Logic of Prediction in Psychology," *Psychological Review,* LI (1944), 210–228.

Savage, L. J. "The Theory of Statistical Decision," *Journal of the American Statistical Association,* XLVI (1951), 55–67.

Schoeffler, Sidney. "A Note on Modern Welfare Economics," *American Economic Review,* XLII (1952), 880–887.

——— "Toward a General Definition of Rational Action," *Kyklos,* VII (1954), 245–273.

Scitovsky, Tibor. "The State of Welfare Economics," *American Economic Review,* XLI (1951), 303–315.

Sebba, Gregor. "The Development of the Concepts of Mechanism and Model in Physical Science and Economic Thought," *American Economic Review,* XLIII (1953), *Proceedings,* 259–268.

Shubik, M. "Information, Risk, Ignorance and Indeterminacy," *Quarterly Journal of Economics,* LXVIII (1954), 629–640.

Simon, H. A. "Logic of Causal Relations," *Journal of Philosophy,* 49 (1952), 517–528.

Smith, N. M., S. S. Walters, F. C. Brooks, and D. C. Blackwell. "The Theory of Value and the Science of Decision," *Journal of the Operations Research Society of America,* I (1953), 103–113.

Snedecor, G. W. "On a Unique Feature of Statistics," *Journal of the American Statistical Association,* XLIV (1949), 1–8.

Somers, Harold M. "A Theory of Income Determination," *Journal of Political Economy,* LVIII (1950), 523–541.

Solow, R. "On the Structure of Linear Models," *Econometrica,* 20 (1952), 29–46.

Spengler, J. J. "Discussion in Seminar on the Development of Economic Thought," *American Economic Review,* XLIII (1953), *Proceedings,* 269–271.

——— "Sociological Value Theory, Economic Analyses, and Economic Policy," *ibid.,* 340–349.

Stone, J. R. N. "Prediction from Autoregressive Schemes and Linear Stochastic Difference Systems," *Econometrica,* XVIII (1949), Supplement, 29–37.

Streeten, P. "Programs and Prognoses," *Quarterly Journal of Economics*, LXVIII (1954), 355–376.

Tarski, Alfred. "The Semantic Conception of Truth," *Philosophy and Phenomenological Research*, IV (1943–44), 341–375.

Theil, H. "Econometric Models and Welfare Maximisation," *Weltwirtschaftliches Archiv*, LXXII (1954).

Thirlby, G. F. "The Economist's Description of Business Behaviour," *Economica*, XIX (1952), 148–167.

Vining, Rutledge. "Methodological Issues in Quantitative Economics: Variations Upon a Theme by F. H. Knight," *American Economic Review*, XL (1950), 267–284.

Walsh, V. C. "On Descriptions of Consumer's Behavior," *Economica*, XXI (1954), 244–251.

Weckstein, R. S. "On the Use of the Theory of Probability in Economics," *Review of Economic Studies*, XX (1952–53), 191–198.

Weisskopf, Walter A. "Psychological Aspects of Economic Thought," *Journal of Political Economy*, LVII (1949), 304–314.

Wold, Herman O. A. "Causality and Econometrics," *Econometrica*, 22 (1954), 162–177.

——— "Statistical Estimation of Economic Relationships," *Econometrica*, 17 (1949), Supplement, 1–22.

Wolfe, A. B. "Neurophysiological Economics," *Journal of Political Economy*, LVIII (1950), 95–110.

Zilzel, Edgar. "History and Biological Evolution," *Philosophy of Science*, VII (1940), 121–128.

——— "Physics and the Problem of Historico-sociological Laws," *Philosophy of Science*, VIII (1941), 567–579.

Unpublished Material

Adams, Robert W. "The Use of Economic Models in Forecasting," Ph.D. dissertation, Massachusetts Institute of Technology, 1951.

Ames, Edward. "Induction and Probability Theories in Economics," Ph.D. dissertation, Harvard University, 1952.

Barnes, Leo. "An Experiment That Failed; An Analysis of Economic Forecasting in American Reconversion, 1945–1946," Ph.D. dissertation, Graduate Faculty of Political and Social Science, New School for Social Research, 1948.

Grayson, Henry W. "Studies in Economic Forecasting by Governments," Ph.D. dissertation, University of Toronto, 1950.

INDEX

Accelerator, nonlinear, 137–138

Accidents, disturbing effect of, 31

Action: nonrational, examples of, 193–196; definition of, 204–205; outcome of, 205; rational choice of, 205–210; complementarity to calculation, 209; combined, 209; example of, 214, 216. *See also* Policy-making

Affirming the consequent, fallacy of: instance of, 38; in inventory theory, 87–88

Agronomy, 22, 40, 43

Anthropologists, economic, 164

Anxiety: avoidance of as governing economic thought, 165–167

Art: definition of, 156–157; economics as, 156, 157–158, 158–162, 179. *See also* Decision theory; Policy-making

Artificial closure: discussion and definition of, 29–31, 40; econometric models as, 106, 132; examples of, 107–111, 136–139; psychological mechanisms producing, 165–169

Artificial factorization: discussion and definition of, 28–29, 40; in Dewey's and Dakin's analysis, 102

Artificial fixation: discussion and definition of, 26–28, 40; examples of, 58–59, 73–75, 78, 95; psychological mechanisms producing, 165–169

Artificial generalization: discussion and definition of, 21–24, 40, 170; in construction of endogenous models, 31; examples of, 63, 68, 69, 88, 95, 102, 117; psychological mechanisms producing, 165–169

Artificial indirectness: discussion and definition of, 37–39, 40; in inventory theory, 87–88

Artificial isolation: discussion and definition of, 32–37, 40, 170; examples of, 68, 72, 75, 82, 83, 129, 139; de-stroys usefulness for policy-making, 135; psychological mechanisms producing, 165–169

Artificial mechanization: discussion and definition of, 18–20, 40, 170; in construction of endogenous models, 30; examples of, 76, 83; psychological mechanisms producing, 165–169

Artificial semiclosure: discussion and definition of, 31–32, 40; examples of, 80, 106, 111–118, 118–125, 125–130, 132; psychological mechanisms producing, 165–169

Artificial simplification: discussion and definition of, 20–21, 40; example of, 72; psychological mechanisms producing, 165–169

Artificial systematization: discussion and definition of, 24–26, 40; psychological mechanisms producing, 165–169

Aspectual nature of economics: as explanation of failures of economics, 7–8

Astronomy, 2, 8, 27, 28, 30, 40, 43, 95, 171

Autonomy of relation, 127

Babson Economic Service. *See* "Overshoot" method

Barnes, Leo: *An Experiment That Failed*, 139–149

Batteries of homogeneous agents. *See* Artificial simplification

Bayes solution, 181

Beckler, Bernard. *See* Business Investment Programs study

Behavior equations: discussion of, 21–24; mentioned, 20n; in econometric models, 104, 119; weakness of, 130–131. *See also* Artificial generalization; Models, econometric

DATE DUE